Lygon St.

MICHAEL HARDEN
STORIES AND RECIPES FROM
MELBOURNE'S MELTING POT

FOOD & RECIPE RESEARCH – MAUREEN MCKEON   MURDOCH BOOKS

Introduction

Lygon Street is one of Australia's well-known streets. Nobody who heard about this project had to ask what or where Lygon Street was, though there were plenty who questioned why you would devote a whole book to it. The most common responses were evenly divided between those who dismissed the iconic street as a clapped-out tourist trap and those who viewed it as a hotbed of violent organised crime.

Such responses possibly highlight the tendency of Australians to dismiss the recent past. Perhaps it is part of being a new country, this desire to brush aside the details and move onto the next big thing, as if we are in a hurry to make up for lost time. But in doing this we can lose the small stories, the individual pleasures, the hardships and heartbreak, the moments of joy and imagination that have helped form part of who we are.

No one is suggesting that tourists and gangsters play no part in Lygon Street's story, but so much else has occurred in the street since it was first mapped out in the 1850s that it becomes slightly infuriating to see how quickly the negative stories are allowed to swamp the positive ones.

Lygon Street is home to the oldest, continuously operating trade union headquarters in the world, the birthplace of the Australian Labor Party and the scene of the first union for women in Australia; it is also the location for the first Salvation Army headquarters in Australia. It was one of the world centres of Yiddish theatre in the 1930s and 1940s and, a couple of decades later became the canteen and watering hole for the writers, actors and directors who formed Australia's first truly alternative theatre scene. Lygon Street was the site of Australia's first espresso machine, its first pizza house, the first produce store to stock extra virgin olive oil and fresh mozzarella cheese, the first wine bar to truly champion the Australian wine industry and the first fully fledged street festival in the country. It was the place where cooking legends like Tony Bilson and Stephanie Alexander honed their skills. There are some who argue it was the first place where Australians tasted truly authentic Italian home-style cooking and others who believe it is the true beginning of east–west fusion food.

Over and above all the firsts, Lygon Street has proved itself to be one of Australia's greatest and most harmonious melting pots. While the Italian story is the one most often told, Lygon Street has also made room for Jewish, Greek, Lebanese, Spanish, Chinese, Indian, German, Thai, Jamaican and Malaysian immigrants. Most importantly, it has done this in a suburb that has always had a majority of Anglo-Irish residents. It may not have been all sunshine and roses, but the tales of harmony far outweigh the ones of conflict. It is a street that gives multiculturalism a good name.

To tell the complete Lygon Street story would require an encyclopaedia. Everybody who has visited, worked, partied or lived in Carlton feels as if they own a part of Lygon Street, and they probably do. Even if they only ever sang along to Skyhooks' 'Carlton (Lygon Street Limbo)' they have a story, a memory, a connection. It is a unique place with a remarkable history that deserves to be remembered beyond the short-term memory clichés. It is a street with a future potentially as fascinating as its past. It is one of Australia's great melting pots.

***

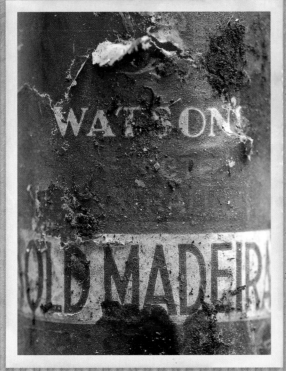

chapter
01
Best-laid
plans

Best-laid plans

Lygon Street makes a great argument for the importance of solid foundations. In the century and a half since it first appeared on the maps of Melbourne, Lygon Street has experienced the full gamut of economic, social and demographic boom and bust. But still it has kept functioning, not just as a major artery of commercial activity but as a generous force, capable of gathering life, energy and a sense of place to the inner-city suburb through which it runs. It may have appeared shabby and ill-used at times, but Lygon Street has always managed to duck and weave the slings and arrows tossed its way by the wider world. And there can be no greater reason for its continued grip on the imagination and its constant success than that it was built on the sturdiest of foundations.

The progressive and visionary way the suburb of Carlton was planned and developed in the mid-19th century is the rock on which Lygon Street was built. Hope and confidence brought it into being and these heady ideals have helped the street retain its integrity even when dark forces from any number of eras — everything from severe economic depression and ravenous developers to misguided social experiments — descended on the street, seemingly intent on stripping it of the very elements that defined its character. Yet Lygon Street has proved that it is made of sturdy stuff.

Lygon Street first appeared on Melbourne city maps in the early 1850s, part of an extension to the original Melbourne city grid that was laid out by Surveyor-General Robert Hoddle. This second grid, originally surveyed and planned by Hoddle, was implemented by Hoddle's successor, Andrew Clarke, and was initially labelled (with a remarkable lack of imagination) the 'City Extension'.

Many of the street names in the new extension were named after eminent British warriors and Lygon Street was no exception. Britain's Inspector General of Cavalry at the time was Edward Pindar Lygon whose ancestors had arrived in England with William the Conqueror and had fought against Napoleon. What Edward Lygon had to do with a newly hewn street in a newly wealthy town in the newish colonies on the far side of the world is probably irrelevant. It seems mere association with a long and proud military history was enough to lend a sense of import, gravitas and pride to the freshly minted street.

It could be argued that Lygon Street was, in many ways, instrumental in defining Carlton, given that it — and other City Extension streets such as Drummond and Rathdowne — actually predate the official naming and delineating of Carlton as a suburb. The name Carlton itself had been bandied around since the 1850s, although until the early 1870s Lygon Street was considered to be part of North Melbourne. Even so, the street had well and truly established its own identity before the mapmakers and bureaucrats caught up.

Certainly Lygon Street's early jump from the blocks to become the area's main commercial centre (Drummond and Rathdowne Streets went for the high-end residential tag) set the tone for the type of businesses and buildings that would, in many ways, come to be seen as definitively Carlton. This was certainly true in the very early days and was something that carried through the following eras.

✳✳✳

The City Extension placed Lygon Street at the centre of the new grid that ran off at an angle from the original city grid. It ran through an area of lightly timbered bushland that, despite the disastrous effect of European settlement on the local indigenous population, still played host to an occasional gathering of the Wurundjeri people. Accounts written during the time the area was being surveyed mention Wurundjeri fires flickering at night in bushland that is now the site of Melbourne University.

One early account in *The Chronicles of Early Melbourne 1835–1852*, written by 'Garryowen' (the journalist and author Edmund Finn), described the pre-surveyed area as 'a nice afternoon stroll from the inhabited portions of the township, amongst the luxuriant gum and she-oak trees beyond the (now) Carlton, spread out as in some old grand park. No one outside a lunatic asylum would think of going into business beyond Lonsdale Street, which was the point of demarcation between town and country.'

This picturesque land was a logical choice for city planners to establish an ordered, well-surveyed expansion of Melbourne. The area was considered rural and uninhabited, despite its proximity to Melbourne, the presence of a basalt quarry and the Collingwood stockade (one of three prisons in Melbourne at the time) and those occasional flickering indigenous fires. With its good elevation and natural drainage, it was always destined to become a source of quality real estate. What made the area suddenly irresistible (and the birth of Lygon Street inevitable) at this point in time was the population explosion that occurred after the discovery of gold in Victoria in 1851.

***

It is difficult to comprehend the extent of the transformation that the discovery of gold brought to Melbourne. Prior to this, Melbourne was a small but successful town that was declared a city in 1847. The state of Victoria had only just become a separate colony in 1851 when the gold rush hit and the pace of growth went from measured to borderline insane. Between 1852 and 1854 an estimated 90,000 people each year arrived by sea, the pace 'slackening' in the following years to a mere 60,000 arrivals per annum. While most immigrants headed straight for the gold fields, it was not long before many of them returned to the city to either spend their fortunes or to find work if their prospecting dreams had not proved fruitful. There was plenty of other work to be had. With the gold rush, Melbourne had become a thriving manufacturing centre, servicing the gold fields and inland towns and it quickly overtook Sydney as Australia's largest city.

13

Building went into overdrive, not just housing but grand public buildings — town halls, libraries, churches, post offices — and, by the mid-1850s, the city was sprouting a series of suburbs that were like villages separated from each other by swamps, ravines and watercourses. It was not until major engineering works to drain swamps and build bridges were commenced in the 1880s that these villages were joined and Melbourne became the metropolis that was deemed 'marvellous'. But many of the inner-city suburbs that were filled with small cottages designed to house workers also began to fill with factories and other non-residential buildings and, with the ever-increasing population, ramshackle housing and a lack of sanitation, these working-class suburbs began to take on the appearance and reputation of slums. Even with 100 million pounds worth of gold flooding the city, there were still many that did not share in the wealth.

In this respect, the timing was good, or lucky, for Lygon Street. A delay in surveying the area that was to become south Carlton meant that the initial population explosion that occurred in the early days of the gold rush — and the unruly and haphazard building boom that came in its wake — was concentrated in suburbs like Fitzroy, Collingwood and Richmond, inner-city areas that attracted working-class people because of their proximity to the factories, markets and building sites near the booming city centre. These suburbs bore the immediate brunt of an increase in Melbourne's population that saw it rise from 23,000 in 1850 to 130,000 in 1858. The subsequent dire housing shortage saw the government so overwhelmed by the number of people suddenly needing shelter that it was forced to open up allotments which fell outside the jurisdiction of its Building Act 1848, (initially put in place to ensure good planning practice and decent building standards for the city). Subsequently, flimsy, low-grade buildings (many of them potential fire traps) were allowed permits and jerry-built houses sprang up like shantytowns in many areas. Delayed by a few months, the City Extension that was to become Carlton was able to come into being with less urgency and with most of the elements of good planning intact.

Surveyor-General Clarke envisaged the City Extension to be a Bloomsbury-like area with wide tree-lined streets delineating a classic grid, land reserved for squares, churches, public buildings and large areas of parkland. The area was planned so that no allotment would be more than two blocks from a park or public square (Lygon Street's Argyle Square was one of these parks). The establishment of the Melbourne General Cemetery in 1853, at what was then the northern end of Lygon Street, and the University of Melbourne in 1854, seems to show that the Bloomsbury model was one shared by more than the Surveyor-General. And can it be just coincidence that a suburb whose model was Bloomsbury, London's artistic and literary suburb, has continuously attracted a stream of bohemian and artistic activity since it was first laid out?

***

In the very early days of Carlton, however, the real art was in securing land. Such was the demand for land in Melbourne that by 1857, just five years after the City Extension first appeared on maps, all the subdivided allotments in the area had been sold and the suburb continued to expand north at a great rate of knots. The initial tent and shanty dwellings that were the first signs of life along the unmade roads of the southern end of the new suburb were quickly replaced by more substantial dwellings — the area, with its proximity to the city, advantageous elevation and semi-rural aspect became a fashionable place to live. The increasing number of businesses setting up shop along Lygon Street was also making the area a more attractive and amenable place for those who could afford it.

Lygon Street had its share of residential buildings but it did not take long for it to become apparent that it was going to be Carlton's commercial heart. From the early 1860s, residential buildings were already being converted into shops, often with a dwelling above where the business owner lived. The seventy-foot road width and twelve-foot deep footpaths, similar in dimensions to the streets on the Melbourne city grid, provided Lygon Street with an ideal, familiar structure for conducting commercial trade. Add the street's location at the centre of the new grid and it would always have appeared to be the most logical and viable place for businesses to set up shop.

The Melbourne General Cemetery

The Melbourne General Cemetery, which runs for seven blocks along Lygon Street from Princess Street to Macpherson Street in North Carlton, opened for burials in 1853. It was the third cemetery in Melbourne, planned in 1849 to alleviate the pressure on the two existing cemeteries that were located at what are now the Flagstaff Gardens and Queen Victoria Market.

The original plan was for a 10 acre site but this was increased to 27 acres in 1851 and then, with the population explosion brought on by the gold rush, was expanded to 60 acres in 1852. In 1858, with the new suburb of Carlton starting to snap at the 'bush' cemetery's heels, the site was further increased to 100 acres.

Melbourne General Cemetery was modelled on the new-style cemeteries springing up in Britain that were favouring a more park-like approach to burial (as opposed to the unfashionable overcrowded churchyard model). It was carefully planned and subdivided, giving the major religious denominations at the time — Anglican, Roman Catholic, Presbyterian and Methodist — the lion's share of the space, with the leftover room originally allotted to 'Other Denominations' — Jews, Lutherans, Quakers, Chinese and so on. One commentator at the time (John Stanley James, writing under the name 'Vagabond') commented archly, that 'even in death [they] must not mingle together'. Aboriginals, who had been allotted space in the original 1849 plans, were dropped off the plan by 1851, apparently not allowed to mingle at all.

One-time director of the Royal Botanic Gardens, Baron Ferdinand von Mueller, was integral in the layout and planting of the cemetery until 1873 and he and his successors were responsible for the cemetery being seen as an aesthetically pleasing place for a stroll during the 1880s and 1890s, despite the increasingly crowded atmosphere.

Above: The entrance to the Melbourne General Cemetery, 1870.

The cemetery was closed to new grave sales in 1904 but, after a long period of neglect and frequent vandalism, new ground was found (the original entry drive) and the cemetery resumed operation until the 1940s when space ran dry again. Unsuccessful attempts to establish a crematorium to keep the cemetery solvent resulted in early grave areas being 'topped up' and sold as family plots. Paths and roadways were also filled in to create fresh ground. Such behaviour has stopped now and Melbourne General Cemetery has come back into favour as a peaceful place for a stroll.

Part of the attraction is, of course, the graves and memorials of the famous. Melbourne General Cemetery's roll of honour includes Victoria's first Governor, Sir Charles Hotham; Australia's first Australian-born Governor General, Sir Isaac Isaacs; two Prime Ministers, Sir Robert Menzies and James Scullin; and sporting stars such as billiard champ Walter Lindrum. In addition to these there are memorials to writer Marcus Clarke, doomed explorers Burke and Wills and even Elvis Presley.

***

And they did. By the early 1860s (by which time Lygon Street had been extended several blocks further north as more land was subdivided) the street had begun to fill with a mix of small businesses, from hotels and greengrocers to chemists and coffee kitchens. By 1870 Lygon Street had become a fully fledged commercial centre, helping to feed and water the locals with four hotels (the Albion, University, Leinster Arms and Carlton Belle), two butchers, two greengrocers, two grocers, a baker, a confectioner, a wine and spirit merchant and a dairy.

In addition to the food businesses, it was also home to an impressive collection of tailors, dressmakers, bootmakers and milliners, while others plied their trade as tobacconists, hairdressers, music teachers, chemists, plumbers, watchmakers and ironmongers. This admirable variety of businesses was slotted in among Lygon Street's prominent public buildings — several churches of various Christian denominations and, on the corner of Victoria Street, the union headquarters Trades Hall — all of which had been granted Crown land by the government when the City Extension was first being planned.

With this mix of public space (in the form of Argyle Square), statement-making public buildings, a wide thoroughfare and an increasingly thriving and diverse string of businesses operating from Victoria Street to Elgin Street, Lygon Street had definitely arrived as Carlton's commercial centre and its most obvious public arena.

Lygon Street's success reflected the early success of this well-planned suburb as a whole. A glowing report written in the late 1870s by the often acerbic Garryowen in his *Chronicles of Early Melbourne* gives the clearest picture of how quickly Carlton had established itself as a viable place in which to work and do business:

I must now rapidly keep moving, and ask my readers to clap on all steam and accompany me across by what was the Prisoners' Stockade, afterwards a branch Lunatic Asylum, and now a State School [now Carlton North Primary School]; and skirting along by the fence of the Necropolis [Melbourne General Cemetery], where some hundred thousand human beings have found a resting place in thirty years, we stand on the highest spot of the

19

palaeozoic hill on which the greater part of Carlton is built. Looking around you, compare it as it now is with what it was not many years ago, when all the country around the Royal Park and the other Hill of Hotham [now North Melbourne], revealed a vista of hill and dale, well wooded and grassed, well suited for a delightful rambling excursion. The perspective now is an untold treasure, planted in the soil, and cropping up in splendid mansions, handsome villas, busy marts, spacious streets, squares, parks and gardens, and stately churches — all these practical evidences of civilisation.

Garryowen went on to say that the 'presently superior appearance' of Carlton 'as compared with other localities, may be attributed to the relatively late period when the greater part of the land was sold, and the judgement evinced by the land speculators in subdividing their purchases'.

When a large portion of Carlton … was put into the market, numbers of people who had saved money from the early gold years (and better still, knew how to keep it), invested it there to advantage. A taste also gradually grew up for dwellings with the comfort and conveniences of English life, and to such causes are to be traced the superior style of building, very generally prevailing.

By Garryowen's account you could be forgiven for thinking that Carlton was some kind of paradise on earth. Certainly there were some substantial and graceful buildings in the suburb and the layout of the streets and parks provided a good foundation on which to build, but the roads remained in a fairly primitive state until the late 1860s when they were transformed. Before then, winter in Lygon Street would see the road turning into a virtually impassable quagmire, making it difficult for businesses and residents alike to be able to move freely and gain access to the goods they needed. A further handicap was that the new grid was initially independent of the original city grid and was in fact separated from the city by a 'ravine' that could only be crossed by a temporary log bridge at the top end of Swanston Street. Carlton was all but cut off from Melbourne's commercial heart.

***

It could be that the increasing commercial clout of Lygon Street worked in its favour as it was among the first of Carlton's streets to be joined to the city grid (joining up with Russell Street) and to receive more 'permanent' street paving which, in turn, allowed water and gas supplies to be connected. These advantages saw an increasing number of diverse businesses opening on Lygon Street throughout the 1870s, 1880s and 1890s. This period of great commercial success for the street saw a mix that included both smaller shops — butchers, dairies, greengrocers, tailors, bootmakers — that catered to the needs of local residents, and larger more diverse stores like Ball & Welch (situated between Lygon Street and Drummond Street) that in their variety of goods — everything from drapes to bicycles — were closer in spirit to modern department stores. These stores began to put the street on the map as a destination for shoppers that provided an alternative to the big stores in the city centre.

It was also during this same period that the commercial prosperity of Lygon Street was reflected in the many significant buildings — both private and public — that were built along the strip, some of which remain intact today.

Perhaps the most impressive of these is the Lygon Buildings, built in 1888 on the corner of Lygon and Grattan Streets. Designed by George de Lacy Evans and developed by the Church of England on land that was originally granted to them by the government, the large, ornate boom-era classic originally contained eighteen two- and three-storey shops and three large private houses. It is the largest and most intact terrace of 19th century shops in Melbourne.

***

At 376–384 Lygon Street the Holdsworth Building, built in 1871, housed undertakers until 1972 before iconic names such as Brunetti's and Café Paradiso moved in. Only some of the building remains now — it was partially demolished to make way for the Lygon Court development at the end of the 1980s — though its facade, with the distinctive arched veranda,

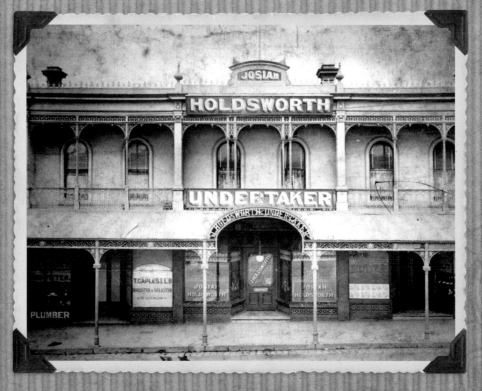

is intact and remains an integral part of the streetscape. Initially made famous for housing the undertaker's shop that prepared local underworld figure Squizzy Taylor for his journey into the great beyond, the Holdsworth Building later became strategic in the 1980s during the great battles over demolition and development of the street.

***

It was actually fitting that Squizzy Taylor, the most famous Melbourne gangster of the time, should have been prepared for burial in a Lygon Street funeral parlour. Squizzy was a common fixture on the street during the 1920s and was linked to some of Carlton's more famous crimes, including the burglary of Trades Hall during which a police constable was shot and killed. On the night he was killed, in October 1927, Squizzy Taylor had been seen visiting a couple of Lygon Street pubs, dressed in his usual flashy, expensive manner. Taylor's activities — robbery, prostitution, race fixing, protection rackets and drug and alcohol dealing — not to mention his sartorial splendour, set something of a precedent on the street for the style and substance of organised crime, a precedent that was taken up with gusto in the 1980s and 1990s by the notorious Carlton Crew.

***

If you strolled down Lygon Street in 1877, there were businesses of every variety to catch your eye, most of them with the iron-posted, corrugated-roofed veranda out the front that had become mandatory in Carlton at the time. The ANZ Bank and State Savings Bank also chose to build impressively solid buildings, something that emphasised the viability and commercial success of Lygon Street.

Along with the more prosaic enterprises — Andrew Griffin the blacksmith, Thomas Sharp the dentist, Mrs Graham the midwife, George Sharp the saddler, William Lewellen the plumber, and A.B. Smith & Co. the real estate agents —

were a host of other shops and businesses that reflected the change from local commercial hub to the forerunner of the kind of shopping strip Lygon Street is today. There were shops selling china, glass and earthenware, a toy shop, a straw-bonnet maker, a photographer, several hairdressers and tobacconists, furniture stores and two confectioners. In 1877 Lygon Street even boasted three 'oyster saloons', one of which, run by a John H. Taylor, also operated as a restaurant.

There were also four wine shops that included Richards Brothers Grocers at 221 Lygon Street, which had been operating since 1863 and had recently been granted a licence. Just over ten years later Richards Brothers sold the business, which was renamed Messrs King & Godfree's Supply Store, a licensed grocer that has only changed hands twice since and still operates as a wine shop and gourmet deli today. Even at its opening King & Godfree was renowned for its level of service and for the quality and range of its goods. Besides a selection of local and imported wines, ales and spirits, there was a wide display of groceries, an impressive variety of imported teas and coffee — ranging from pure grounds to coffee mixed with chicory — that were blended and roasted at the shop. The grocery store was also renowned for its dairy produce, much of which was selected from among the blue ribbon winners at Melbourne's annual agricultural show.

King & Godfree was one of a number of shops mentioned in a five-page feature on Carlton businesses that appeared in the *Weekly Times* in August 1896. The article praised the suburb as a shopping destination, recommending it particularly to its country readers because of the variety of businesses in Lygon Street and the surrounding area — smiths and saddle-makers next to drapers and fancy goods emporiums meant that both farmers and their wives could take care of business along the same strip. The *Weekly Times* supplement also mentioned the bigger stores like Ball & Welch with its twenty-five departments over three levels, and draperies like J.L. Dick & Co. that emulated the style and variety of city shops and played a big part in attracting shoppers to Lygon Street from beyond the boundaries of Carlton.

Trades Hall

The impressive bluestone building sitting at the corner of Lygon and Victoria Streets is the oldest continuously occupied trade union headquarters in the world. But there is more to Trades Hall than its role as home base for Victoria's union movement. The building at the entrance to Lygon Street has seen the birth of a major political party and tertiary institution, has helped conserve the architectural integrity of Carlton, run its own radio station and art school, and was the scene of the only murder of a policeman in the history of Carlton.

The idea for a Trades Hall in Melbourne had its genesis in the union victory that followed the 1856 struggle for the eight-hour working day. Unions decided to mark the historic victory with the establishment of a 'workingman's parliament' where they could not only hold meetings but also attend lectures, borrow books and generally improve themselves with educational pursuits.

In 1858 an acre of Crown land was granted to the organising committee of the Melbourne Trades Hall and Literary Institute by the government, with the condition that it would never be traded for gain (interestingly, a condition not forced upon the churches who were granted land around the same time — the Anglicans, for example, developed their patch of Lygon Street turf into the commercial and residential Lygon Buildings). Through fundraising, loans and donations the unions were able to construct a relatively modest iron-roofed timber building consisting of a large hall and four committee rooms that opened on 29 May 1859.

While its main function was to provide a headquarters for the local unions, Trades Hall also fulfilled the educational part of its original charter by providing lessons for the working class in mathematics, English, economics, public speaking, history and politics. In 1867 an Artisans School of Design was established that taught painting to a generation of student painters that included Frederick McCubbin and Tom Roberts. The idea of a Working Men's College also came from Trades Hall and resulted in the establishment of the Royal Melbourne Institute of Technology (RMIT) in 1887.

The growth of the union movement was such that by the 1870s decisions were made to demolish the original building and build a larger, more impressive

Trades Hall. Architect John Reed from the firm Reed & Barnes, whose CV included the Melbourne Town Hall and the Public Library, was commissioned and the first part of the new building was completed in 1875, followed in 1882 by the extension that fronts Lygon Street today. A further extension in 1884 encompassed the Female Operatives Hall, built following the successful action by women in the clothing industry to form the Victorian Tailoresses Union, the first union for women in Australia and one of the first in the world.

Trades Hall was the birthplace of the Australian Labor Party, which emerged from the Progressive Political League, a party formed after defeats suffered by unions during the Great Strikes of the 1890s. It also played an integral role in the defeat of a 1916 referendum on conscription, ran soup kitchens during the Great Depression, and radio station 3KZ, which began operating from Trades Hall in 1930, was the first to broadcast the news of the surrender of Japan that ended World War II. In the 1960s, Trades Hall, in particular the Builders Labourers' Federation, teamed up with the newly formed Carlton Resident's Association to play a vital part in the fight against the proposed levelling and rebuilding of great swathes of Carlton.

A less salubrious incident — the murder of policeman David McGrath — occurred in 1915 during a burglary at Trades Hall. McGrath and another policeman caught three men in the act of breaking into a safe and, in the ensuing gun battle, McGrath was shot and died of his wounds. One of the burglars, John Jackson, was found guilty of the murder and had the dubious honour of being the last man to hang at the Old Melbourne Gaol.

Trades Hall remains the headquarters of Victoria's union movement today and it also continues its affiliation with the arts, playing host to theatre productions throughout the year and providing venues and a bar during the Melbourne Comedy Festival.

Trades Hall may seem like a separate entity on Lygon Street, somewhat removed from the commercial activity further north, but with its affiliation with the working class and the arts, it could also be seen as a very Lygon Street kind of place.

***

Lygon Street also became something of an evening shopping destination after gas lights were installed along the street during the 1880s, with shops staying open as late as 11 pm on Saturday nights. Many of the late-night patrons would have taken refreshment at William Hart's mobile coffee stall which was located at the corner of Lygon and Faraday Streets and sold coffee, dispensed from a four or five gallon polished and nozzled tin, and snacks such as sandwiches and cakes.

Evening shopping was, however, a short-lived phenomenon on Lygon Street. Keeping shops open for as long as there were customers about meant that shop assistants were working ridiculously long hours — sometimes up to eighty hours per week. For a street that boasted the world's first union headquarters at its entrance, this sort of exploitation would not do, and in June 1881 most shops in Carlton agreed to close their doors at 7 pm. A gradual reneging on the agreement saw more and more shops returning to late-night hours until legislation was finally brought in towards the end of the 1880s forcing them to close at 7 pm; a welcome relief for workers but a blow to those who enjoyed the charming night vibe of the street.

While there is little doubt that the businesses on Lygon Street at this time were mainly serving locals, as the suburb expanded northward, the shops on Lygon Street also became a destination for those on their way to and from work in the city. But, if public transport is anything to go by, it seems Lygon Street had been a destination almost from the time it first came into being.

As early as 1860, the City of Melbourne proclaimed that particular stands for hackney cabs, or horse-drawn carriages, in the centre of Melbourne were to be reserved solely for the use of cabs travelling to and from Carlton, to Lygon Street's commercial and retail centre in particular. All other hackney cab stands were deemed for general use, which seems to suggest that there was a certain volume of traffic travelling to and from Carlton's commercial heart on a frequent basis.

In 1869, the Melbourne Omnibus Company was running horse buses from Flinders Street Station (called the Hobson's Bay railway at the time) to Fitzroy and Collingwood, via Lygon Street, at the rate of one bus every five minutes. A year later, a service was introduced that exclusively targeted Carlton (to Rathdowne Street, via Lygon Street) making the area easily accessible from the city. In 1898 the North Carlton cable tramway opened, confirming and securing the commercial viability of Carlton's main business strip. When cable trams were ditched in favour of electric trams in the 1930s, the Lygon Street tram line was replaced by buses and the tram tracks removed. Those wishing to travel by tram through the area now would have to use the electric lines on Swanston or Nicholson Streets.

***

It is interesting to note that while Lygon Street's prosperity continued on the up and up, the suburb around it was not faring so well. From the 1870s onwards, the wealthier residents of Carlton had begun to move to the rapidly expanding suburbs, particularly those south of the Yarra River. While parts of Carlton remained fashionable for another decade or so, the rapid development of the suburb had begun to thwart much of the careful early planning.

Blocks of land that were to have contained ten allotments were being sold by developers and then divided into as many as seventy-two allotments. Frail, flimsy buildings were being jammed into every conceivable space to house an ever-increasing number of workers, drawn to the area not only because of its proximity to the city with its factories and other places of work but because slum housing was all many people could afford.

It is little wonder that those who could afford to move were abandoning Carlton for leafier suburbs like Kew and Hawthorn in the east or St Kilda, Prahran and Brighton in the south. Overcrowded, badly built, terribly ventilated slum housing was bad enough but Melbourne as a whole was lagging far behind other capital cities like Sydney and Adelaide in terms of sanitation. Despite — or perhaps because of — Melbourne's population explosion there were no sanitary engineering works even contemplated until 1891 and so by the 1880s Melbourne was literally wallowing in its own filth. A visiting Sydney journalist commented that 'Marvellous

Melbourne' should probably be re-named 'Marvellous Smellbourne'. As well, Melburnians at this time were experiencing much higher rates of infectious diseases such as typhoid fever than comparable 19th century cities and in areas like Carlton, where the poverty-stricken working class were lured by textile and clothing workshops, Carlton Brewery, hotel and retail jobs, brickworks and building work the stench and disease were amplified. The more spacious suburbs, made increasingly accessible by a rapidly expanding public transport system, provided some respite from the often hideous conditions of many parts of Carlton. The dream of such an escape was a recurring one for many Carlton residents, new and old.

As early as 1868, a writer from *The Argus* newspaper was noting that 'a whole district of the city naturally pleasant and healthy' was being transformed into something 'noisome and pestilential through overcrowding'. The economic depression that hit in 1891, throwing Melbourne's financial and property industries into chaos, exacerbated the fall in Carlton's fortunes. Slum growth accelerated and poverty and misery were commonplace.

During this time much of Carlton was gaining a reputation as a hotbed of drunkenness and crime. The reputation was not so surprising really when you consider that in the years 1890–1892 there was an average of one arrest for every 5.6 Carlton residents. Most of the arrests were for crimes that contributed to public disorder like drunkenness, obscene language, vagrancy and general disorderly conduct. There were people arrested for prostitution, gang violence and property offences, crimes that the newspapers were quick to report on in salacious detail which further accelerated the demise of the suburb's once shiny reputation. It was not as if these criminal activities were exclusive to Carlton. The centre of Melbourne during this final decade of the century was described by artist Norman Lindsay as being 'the era of the larrakin gangs, of street garottings, of opium dens in Little Bourke Street's China Town, of pubs open all hours, and at night in Bourke Street, a promenade of whores openly soliciting custom'. But people seemed to expect bad behaviour in the city, whereas Carlton was founded on much higher ideals and so its demise seemed that much more shocking. And so, around this time even the large homes in the more fashionable parts of Drummond Street were being abandoned by the wealthy and divided up into increasingly dodgy boarding houses. It appeared that Carlton was sliding away from the grand ideals on which it had been founded.

***

Lygon Street, of course, was not immune to the struggling economy and the falling fortunes of the suburb around it. While much of the street went on with business as usual, many of the restaurants, fancy goods stores and oyster saloons disappeared, reflecting a growing middle-class apprehension about the area's safety. This was fuelled in no small part by the continuous, lurid reporting of crime in Carlton by the newspapers of the day.

But the reality was that things had changed. Parts of Lygon Street became notorious for the number of brothels that operated there. The existence of charitable organisations, such as the Working Women's Home of Rest that mainly looked after female ex-prisoners also did nothing to dispel the idea that Carlton was a place for the destitute and desperate.

It was certainly a case of changed circumstances for Lygon Street but it seems that changed circumstances was something Lygon Street would become accustomed to dealing with. That the street and the suburb through which it served as a major artery were able to keep functioning — and even thriving — in such times says something about the solid foundations on which they were built. Even with rougher than usual handling, Lygon Street was well equipped to survive.

***

The pot begins to simmer

chapter 02

The pot begins to simmer

From the time it was laid out across the bushland to the north of the Melbourne city grid, Lygon Street became a melting pot. Even in its earliest days, the days before the distinct waves of Jewish and Italian (and, to a lesser extent, Greek, Lebanese and Spanish) immigrants washed over Carlton, the people who lived, worked and owned businesses on the street came from many different ethnic backgrounds and economic circumstances. There was never anything homogenous about Lygon Street and that was part of its attraction and charm. It was — and continues to be — a street capable of making room for all.

If you look at the names of the people who owned businesses on Lygon Street at the end of the 19th century there is an unsurprising predominance of Anglo-Irish names, a reflection of the ethnic make-up of Melbourne at the time. But if you look beyond the names like Edward Ryan, the hairdresser, David Pope, the confectioner, and Miss Emma Lewellan, the dressmaker, you will find H.E. Kugelmann, the herbalist, Abraham Soloman, the bootmaker, A. Borzoni, the confectioner, and Francis Luce, the fruiterer and confectioner. Their names provide evidence of the much greater diversity of nationalities in Carlton than a cursory glance at the business registers might first imply. The fact that many immigrants from Europe anglicised their names to make commercial and social life among the predominant culture a little easier also helps to throw a veil over the real diversity of the community that surrounded Lygon Street.

Of course, diversity of community was not uncommon in this neck of the woods. The 1850s gold rush had turned the whole township of Melbourne into one big melting pot of fortune seekers from all over the globe who arrived in their droves, drawn together by a common dream of great and instant wealth. As with all gambling, the dream of immediate fortune did not quite match the reality and most of the arrivals had to settle for a more mundane way to make their money. Simply stuffing their pockets with the plentiful gold nuggets that rumour had lying on the ground for the taking was, unfortunately, never an option for most.

The newly created suburb of Carlton had plenty to offer new migrants recently divested of their get-rich-quick fantasies. It was close to the business centres of the city and to the flour mills, breweries, joinery works, timberyards and the confectionery, footwear and textile factories in neighbouring Fitzroy and Collingwood and, in the early days at least, the suburb attracted both wealthy business people looking to escape the increasingly crowded city centre and working people — mostly men — who could find accommodation in the many boarding houses and tiny cottages that had sprung up in response to the booming population.

Migrants the world over always initially congregate in areas where people with similar cultural backgrounds — their own kind, their own language — have already established homes and businesses. This urge to herd is understandable, particularly in a place as far-flung, strange and isolated as Melbourne in the second half of the 19th century must have appeared. The few culturally similar individuals who had already established themselves must have always looked like the best and safest option when setting up in such a place. This was certainly the case in Carlton.

It is interesting to note that the two main groups who would have the largest impact on Lygon Street's identity in the following century — the Jews and the Italians — put down their roots in Carlton very early on. These two groups may not have been numerically significant at the time in comparison with the population as a whole, but the fact that they grouped together and started businesses in commercially visible places like Lygon Street meant that they became an obvious and comforting beacon for those who followed.

The first Jewish residents to settle in Carlton were mainly from England and Germany, many of them business people who had made money directly or indirectly from the gold rush and had then moved into the more salubrious southern parts of the suburb. This initial group was joined in the 1880s and 1890s by greater numbers of Yiddish-speaking immigrants from Eastern Europe who came to the *Goldene Medina*, or 'Golden Land', (as Australia with its slightly overblown gold rush-driven reputation was known), to escape the violent anti-Semitic Russian pogroms. This influx of migrants from Eastern Europe — from Russia, Romania, Hungary, Poland and Galicia — settled in Carlton in increasing numbers just as the established original Jewish families were starting to head south towards the more affluent areas around St Kilda. Many of these newer arrivals were impoverished and so working-class Carlton, with its cheaper rents, access to jobs and small but noticeable number of Jewish-owned shops along strips like Lygon Street, was the logical place to take shelter.

Italians were also a small but distinct early presence in Carlton, though their numbers in the late 19th century were even less than the relatively small population of Jews. In 1891 there were only 232 Italian-born people living in the City of Melbourne (which included Carlton), constituting about one per cent of the local population. In terms of their immediate effect on Carlton and Lygon Street, the Italians of the time could probably be considered to be punching above their weight.

Most of the Italians who moved into Carlton at this time would have done so because of close proximity to readily available manual labour — on the wharves, in the stonemasons' yards and in market gardens that were scattered across the city. But among the Italian immigrants were craftsmen who worked on many of Melbourne's mansions (including the enthusiastically florid 'Benvenuta' in Drummond Street) and other grand buildings of the gold rush boom. A sizeable number of these were being built in the Italianate style that was all the rage in 19th century 'Marvellous Melbourne' (a term coined by visiting English journalist George Augustus Sala to express his delight and surprise at a city that 'teems with wealth as it does with humanity', even though it was not yet fifty years old).

The Italians also had a sizeable presence on the Melbourne music scene of the time and were integral in bringing opera to the colonies through touring companies such as the Cagli-Pompei Royal Italian Opera Company.

There was certainly a strong musical presence among the Carlton Italians, including Alberto Zelman, who settled in Melbourne after arriving in Australia in 1871 with Cagli-Pompei. The company had toured throughout Australia and New Zealand, playing not only in the town halls and theatres of the cities but on more rudimentary stages in country towns. Alberto lived in Carlton and became a leading conductor, composer and teacher. His eldest son, Alberto Victor Zelman, founded the Melbourne Symphony Orchestra.

Lygon Street had its own Italian musical presence, though it was fittingly less highbrow and more populist than in other areas of the suburb. A group of travelling musicians — harpists and violinists mainly, many of them trained in Viggiano — had begun settling in Melbourne in the 1890s. In the early years of the 20th century many of them played with the popular Di Giglio Band, which was based at 62 Lygon Street and catered for occasions such as weddings and dances. Band members were also known to busk in the streets. Most of these musicians lived in Carlton (many of them clustered around Lygon Street's Argyle Square) and so the suburb became known for its musical Italian population.

✳✳✳

As the economic collapse of 1891 stomped on the last of Carlton's fashionable middle-class credentials, there were small but well-established Jewish and Italian communities in Carlton, and a smattering of Jewish and Italian businesses on Lygon Street. Already teetering on the edge of slumdom and home to some of Melbourne's poorest residents, the area could only benefit from their presence as the depression hit Carlton like a ton of bricks. The immigrant groups, with their strong community ties and cultural traditions, attracted more like-minded migrants into the area and helped bolster the community, keeping commercial areas like Lygon Street viable and giving the suburb a focus apart from the terrible hardships that were being suffered by the hundreds of people who could no longer find work.

While the 1890s and 1900s saw Lygon Street maintaining its position as the commercial centre of Carlton, the street also attracted an impressive amount of charitable work. Churches and benevolent societies moved into the area (both before and after the 'great crash') determined to feed, clothe and shelter those who were no longer able to fend for themselves. Women and children were the main focus of this philanthropic attention because many families were left to fend for themselves as their desperate husbands and fathers headed to the bush, chasing rumours of work on the land. But the charitable organisations that set up on Lygon Street had numerous and wide-ranging goals, attempting to tackle and put to right many of the area's perceived social ills, from drunkenness to troubled youth.

Lygon Street was the first place the Salvation Army set up a permanent base in Australia when it opened the Prison Gate Brigade Men's shelter in 1883. In 1891, the Women's Christian Temperance Union established the Working Women's Home of Rest in Lygon Street, catering mainly to female ex-prisoners, while, at the height of the depression, the Melbourne Ladies' Benevolent Society was assisting up to 350 families a week from a relief depot set up on Lygon Street. The Carlton Creche was opened in a private house on the street in 1900 and the Reverend George Cole of the Lygon Street Primitive Methodist Church held 'bun and banana' nights to attract the area's notorious larrikin youth in an attempt to transform them into useful, productive and God-fearing citizens.

The Primitive Methodist Church was also the home of the Wesley Central Mission, the distribution point for loads of rabbits sent down by supporters in the country to help feed the undernourished poor. A Sister Zelma, who worked out of the mission, distributed the rabbits from a wheelbarrow she pushed through Carlton's slum-like back lanes. The Mission continued to operate from Lygon Street until the 1950s, though by then the need for distributing rabbits from a wheelbarrow was no longer necessary.

***

Rabbit Stew

Serves 6

✳✳✳

2.5 kg (5 lb 8 oz) farmed white rabbit, cleaned
4 tablespoons plain flour
4 tablespoons olive oil
2 brown onions, thinly sliced
4 carrots, sliced
2 parsnips, chopped
4 celery sticks, chopped
3 bay leaves
3 large potatoes, halved

✳✳✳

This recipe was written by Mary Graham, born 1922, who was a young girl living in Melbourne in the depth of the Depression. She remembers vast numbers of unemployed people knocking on the door of the family home looking for work and food. Meals were often provided for people in need and it was not unusual in those days for men from the country to bring rabbits into town where they were soaked and stewed to feed the needy.

Wash the rabbit under cold running water and pat dry with paper towels. Cut the rabbit into six serving portions by removing the forelegs and the back legs following the bone structure. Cut the saddle into two pieces through the ribcage, discarding the flap of belly. Season the flour with salt and freshly ground black pepper, and toss to coat the rabbit pieces.

Heat the oil in a large heavy-based saucepan over high heat. Add the rabbit and cook for 10–12 minutes, turning until brown all over. Set aside on a plate.

Add the onion, carrot, parsnip and celery to the pan, reduce the heat to medium and cook for 5–6 minutes, or until the vegetables are tender. Return the rabbit to the pan and add enough water to just cover. Add the bay leaves, season with salt and pepper and bring to the boil. Reduce the heat to low, cover, and simmer for 30 minutes. Add the potatoes, cover, and simmer for a further 30 minutes, or until the potatoes are cooked through. Remove from the heat and serve immediately, sprinkled with the parsley and thyme.

Despite the economic hard times, the presence of homeless shelters, grog shops and brothels, and a reputation for crime and vice (exacerbated no end by the increasingly visible presence of strange clusters of people from foreign lands), Lygon Street continued to hum along nicely. Its mix of businesses may have started to shift and change as more migrants moved in, but still the street functioned like any village commercial centre, servicing the local community and those who were passing through on their way to and from the city.

Despite Carlton's reputation as a hotbed of crime, the number of arrests for misdemeanours such as drunkenness and vagrancy actually declined in the new century. It may be drawing too long a bow but it could be mooted that the increasing numbers of migrants looking to build a new life for themselves and their families, who came from cultures where drunkenness was not the norm, might have contributed to the falling arrest rate, along with the organised relief efforts. There may not have been too much co-mingling between different ethnic groups at the time but the first benefits of the melting pot were undoubtedly beginning to be felt.

***

The first three decades of the 20th century saw parts of Carlton and Lygon Street begin to take on a distinctly Jewish flavour. It was the migratory snowball effect in action. As more Jews from Eastern Europe arrived at the wharves in Port Melbourne, they were met by relatives or friends or, later, by the Jewish Welcome Society, who would take them back to the rectangle of Carlton bordered by Lygon, Faraday, Nicholson and Park Streets. This was home to the majority of the Carlton Jewish community. It was only logical for new arrivals to look for places to stay nearby and so the community continued to swell. It is estimated that during the 1920s nearly two-thirds of Melbourne's Jewish population lived in Carlton with a census in 1933 putting the number at about 2800.

To many newly arrived Europeans, the streets of Melbourne they passed through on their journey from Port Melbourne would have seemed strangely quiet and deserted compared to what they were used to in the Old World. So to be immediately brought among Yiddish speaking people who understood the dislocation they were feeling would have been a wonderful relief.

This feeling must have been particularly strong during the 1920s and 1930s when Carlton's Jewish community really shifted into gear. After landing in Melbourne, often traumatised from fleeing anti-semitic violence in their homelands, the latest arrivals found a place where there were Jewish grocers, butchers and bakers, kosher restaurants and cafés, bookshops containing religious books and texts in Yiddish, and Yiddish theatre productions featuring some of Europe's most acclaimed actors. There were synagogues, welfare groups, political associations, community newspapers, sports and leisure facilities and classes in Yiddish and Hebrew language and religion. New migrants without any English could go about their business — shopping, looking for work, catching up on news from home — with very little trouble. Sure, the community was relatively small, but the Jews who lived in Carlton certainly ensured that the best adjective for their *shtetl*, or village, in Carlton was 'thriving'.

At the heart of Carlton Jewish life was the Kadimah. Founded in the city in 1911, it moved to Drummond Street in 1915 and then to a purpose-built building in Lygon Street in 1933. Cultural, political, theatrical and social events were held at the Kadimah and it was a symbol, not only of the strength of the Jewish community in Carlton, but of the community putting down serious and committed roots in its adopted land.

***

Kadimah

✶✶

In Hebrew, Kadimah means 'progress' or 'forward' and Lygon Street's Kadimah certainly lived up to its name. Though it also played an important role in Jewish political and social concerns, the Kadimah's primary role was a cultural one. It provided context, meaning and a sense of belonging for newly arrived Jewish immigrants, allowing them to settle more quickly and successfully and to progress more smoothly into the way of life of their adopted country.

The first meeting of the Kadimah was held in Bourke Street in the city centre in 1911 and was attended by fourteen Polish Jewish immigrants who began establishing a library of Jewish books, periodicals and newspapers. By 1915, the Kadimah had moved to Drummond Street in Carlton, reflecting both the area's increasing Jewish population and the particular make-up of that population — Yiddish-speaking Jews from Eastern Europe.

In the 1920s the Kadimah started the tradition of bringing out 'shining lights' of the European Yiddish literature and theatrical worlds to lecture or perform; something that drew further attention to the establishment and increased membership.

The Jewish Welcome Society (JWS) was founded within the Kadimah and had its headquarters there. The aim of the Society was to meet every new Jewish immigrant at Station Pier, bring them to Carlton, find them housing and work and give them enough of a grasp of English to get by in the wider world. In 1926 the JWS met twenty-six different ships that offloaded Jewish passengers in Port Melbourne.

The increasing influx of Jewish immigrants began to strain the Drummond Street Kadimah's resources and so, at the end of the 1920s, an appeal was launched to raise money for a new building. In March 1933, the new, purpose-built Kadimah opened at 836–840 Lygon Street in North Carlton.

The new Kadimah, with its 400-seat capacity theatre hall and library, was then called the Kadimah Jewish Cultural Centre and National Library and took its cultural brief seriously. The first Yiddish book to be published in Australia, *Der Oytalisher Almanach* (*The Australian Almanac*), came

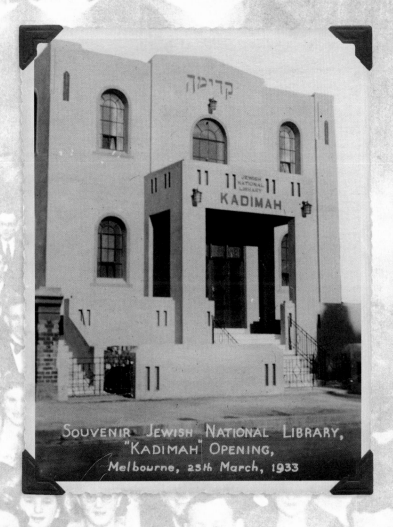

SOUVENIR JEWISH NATIONAL LIBRARY,
"KADIMAH" OPENING,
Melbourne, 25th March, 1933

from the Kadimah in 1937. It was also a strong supporter of writers such as the renowned Pinchas Goldhar who published stories, edited the Yiddish weekly newspaper and even translated some Henry Lawson short stories into Yiddish. There were also many non-Jewish Australian artists and writers invited to talk at the Kadimah to help introduce immigrants to Australian culture.

The Kadimah had always mounted productions of Yiddish plays that were successful and popular but after World War II, when Melbourne became the second highest per capita home of holocaust survivors after Israel, the sometimes amateurish productions became more professional, aided by the arrival of some of the Yiddish theatre's greats who were fleeing a Europe that no longer existed.

***

49

Above: The Rosenthal musicians perform at the Kadimah on Lygon Street n.d.

In 1950, when the Kadimah had 1000 members, the Dovid Herman Teater by der Kadimah (David Herman Theatre Company) was formed and world-renowned Yiddish actors and actresses such as Jacob Weislitz and Rachael Holtzer (apparently 'the Nicole Kidman of Jewish Theatre') began to appear. This was Yiddish theatre of the highest order, according to one writer in a Jewish journal at the time:

I have often remarked the curious atmosphere about a Yiddish theatre that is never to be found elsewhere. One fact that strikes the newcomer rather forcibly is the way the audience reacts to the emotions of the actors. The excellence of an actor on the Yiddish stage is usually measured in fact by the volume of sobs and tears he elicits from the audience. Jewish theatregoers can be heard to remark: Mr So and So last night was simply wonderful. His acting was so superb that a woman actually fainted. They had to carry her out. You should have heard how the audience sobbed.

Victor Hecht, owner of a fruit shop on Lygon Street and a holocaust survivor, said that he never missed a play at the Kadimah.

'I sometimes went to English plays and I found it hard because I couldn't understand all the words,' says Victor. 'But the plays in Yiddish were good because for me the language cut deep.'

Above: The Green Fields Kadimah production at the Kadimah n.d.

The Kadimah was known worldwide at this time as an important centre of Yiddish and Jewish life. With its often volatile politics, constant series of plays, lectures and recitals, well-resourced library (a paid librarian had to be engaged in the 1950s because of growing demand for books and newspapers) and string of balls, fundraisers and dances, it is little wonder the Kadimah figured so largely in so many lives and made the building on Lygon Street the cultural heart for many in the community.

Allan Wynn, son of the winemaker Samuel Wynn who was president of the Kadimah twelve times, says that 'for many newcomers unable to read English, it was an oasis at which they could renew their contact with an intellectual life without which they would have been like lost souls'.

Others said it helped them so that they 'didn't feel entirely lost in a big country'.

The decline in the Carlton Jewish population as more and more people moved to St Kilda and Caulfield also saw the relevance of the Kadimah in Lygon Street diminish. In 1968 the Kadimah relocated south of the river. Fittingly, given the changing face of Lygon Street, the Kadimah building became headquarters to the Eolian Islands Society, the oldest Italian regional association in Melbourne. It still occupies the building today.

***

Of course, to the wider community it may have seemed as if the Carlton 'slums' were now also harbouring insular ghettoes of immigrants. But the successful blend of businesses on Lygon Street — kosher butcher shops sharing the street with those run by Anglo–Australians, pharmacies run by Jews, Italians and Australians, cake shops offering both 'Australian' and 'Continental' varieties of sweet stuff — proved once again (at least to those who were living among it) that the street was a pot into which anyone could melt.

In her book *Broken Biscuits, The Changing Face of Carlton*, Mary Fisher describes some of the local atmosphere on the street at the time, specifically how a grocery shop in Lygon Street not only affected the life of a young Jewish girl who lived in Carlton, but how it came to be an integral part of the life of the Jewish community in the 1930s. The shop, A. Boltin & Son Grocers, was located at 362 Lygon Street, next door to the Albion Hotel and across the road from King & Godfree:

Mostly [this story] is about a magical shop and the man behind the counter. A man of middle age, middle height, receding hairline and closely cropped moustache. An ordinary sort of man until he smiled. Then a transformation took place. A mischievous twinkle crept into his eyes when dealing with kids and when he listened to some kinsman in trouble, his look took on one of compassion.

... A warm feeling comes over me as I think about that shop — a magical shop we called it. It was the first shop in Carlton to sell home-made ice cream, sour cream, salt herring, everyday groceries, confectionary and broken biscuits. For newcomers it was a bit of home; nostalgia. It also served as a meeting place, to exchange news from home and local gossip ... I remember the scuffle which usually broke out between Izzy and me whenever Mother needed something from that shop. 'It's the only time you two are eager to do messages,' she laughs at us. She knew our secret. The dispute would be settled by both going separately. I would buy the quarter pound of butter, Izzy the pound of sugar.

Oh the smell that hit you as you entered the shop. The large open barrels of salt herring, a smaller container of anchovies packed in salt, another container with sprats swimming in their salty brine, rolled back bags of sugar, rice, flour, each with its own scoop. There were none of the packed goods we buy in supermarkets today. On one end of the counter stood the highly polished scales and on the other, a slab of butter and one of cheese. The customers were all poor and lived from hand to mouth, so buying a quarter pound of butter and a pound of sugar was the norm.

He would weigh the butter, pack it neatly with the wooden pats, wrap it and hand it to me. I would stand and wait. 'Is there anything else, Shaindele?' he would ask. Then I would panic. He was not going to give me a biscuit. I would be close to tears as I answered 'No' and would move towards the door. 'Shaindele, you have forgotten your biscuit.'

I would see mischief in his eyes as he handed me the precious biscuit. Each time I would examine it carefully. If I was in luck it would be a teddy bear with only one ear missing or perhaps a toe.

The shop was a kind of institution; everybody came there at some time or another, everybody depended on it. The man with the long white apron was everybody's friend. Women came to him with their family troubles, small manufacturers came on Thursday to borrow money to pay their workers' wages. They would pay him back on Monday so that he could purchase his goods on Tuesday. When a family was in strife he would wipe off the debt, but woe betide anyone who tried to take him down.

***

Shops like these were integral in making Lygon Street feel like a village; a home away from home. They provided something familiar and reassuring in an unfamiliar city that was not overtly hostile but certainly suspicious and resentful of these strange newcomers with their foreign tongues and unfamiliar habits.

Another well-known Jewish business on Lygon Street at this time was the Monaco Cake Shop, run by Joseph and Pearl Levine. The story of Joseph's journey to Australia was typical of many of the Jewish immigrants who had settled in Carlton.

Joseph owned a restaurant in Russia but moved his family to Poland after the revolution because he feared the new regime. He had had two pianos confiscated from his restaurant and knew that he would lose his entire business if he stayed. He took the family recipe books with him to Poland and the family settled in Bialystok for a time before moving to Palestine. He left his family in Palestine while he travelled to Perth, arriving in 1927. Once he had arrived he sent for his family and, soon after they arrived in 1928, they all moved to Melbourne, settling in Carlton.

Joseph started the Monaco Cake Shop in a two-storey building on Lygon Street in a single-fronted shopfront that later became part of Jimmy Watson's Wine Bar. He made European-style kosher cakes from the old family recipes he had brought with him from Russia. The family lived above the shop and stayed there until 1938 when Joseph and Pearl followed a well-trodden path for many in the Carlton Jewish community, selling the Lygon Street shop and moving south of the Yarra to start another cake shop in Acland Street, St Kilda.

Just around the corner from Lygon Street, on Drummond Street, were a couple of other businesses that played a vital role in the Jewish community's wellbeing. In the 1920s, Zal Markov, who was a fully qualified chemist from Russia, opened the Markov Chemist Shop on the corner of Drummond and Elgin Streets. Markov's gained a reputation among the local community as a place where you could be diagnosed for what ailed you, free of charge. One customer, Victor Hecht, who owned a fruit shop on Lygon Street at the time, recalls that 'the old man, Mr Markov, would look at you and see what you needed and just mix up something and give it to you'. One of Markov's apprentices, Abraham Horowitz, went on to open his own pharmacy in Lygon Street though, by all accounts, he ran a more traditional business, leaving most of the diagnosing to the doctors.

Just up the road from the Markov Chemist Shop were two kosher cafés, places where new arrivals and established residents could gather, share news and eat the food they remembered from Europe. On one corner there was the Café Tel Aviv, opened by the father of distinguished journalist

Sam Lipski, which had rooms upstairs where those fresh off the boat could board. On the other corner was Sam Cohen's Continental Café (later to become the acclaimed Donnini's restaurant and, in more recent times, the equally acclaimed Three, One, Two). Cohen's was another kosher café that was the first point of call for many Jewish immigrants. It too had rooms above the restaurant where people could stay for a few days before they found permanent accommodation. Some remember the food at Cohen's as plain and traditional. There would be a chicken broth with noodles, a piece of meat, a compote of fruit and a cup of tea. Sometimes there was cake and, on Fridays, there would be fish.

In an article in *The Age* newspaper in 1988 entitled 'Our Ethnic Founding Fathers', Sam Lipski recalls Cohen's as a place that introduced staff and students from the University of Melbourne to a style of food they had never seen before. 'Professor Goldman, the first professor of Semitic Studies at Melbourne University, was a large man who liked good food and cigars. He used to bring a large circle of academic friends and writers to Cohen's Kosher Café. It was famous for borscht and potato dishes, veal schnitzel and stuffed veal, meat soups and chicken soups with noodles.'

Cohen's was still operating at the end of World War II and it became, for a time, a regular hangout for a group of recent refugees from Europe, young men without any family who gathered together in quiet groups and were often simply referred to as the 'Buchenwald Boys'.

Another Jewish business on Lygon Street at the time was a kosher butcher shop started by three Ukrainian brothers called Smorgon who used meat as a stepping stone to a vast and successful business empire. Then there was Mattison's bookstore that carried a large stock of prayer books and, further up the street in North Carlton the textile factory Fetter's Knitwear that manufactured socks and jumpers, a fruit shop run by a man called Schwartz and a Jewish bakery called Ernest's Bakery.

***

Matzo Kneidlech

Serves 8–10

***

4 eggs
4 tablespoons coarse matzo meal (see note)
4 tablespoons fine matzo meal
3 tablespoons schmaltz (see note) or olive oil
a small pinch of ground ginger

***

These Jewish dumplings are traditionally made during Passover, the festival that commemorates the exodus from Egypt and the journey from slavery to freedom. No leavened bread is eaten during Passover, in remembrance of the haste with which the Hebrews left Egypt — in such haste that their bread had no time to rise!

Whisk the eggs well, then add the coarse and fine matzo meals, schmaltz and ginger. Season with salt and freshly ground black pepper, stirring thoroughly to combine. Set aside for at least 4 hours (the mixture will be too soft otherwise).

Using your hands or a small spoon, shape the mixture into small balls, about the size of a walnut. It is easier to work with wet hands, and the spoon should be rinsed in water as you work. You should make around 24 balls in total.

Bring 6 litres water to the boil in a large saucepan. Add salt to the pan once the water boils, then add the dumplings. Reduce the heat to low, then cover with a lid and simmer gently for about 40 minutes — the dumplings will be larger, white and fluffy when they are cooked.

Lift the dumplings out of the water with a slotted spoon. Kneidlech are traditionally served in chicken soup (see recipe page 57). They can be reheated in the simmering broth.

Note: Matzo is unleavened bread. It can be finely or coarsely ground into crumbs, known as matzo meal, and is commonly used in Jewish cooking. Schmaltz is dripping or lard, usually rendered chicken fat. It is available from Jewish and Continental grocers or delicatessens.

Chicken Soup

Serves 8

***

1kg (2 lb 4 oz) whole chicken, preferably a boiler
4 chicken carcasses
6 chicken wings
2 brown onions, unpeeled
2 large carrots, peeled and halved
1 parsnip, peeled and halved
2 celery sticks, halved

***

A classic of the Jewish kitchen, this chicken soup should be made in advance so that the fat can rise to the top of the chilled broth and be removed. The soup can be frozen successfully for up to 3 months.

Rinse the whole chicken, carcasses and wings under running water. Place in a large saucepan or stockpot and cover with water. Bring to the boil, skimming off any froth that comes to the surface. Add the vegetables and 1 tablespoon salt and simmer over low heat, partially covered, for 2 hours, or until the vegetables are very tender.

Allow to cool, then remove and discard the chicken, carcasses, wings and vegetables. Strain into a large bowl and refrigerate overnight to allow any fat to rise to the surface. Remove the fat, then gently reheat the soup over medium heat, seasoning with salt and freshly ground black pepper, as needed.

Serve with soup noodles or dumplings, such as matzo kneidlech (see recipe, page 56).

Many of the businesses in the occasional clusters of shops on the North Carlton stretch of Lygon Street were Jewish, including the Saffer Grocery Store that stocked pickles, herring and, around Passover, plentiful supplies of matzo. Just off Lygon Street was Pahoff's Dairy, where locals would arrive with billycans to get their milk. When children were sent to collect milk from Pahoff's, the owners usually rewarded them with a piece of barley sugar.

Near the corner of Lygon Street and Pigdon Street was the practice of a doctor by the name of Mark Ashkenazy who became something of a local celebrity during World War II. Mark served as a medical officer in the Australian Armed Forces and, during his service, he became well known for inventing a portable transfusion machine.

For all that it may seem that the Jewish community forged its own separate path in Carlton, creating an all-embracing *kehillot*, or community, that could look after its members from cradle to grave, it is obvious that such a small community would necessarily have to engage with the wider population. And it was in places like Lygon Street that immigrants could mix, both with immigrants from other places and with the Australian-born community. One of the best examples of this mingling was at the licensed grocers, King & Godfree.

King & Godfree has been operating on the corner of Faraday and Lygon Streets since 1884. It was originally owned by the Richards Brothers who started in the grocery business on Lygon Street in 1863, moved to the current corner location in 1871, gained a liquor licence in 1876 and sold to Mr Edward King and Mr George Godfree in 1884. King & Godfree acquired three other grocer shops in their sixty-three years in the business but the shop on the corner of Lygon and Faraday Streets remained the headquarters and the template from which the other stores took their cues.

In the 1930s, King & Godfree was run like many other grocery stores at the time, though it was also slightly different given that it had a licence to sell alcohol. Long-term employee, David Campbell, who started work at King & Godfree in 1938 at the age of fifteen and retired in 2001, gives a good account of how grocery stores were run before the days of self-service:

These were the days of customer service ... The customer would come to the counter, ask for goods and away you'd go to get them from the shelves, a couple of things at a time, until the order was completed. In the meantime, between the tos and fros, you'd ask after the kids, discuss the weather, did Carlton win, Bradman make another century or whatever.

Anyone not serving would weigh and wrap sugar, rice, flour; you name it, we packaged it ... There are many things today to make things easy, which we take for granted. Just imagine a day without staples, cellotape, plastic carry bags, cardboard boxes, registers which do the adding up and so on. Placing a large sheet of paper on the counter, then building the weeks' groceries into a shape around which the paper could be folded and tied with string was quite an art.

Despite the slightly (by today's standards) exotic sounding form of service and intricate wrapping of goods in paper and string (emulated now in more upmarket, designer food establishments), the scene at King & Godfree would have been similar to many quality grocery stores throughout the country. But there was a point of difference at this time that not only revealed a store that was keeping an eye on what was good for business amongst its local customers, but recognised that the Jewish presence on Lygon Street and in the surrounding community was strong enough to warrant non-Jewish businesses tailoring parts of their business to meet specialised needs.

Grahame King, grandson of Edward King, remembered working in the shop when he was a schoolboy in the late 1920s, helping with weighing and packing sugar and tea during the school holidays. He also remembers the kosher shop that King & Godfree established at this time and 'the old Rabbi watching everything and stamping the goods kosher. Many of these goods were then packed up and sent all over Australia.'

Advertisements in the Carlton-oriented newspaper *Australian Jewish News* show King & Godfree's pitch for the business of local Jews, pushing its credentials as 'The Only Authorised Kosher Grocer'. One ad from June 1929 reads:

61

Other ads from 1934 announced that King & Godfree was a 'Kosher Grocer appointed by the Melbourne Beth Din for the supply of groceries for the Passover' and alerted customers when 'Palestine wines and liqueurs had just landed'.

King & Godfree was a business that kept up with the times, no matter how the times changed. In 1955, when Lygon Street was beginning to take on a distinctive Italian flavour, the shop was bought by the Valmorbida family and subsequently began to position itself to take advantage of a whole new set of market forces.

Though immigrants from Italy living in Carlton still only numbered in the hundreds up until the 1920s, there were forces afoot that were going to change the face of Lygon Street permanently. And, in some ways, much of the change in the street stemmed from decisions made in the United States.

From the beginning of the 20th century the unrivalled destination of choice for most European migrants was America. Australia was too far-flung and too unknown to be top of any self-respecting potential immigrant's list, particularly in the face of the 'land of opportunity' spiel coming from the States.

However, by the 1920s, Americans were becoming increasingly uneasy about the success of their message, which had seen a huge and constant flow of migrants from war-ravaged Europe landing on their shores. Responding to the ever more strident anti-immigration arguments that were being trotted out on all sides, the US Senate responded in 1924 with a bill that slashed the intake of migrants, effectively closing the door to America for many Europeans. Alternatives were sought and the fledgling Italian and Jewish communities in Australia, aided by the more amenable migration conditions, began turning heads — and dreams of a better life — towards Australia.

The new-found interest saw Italian liners establishing regular shipping routes to and from Australia in the 1920s and 1930s (most ships would come via Perth and then onto Melbourne), resulting in a noticeable increase in the number of Italians arriving in Carlton, a good proportion of these escaping the rise of fascism in Italy. Even so, the numbers were still measured in hundreds rather than thousands, making it something of a practice ripple for the larger wave of Italian immigration after World War II.

For all the changes that new waves of immigrants were bringing, Lygon Street at this time — physically at least — was not changing much at all. The Victorian era buildings that defined the streetscape were perfectly suited to the needs of both traders and customers and so remained pretty much unchanged — if a little shabbier — from their heady days at the centre of a reasonably wealthy middle-class suburb. Double-storey terraces with ornate wrought-iron detailing lined the wide street and, up until the 1930s, much of the traffic on the streets was still horse-drawn.

David Campbell, the grocery assistant who was born and raised in Carlton and worked all his life at King & Godfree, gives a particularly vivid account of the kind of traffic and road conditions on Lygon Street before the dawn of mass car ownership:

Much of the traffic on the roads was horse-drawn. Apart from private jinkers, there were hansom cabs, brewery wagons, council garbage carts, road workers' lorries and road watering drays, furniture removalists, butchers, bakers, rabbitoes, fishoes, grocers vans [and] milk carts.

65

In Faraday Street, between Lygon and Drummond Streets, a line of wagons formed in the middle of the road each day and were for hire for any job, just like a taxi rank. The bakers cart had two levels in the storage area. There was a small step about four inches square at the rear of the cart for the baker to stand on to reach the higher level. We used to run behind the cart, hop onto the steps and get a ride. This was known as 'whipping behind the cart'.

During very hot weather the bitumen on the road was liable to soften and the council carts loaded with sand would come around and a couple of chaps with shovels would swish sand across the road. On the footpath outside all hotels was a horse trough for watering with an automatic filling action similar to a toilet cistern so the water didn't fall below a certain level.

Carts that were on the road all day carried a hessian bag of chaff and when the driver stopped for a lengthy period he would hang the bag from the horses head and the horse could munch away. In Carlton, it wasn't uncommon for a herd of sheep to be driven through the streets on their way to the abattoirs by a drover and a couple of dogs.

***

Given such conditions, in a run-down suburb that many of those on the outside (and some of them in) saw as a slum, it is little wonder that many people arriving from the Old World would sometimes question what they had achieved by moving so far from home. Yiddish writer Pinchas Goldhar described how newly arrived immigrants would greet each other with '*Shalom Alcheichem*, ask about each other's livelihood and joke about the Golden Country, Australia'. But the long wide stretch of Lygon Street was taking it all in, accommodating newcomers alongside old timers, almost as if it was gathering its strength to prove that its potential was not a thing of the past. Lygon Street was already etching itself into history as one of Australia's great melting pots. It was just waiting for the next stage to bring its message to a wider audience.

***

67

Herring Salad

Serves 4

***

3 or 4 schmaltz herring fillets (see note)
1 thick slice stale white bread (challah is best), soaked in water for
5 minutes and squeezed dry
1 tablespoon white wine vinegar
1 small brown onion, peeled and finely grated
1 granny smith apple, peeled, cored and grated
2 hard-boiled eggs, grated
white pepper, to taste

***

Herring salad is usually served as one of the *vorspeise*, or appetisers, that are the European-Jewish version of antipasto.

Chop the herring very finely and mix with the soaked bread in a bowl. Add the vinegar, onion, apple and egg and mix well. Season with white pepper, to taste — you may need to add a little more vinegar, or some of the oil from the schmaltz herring.

Cover with plastic wrap and store in the refrigerator until ready to serve. Serve with rye bread, dill pickles and fresh tomatoes. Herring salad is best served on the day it is made, although it can keep for 1–2 days in an airtight container in the refrigerator.

Note: Schmaltz herrings are herrings in oil. They are imported from Germany or Holland and are available from Jewish and Continental grocers or delicatessens.

Potato Kugel

Serves 8–10

✳✳✳

2 kg (4 lb 8 oz) all-purpose potatoes, such as desiree
1 brown onion, grated
2 eggs, lightly beaten
2 tablespoons plain flour
1 tablespoon potato flour
160 ml (5¼ fl oz/²⁄₃ cup) peanut or safflower oil

✳✳✳

Kugel is a Jewish baked 'gâteau' that is traditionally made with rice or noodles. This recipe uses potato and makes a wonderful side dish to most chicken, veal or beef dishes.

Preheat the oven to 180°C (350°F/Gas 4). Grease a deep 20 x 20 cm (8 x 8 inch) baking dish.

Grate the potatoes, then place in a colander and press lightly to squeeze out any excess liquid. Transfer to a large mixing bowl and add the onion, eggs, flours and oil and mix well. Season with salt.

Put the potato mix into the prepared baking dish and bake for 1 hour 30 minutes, or until golden brown on top. There should be no resistance when it is pierced with a skewer or sharp knife. If there is, return to the oven and cook for a little longer. Cut the potato kugel into squares and serve hot.

Gefilte Fish

Serves 8–10

***

FISH STOCK
Murray Perch bones (see below)
1 carrot
1 brown onion, unpeeled
1 tablespoon sugar
½ teaspoon white peppercorns

1.5 kg (3 lb 5 oz) Murray perch, gutted, scaled, filleted and skinned
(bones reserved for stock)
500 g (1 lb 2 oz) boneless, skinless flathead fillets
250 g (9 oz) skinless perch fillets
2 brown onions, finely chopped
1 tablespoon sugar
3 eggs, lightly beaten
55 g (2 oz/⅓ cup) fine matzo meal (see note, page 56)
white pepper, to taste

***

This is a traditional Eastern European dish. Sometimes the fish mixture is placed inside a whole fish, but more usually, it is formed into balls, poached, decorated with carrot slices and served chilled. This is a Polish version of gefilte fish, as can be seen by the addition of sugar. Polish Jews preferred their fish sweet, a practice not shared by Russian Jews.

Fish can be minced in the food processor, but be careful not to overmix. Some fishmongers will mince fish on request. Ask for the fish bones and heads so they can be used for making the stock.

To make the stock, put the fish bones, carrot, onion, sugar and peppercorns into a stockpot with 2 litres (70 fl oz/8 cups) of water. Bring to the boil, then reduce the heat and simmer for 30 minutes. Remove from the heat, allow to cool slightly, then strain, discarding all the solids except the carrot to use as a garnish. Set aside until needed.

Using a meat grinder or food processor, mince the fish fillets, in batches if necessary, then transfer to a large bowl. Add the onions, sugar, eggs, matzo meal and 3 tablespoons water in a large bowl. Season with white pepper and salt, to taste, and mix, using a large wooden spoon, until everything is well combined. Cover with plastic wrap and refrigerate for 3 hours, or until chilled.

Using your hands or a spoon, form the mixture into balls about the size of a large egg — it will be easier if you wet your hands frequently. Flatten the balls slightly. The mixture will probably make around 20 balls, depending on size.

Bring the fish stock to a boil in a large saucepan. Add the fish balls and simmer gently for 1 hour — when cooked the fish balls will be pale in colour. Allow to cool a little in the stock (they will be less likely to fall apart), then remove from the stock and place in a deep, wide serving dish. Cut the reserved carrot into thin rounds and place a round on top of each fish ball. Strain the stock over the fish balls, not quite covering them, and chill. Serve cold.

Hungarian Gugelhopf

Serves 12

***

500 g (1 lb 2 oz/4 cups) plain flour
½ teaspoon salt
60 g (2¼ oz/¼ cup) caster sugar
2 tablespoons dry yeast
2 large eggs, lightly beaten
100 g (3½ oz) unsalted butter, melted and cooled
310 ml (10¾ fl oz/1¼ cups) milk, heated until lukewarm
400 g (14 oz/2¾ cups) chopped dark chocolate, melted and cooled

CHOCOLATE GLAZE
150 g (5½ oz/1 cup) chopped dark chocolate, melted
2 tablespoons unsalted butter, softened
1 tablespoon light corn syrup

***

Gugelhopf is from the Austro–Hungarian Empire and is also known in Germany. It is a yeast cake traditionally served with afternoon coffee. The cake is baked in a special high-fluted cake tin (gugelhopf) with a central chimney which distributes heat evenly. It may be served dusted with icing sugar or a delicious chocolate glaze.

Sift the flour and salt into a large mixing bowl. Stir through the sugar and yeast. Add the beaten eggs, cooled melted butter and lukewarm milk, stirring until well combined.

Turn the mixture out onto a lightly floured surface and knead for 5 minutes, or until soft. Return the dough to the bowl, cover with a clean tea towel and leave in a warm, draught-free place for 30–60 minutes, or until the dough doubles in size (this will vary depending on the temperature of the room).

Preheat the oven to 200°C (400°F/Gas 6). Lightly grease a gugelhopf. Turn the dough out onto a lightly floured surface and knead for a further 5 minutes. Roll out to 30 x 40 cm (12 x 16 inch) rectangle, about 1 cm (½ inch) thick.

Spread the dough with the cooled melted chocolate. Roll the dough into a cylinder starting from the longest side to form a roll, similar to a Swiss roll. Place the roll around the inside of the tin, tucking the two ends together where they meet. Cover the tin with a clean tea towel and leave in a warm place for a further 30 minutes for the dough to rise again.

Bake for 30–40 minutes, or until the cake is a light golden colour. Cool in the tin for 10 minutes before turning out onto a wire rack to cool completely.

To make the chocolate glaze, beat all of the ingredients together until smooth and pour over the cooled cake.

Variation: Try mixing 200 g (7 oz/1⅔ cups) sultanas soaked in 2 tablespoons dark rum or 100 g (3½ oz/⅓ cup) blanched almonds with the dark chocolate used for the filling.

79

The right ingredients

chapter 03

The right ingredients

You could argue that much of Australia's culinary metamorphosis from monolithic steak-and-eggs kind of territory to one of the most diverse and interesting restaurant cultures in the world can be traced back to the changes happening in Lygon Street from the 1930s onwards. These changes, particularly from the 1930s until the post-war late 1940s, were not so much seismic as gradual. Before the 1950s, after which large numbers of migrants made the pace of change faster and more noticeable, the moves afoot in Lygon Street would have been largely invisible to the wider population. Things were moving, but the pace was like that of a large ship turning around — nothing seems to be happening until you suddenly notice that the bow is pointing in a different direction altogether.

If you were able to walk down Lygon Street during the 1930s with your 21st century sensibilities intact you might wonder how anything momentous could come from this quiet wide street lined with grocers and butchers and fruiterers — much like any other suburban shopping strip at the time — where the pubs closed at six and every other door was shut by eight o'clock in the evening. Certainly, there was a mixture of names that demonstrated a multicultural mix of business ownership on Lygon Street — Jewish, Italian, Greek, Chinese, Lebanese, German alongside the numerous Anglo names — but the businesses they were attached to simply and mundanely reflected that this shopping strip mainly sold the goods and provided the services that the local community needed: groceries, haircuts, clothing, hardware, medicine, newspapers and laundry.

If you could detect any signs pointing to the remarkably influential food culture that Lygon Street was to support in years to come, they would be few and far between and not particularly encouraging. Those hospitality businesses that were there — a few pubs like The University and The Albion, some seedy sawdust-strewn wine saloons that spilled staggering drunks onto the streets every evening at 6 pm and one shabby steak-and-eggs café called the Mexican Café — would not exactly inspire great confidence in a bright and shining gastronomic future. Or a bright future of any kind, really. But despite all appearances to the contrary, the building blocks for a future food revolution were being laid.

Of course, much of the run-down ambience of Lygon Street at this time could be attributed to the effects of the Great Depression. All of Australia was affected by this major economic collapse and, in a largely working-class suburb like Carlton, the effects of unemployment and poverty were keenly felt. Down at the southern entrance to Lygon Street, the soup kitchen run by the volunteer Relief Committee at Trades Hall was the scene of regular queues that ran along the street and around the corner into Victoria Street. Men, women and children lined up every day for their portions of soup and bread. It was reported that the theft of food and clothing became more common in Carlton at this time. The theft of a case of butter and a package of tea from Philip Cohen, who peddled groceries from a cart on the corner of Lygon and Faraday Streets, was typical of the petty crimes that pointed to the desperation of the times.

✳✳✳

Carlton's slum pockets were again attracting increased attention for their squalid conditions. These had been exacerbated by the depressed economy and the once grand terraces of Lygon Street became shonky, cut-price boarding houses, their verandas roughly closed in and their large rooms partitioned to maximise the rental potential. The suburb's already existing reputation for poverty, crime and vice grew ever stronger and much of middle-class Melbourne kept its distance.

But, despite the tough times, Lygon Street continued as the solid, central commercial core of a suburb that was surviving, if not exactly thriving.

The mix of shops along the street shifted and changed slightly. The increase in pawnbrokers and money lenders setting up shop reflected the economic times but people still needed to buy groceries, vegetables, meat, milk and bread, and so Lygon Street provided and the lights stayed on.

If there was any sort of upside to the general doom and gloom of the Depression and its effect on the working people of Carlton, it could be that the low rents and lowered expectations of the area drew an increasingly eclectic population into the mix. Not only did the immigrants — most noticeably Jews and Italians — keep arriving, but the cheap living conditions also attracted a bohemian vibe to Carlton as artists, students, young academics and others with little money to spend settled in the area alongside low-income working families. This mix of ingredients surrounded not just the parts of Lygon Street that ran from the southern city border to Elgin Street, but followed its course that had now expanded all the way through North Carlton and into East Brunswick. Such a long, eclectic expanse of population probably helps to explain Lygon Street's future ability to appeal to all walks of life.

***

It is probably not surprising that many of those who experienced the Depression as children recall little pain and suffering during the period. Not having the responsibility of scraping money together to feed a brood of children when a quarter of the working population weren't working could have something to do with the sunny memories. A less cynical observation could have these ungloomy memories showing that Lygon Street faced the Depression as it had faced other challenges — with a stoic, business-as-usual approach.

Victor Smorgon was born in Russia and migrated to Australia with his family in his early teens. They settled in a house in Lygon Street, North Carlton and his father and uncles opened a butcher's shop at 366 Lygon Street in 1927. In an interview for Film Australia's 'Australian Biography' series, Victor recounts how little the Depression impacted on him, his family and Carlton's Jewish community in general:

85

I learned about [the Depression] when I was much older. I didn't know. For us there was no Depression. For any immigrant there was no Depression because you come with nothing and every time you make a penny you're already better off than you were yesterday. Where people that had money during the Depression lost it, for them it was very hard … My father didn't know there was a Depression on. It was no Depression because it was a separate business, the Jewish kosher business. The immigrants were coming in and they were the same, they immediately got some job — to do something if they wanted to …

At the time it was a different standard of living. You've got to understand the standard of living was very low too … you didn't have to have anything except possibly a roof over your head, somewhere to live. Because you can pick up of the trees, you can pick up any food very, very cheap … It all depends where you are, where do you live, where do you measure the living standard … It all depends on the context of where you are at the time and where you're starting from.

While it may be difficult to view arriving penniless and possessionless in a foreign country as any kind of advantage, the Smorgon family, who hung out their Lygon Street shingle just before the Depression hit, lived to tell a very successful tale, showing that many immigrants were simply too busy trying to establish a new life to notice the parlous fiscal environment around them. Coming from impoverished backgrounds, they didn't see the conditions in Carlton as any worse than those they had already experienced.

But what about the non-immigrants? Those who had a knowledge of better times before to compare with what came after? David Campbell, the man who worked as a grocery assistant at King & Godfree all his life, was born in Carlton in 1923 and so was old enough to remember some aspects of living through the Depression. In hindsight he is able to marvel at how his father, who ran a boot repair shop in Carlton and was left a widower at the age of fifty with six children (including a one-year-old), was able to hold the family together. David's understanding and experience of the Depression was not dissimilar to that of Victor Smorgon:

Because I knew no other conditions but these, I was not aware of doing without anything. I feel that I lived in a cheerful environment, always had mates to play with and had food when I wanted some.

Looking back now I know that most of the time what we ate was governed by the rule of the most you could eat for the lowest outlay. Mince meat with onions for flavour made into rissoles, sausages, stews, rabbits, tripe, steak and kidney pies, saveloys, cottage pies and always potatoes which could always be bought cheaply and were the backbone of our diet. Friday night was always fish and chips. Canned sardines on bread was a back-stop for lunchtime snacks [and] in schooldays, coming home each lunchtime I could eat bread and bananas with a sprinkling of sugar.

Coming home after school I would usually look for something to eat before going to sell papers. Usually it would be a slice of bread and plum jam or bread and dripping sprinkled with salt. The dripping from all cooking was always carefully poured into the dripping basin.

***

Many of the oral accounts about Lygon Street at this time come from people such as David Campbell, who experienced the street as children, so there is a preoccupation with food, after-school jobs and games of cricket played in the middle of sparsely trafficked streets. Such a perspective allows an interesting insight into Lygon Street's social institutions, such as the pubs that, in more conventional accounts, usually come across as dark and dangerous places full of men getting tanked as fast as they could before 6 pm closing time rolled around. Admittedly, not much good can come from unleashing hordes of drunken men onto the streets all at the one time, but the accounts of the children who grew up around pubs and were not unduly affected by them show there was more to these watering holes than underlying violence and social ills.

The Rising Sun Hotel in North Carlton (now the home of the sleek Italian produce store, restaurant and wine bar, Enoteca Sileno) featured prominently in many young boys' lives, as it was one of the main places to sell afternoon newspapers. There was also a tram stop just outside The Rising Sun where the paper-round boys would flock to sell newspapers to commuters in the mornings.

David Campbell tells of the competitive nature of the paper rounds and relates scenes of boys tearing through the streets, stacks of afternoon *Heralds* under their arms, aiming to get into the pub first and so have 'first go at the bar full of fellows having the daily after-work sip'.

The men always had a soft spot for the paper boys and there would usually be some banter and sometimes a glass of lemonade or a dry biscuit and a piece of cheese from the plates placed around the bar for the drinkers to help themselves. On Saturday evening during the football season, plates of small pies and pasties were put on the bar for the drinkers and after the hotel closed at six o'clock Mr Drear, the publican, would call the paper boys down to the hotel residence door and hand out a couple of plates of pies and pasties. Another service for the Saturday drinkers was the horse and cart, which came around selling Sydney Rock Oysters for about five cents a dozen. The man would open the oysters on the spot.

The pies and pasties served at The Rising Sun probably came from Mack's Pie Shop, which was a little further along Lygon Street. Mack's was one of a number of home-made pie shops that started to open in Carlton at the time. Pies were made and baked in the shop and were served to customers straight from the oven.

Several years after David Campbell had given up the paper round and started working at King & Godfree, The Rising Sun-centred paper round was still going strong and was as competitive as ever.

One of the new generation of paper boys was seven-year-old Heymie Wald. Heymie was born in 1937, the 'reunion baby' in a family of Polish Jewish immigrants who managed to get out of Europe before the beginning of World War II. His father had travelled to Australia first and then sent for his wife and two daughters once he was established. Heymie talks of his family as being 'one of the lucky ones' despite the fact that his father died when Heymie was only 18 months old.

Being so young, his paper round was 'not a serious run', just an afternoon allocation of twenty newspapers that he carried with the help of a leather strap. He still ventured into The Rising Sun though and remembers vividly the 'six o'clock swill', when 'the inevitable drunks would ply themselves with as much as they could before the bell rang to signal the approach of closing time. Then they would order six more drinks because they were allowed to stay after six but not buy any more'. Heymie also sold papers to commuters on the Lygon Street tram for 2p a piece, leaping on at the stop outside The Rising Sun and travelling several stops south before hopping off again. The paper boys had strict allocation of territory and sometimes, if Heymie ventured one stop too far, he would be yelled at and told to get back to his own turf. Heymie never told his mother about the tram part of the paper round, knowing that she probably would not have been overly pleased with her seven-year-old son, leaping on and off trams weighed down with papers and a money belt.

The paper run along Lygon Street also gave Heymie ample opportunity to see what was happening in the neighbourhood. He recalls that during World War II, when there was much talk of a Japanese invasion after the bombing of Darwin, the windows of shops and houses in the suburb were blacked out at night and trenches were built as air-raid shelters in a reserve alongside Melbourne General Cemetery. As Heymie recalls, these trenches, which ran off Lygon Street and zig-zagged up Hardy Reserve on McPherson Street on the cemetery's northern boundary, were apparently built to accommodate most of the suburb and so made superb venues for games of hide and seek with other kids in the neighbourhood.

Heymie also recalls the house of a violin maker in the North Carlton stretch of Lygon Street, near The Rising Sun Hotel. The violin maker lived in a 'beautiful Victorian house with two enormous palm trees in the front yard, one on either side of the house'. Twice a year, when the violin maker had completed making a certain number of violins he would 'varnish the violins and then hang them from the palm trees to dry — I can always remember walking past and seeing these two huge trees hung with all these shiny violins'.

The existence of these violins, slowly spinning under the shelter of the palm trees seems a good indication that Lygon Street had continued to foster the music and musicians that had first appeared in the street with the arrival of Italian musicians in the late 19th century. Just a few blocks from the violin maker's house was the Jewish cultural centre, the Kadimah, the scene of regular concerts and choir recitals, while further south in Carlton buskers continued to make their presence felt in the street.

Robert (Bob) Watts is the proprietor of Watts Corner Shoe Store, on the corner of Lygon and Grattan Streets, which his father bought from the original owner Mr Luttgen in the 1930s. Bob says that his father used to tell him about the groups of musicians that would play on Lygon Street, most notably a group of Lebanese musicians that used to busk near their shoe shop and 'would get stuck into one another' if any of them played a wrong note.

✳✳✳

Allan Watson, son of famed Lygon Street wine bar owner Jimmy Watson, moved to Lygon Street as a toddler, living above the wine bar at 333 Lygon Street. He too can remember buskers in the street, particularly one with a pedal organ who used to play outside the shop. Allan remembers him because he joined the busker on several occasions 'standing next to him with a toy saxophone I had and pretending to play along'.

Lygon Street was also home to Felice Gagliardi and his 'violin hospital'. Felice was not only famed as Melbourne's only violin surgeon — his Lygon Street shopfront was constantly crowded with violins, cellos, basses, guitars and harps which had been sent from all over the country to be repaired — but was also a well-known violin player with a contempt for wind instruments, which he thought of as 'music murderers, not music makers'. Felice had played on the Tivoli circuit and in theatre orchestras during the era of the silent movies and used to hold regular salons at his shop for like-minded music lovers — he would play his 200-year-old Guarnerius fiddle, drink red wine and talk music and life into the night. He is another of the ingredients that added to Lygon Street's unique mix, contributing to the depth and attraction — the difference — of the street that was always there below the surface for those who cared to find it.

Whether or not the wine that was flowing at Felice Gagliardi's musical salons, held amidst the recuperating string instruments, came from Jimmy Watson's Wine Bar will always remain unknown. But, in terms of synchronicity of views and approach, you would certainly like to think that one like-minded business would support another.

The opening of Jimmy Watson's in 1935 was the signal of a different way of doing things on Lygon Street, a reflection of the European influences that had come to the area, but also a desire to break away from preconceived ideas about where, why and what people drank. It may seem like heavy baggage for a small double shopfront on 1930s Lygon Street to carry, but when Jimmy opened the doors late in 1935, a modest yet major player in the establishment of a mature wine drinking culture in Australia had arrived.

Jimmy Watson came from a family of wine bar owners and musicians. His Australian father and Italian mother ran a wine bar in Gertrude Street, Fitzroy, and the wine bar tradition went back further on his mother's side. The whole Watson family played musical instruments — his father, also called Jim, played the flute, his mother Giselda and his sisters played mandolins — and when Jimmy was fourteen he began learning the flute with the ambition to make music his career.

This seemed possible at first because musicians were in demand in Melbourne at the time, both in theatrical productions and to supply the soundtrack for the era's silent movies. During the day Jimmy would help out in the family wine shops (his sister Grace had married Rinaldo Massoni who had a wine shop in Elgin Street and later established the renowned city restaurant, Café Florentino) and would then play music at night. But with the coming of the 'talkies' in the 1930s, the amount of work for musicians

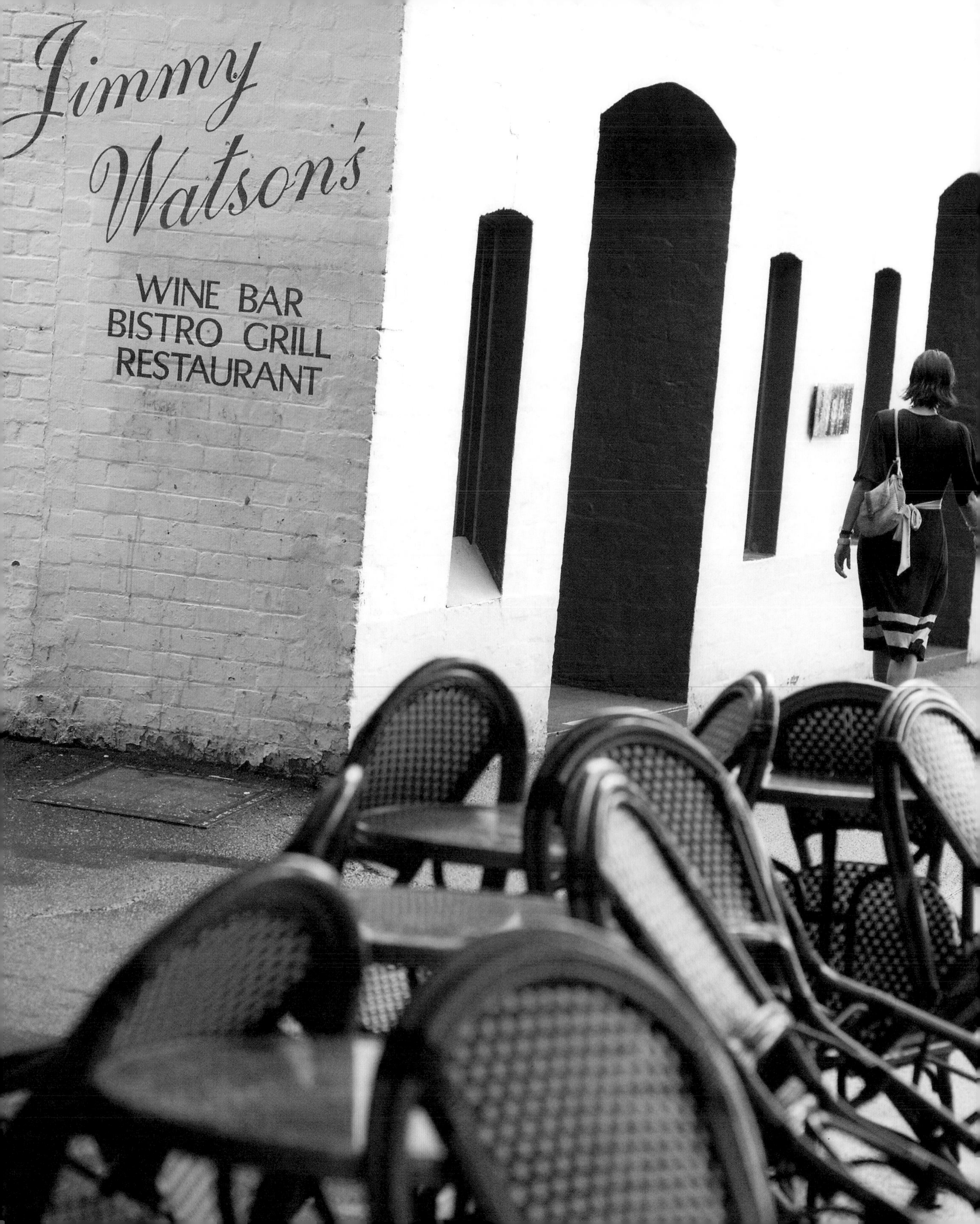
Jimmy Watson's
WINE BAR
BISTRO GRILL
RESTAURANT

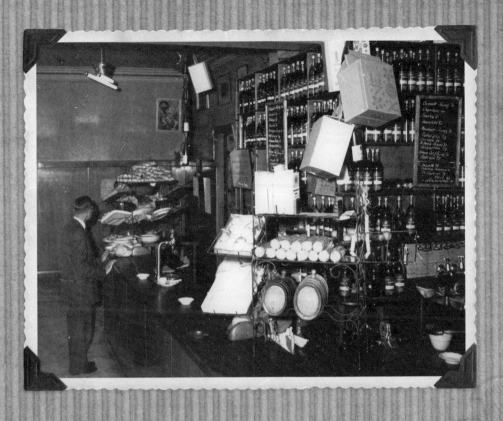

decreased dramatically as they were now only needed to play some music before the show and a rendition of 'God Save The King' when the movie had finished. Having married in 1931 and expecting his first child in 1934, Jimmy decided he needed to have, as his son Allan puts it, 'a fall-back system'. So, when a long-established wine bar at 333 Lygon Street became available, he jumped at the chance and set up J.C. Watson Wine Merchant.

The business he had acquired consisted of two shopfronts with a residence upstairs where Jimmy, his wife and their new son, Allan, lived. The wine bar had a colonial wine bar licence, which meant the shop was only able to sell Australian wine; no beer, no spirits and definitely nothing from overseas. At the time, the general reputation of Australian wine — and the wine bars that sold it — was pretty dismal. Most of the wine drunk by Australians, if they drank it at all, was usually of the sweet fortified variety and was more usually associated with pathetic drunks getting pissed on the cheap than with folk who appreciated the finer things in life. The other wine bars on Lygon Street (including the one Jimmy Watson moved into) did nothing to dispel the reputation of wine bars as low-life dens of iniquity, especially at six o'clock closing time when glaze-eyed drunks were shoved out onto the street, often falling asleep in shop doorways before being moved on by the police.

From the day he opened J.C. Watson, Jimmy was determined to improve the image of wine bars and increase people's knowledge of how good Australian wine could be. The crowd of rusted-on regulars who had been drinking in the bar for years was thinned by Jimmy's policy of no service to anybody who was already drunk. On the other hand, any drinker who behaved according to his unspoken but quickly enforced rules and code of conduct was allowed to stay. In fact, Jimmy worked out a way to keep the older drinkers who sat in the bar all day from getting too drunk. He organised euchre tournaments among the regulars with a prize of one pound or a bottle of Madeira. This, as his son Allan remembers, 'gave them something to concentrate on other than drinking'.

Jimmy was just as determined to kick against the uncivilised early closing laws. He didn't exactly flout the laws, which were heavily policed, but found his own way to work around them.

'Dad hated the six o'clock swill,' recalls Allan Watson. 'And so he would close the doors at six and just keep going. He wouldn't sell anything, but if someone had a bottle of wine he wasn't going to hurry them up and throw them out. There were no sales, so if someone did want another drink he would just give it to them.'

Word spread among wine drinkers that Jimmy Watson's was a different kind of wine bar, one where cheap plonk was not the *raison d'etre*. Allan recalls that the mix of clientele was 'pretty multicultural' from the beginning, with plenty of immigrants from Europe appreciating a place that could provide a decent glass of wine and an alternative to the beer-centric pub culture. The bar became a favourite of academics and students from nearby Melbourne University and, because of Jimmy's links to the musical world, there was a steady stream of musicians through the place. Jimmy would often bring musicians back to the wine bar after they had played their pre-movie set at the cinemas. They would drink wine and play cards in the bar before racing back to the cinema in time to play the national anthem.

Jimmy's mission to spread the word on good Australian wine not only saw him stocking varieties that were not particularly fashionable with wine drinkers at the time — both white and red dry, European-style table wines — as well as the more 'acceptable' fortifieds from areas like Rutherglen in Victoria's north-east. In 1940, he began organising day trips to wineries like All Saints in Wahgunyah and would also bring local and international winemakers and suppliers into Jimmy Watson's to talk to his customers. Such a strategy is commonplace in wineshops and bars today, but at a time in Australia when most wine was referred to as 'plonk', such a move was nothing short of visionary.

The reputation of Jimmy Watson's had grown so much that during World War II, when wine was rationed and the shop only opened on Saturdays, Lygon Street saw long queues of people lined up outside. At the time it was bottle sales only and the demand was so great that as soon as the doors opened at 9 am, the shop would be rushed, cleared out and closed again two hours later.

***

Cured Ocean Trout with Pickled Vegetables

Serves 6

***

750 g (1 lb 10 oz) boneless ocean trout fillet, skin on
300 g (10½ oz) caster sugar
finely grated zest of 2 lemons
finely grated zest of 2 oranges
2 star anise, crushed
1 cinnamon stick, crushed
2 fresh or dried bay leaves, crushed
1 tablespoon olive oil, to serve
lemon wedges, to serve

PICKLED VEGETABLES

250 ml (9 fl oz/1 cup) sherry vinegar
1 tablespoon mustard seeds
1 tablespoon cumin seeds
1 tablespoon coriander seeds
1 tablespoon caster sugar
1 baby fennel, thinly sliced
8 small French shallots
12 caperberries
8 pickled gherkins, halved

***

Initially food was not available at Jimmy Watson's, but by the 1950s you were able to buy meat locally and cook it on the barbecue in the courtyard. In the 1960s the building was renovated to include a kitchen. The menu may have changed over time, but the idea of providing quality food to match the wine, remains the same. This cured ocean trout needs to be prepared a day in advance.

Take out any small remaining pin bones from the fish fillet using strong tweezers or small pliers. Line a shallow container with plastic wrap, making sure there is enough of an overhang over two sides to enclose the fish.

In a bowl, mix together 300 g (10½ oz/1 cup) salt with the sugar, citrus zests, star anise, cinnamon and bay leaves. Sprinkle half of this mixture evenly into the base of the container. Place the fish over the spice mix, skin side down, and cover with the remaining mixture, making sure the fish is well coated. Cover with plastic wrap, to seal, and place in the refrigerator to cure for at least 12 hours, but no longer than 24 hours.

Meanwhile, make the pickled vegetables. Put the vinegar, spices, sugar and a pinch of salt in a large saucepan over medium heat. Add 250 ml (9 fl oz/1 cup) water, bring to the boil, then remove from the heat. Combine the fennel, shallots, caperberries and gherkins in a large bowl, pour over the hot pickling liquid and allow to cool. Cover with plastic wrap and refrigerate overnight to allow the flavours to develop.

Rinse the trout under cold running water to remove the curing mixture, then pat dry with paper towels. Wrap the fish in plastic wrap and return to the refrigerator for a further 3 hours. Using a sharp knife, thinly slice the trout, on an angle.

To serve, strain the pickled vegetables, discarding the liquid. Arrange the trout on four chilled serving plates in an even layer. Scatter a handful of pickled vegetables over the top of each plate and drizzle with olive oil. Garnish with a lemon wedge.

Taleggio Cheese Soufflé

Serves 4

***

SOUFFLÉS

1 tablespoon truffle oil or good-quality extra virgin olive oil
50 g (1¾ oz) unsalted butter
50 g (1¾ oz/⅓ cup) plain flour
100 ml (3½ fl oz) milk
50 g (1¾ oz) Taleggio or Fontina cheese, chopped
1 tablespoon Dijon mustard
2 eggs, separated
12 fresh basil leaves, to serve

SLOW-COOKED TOMATOES

2 firm vine-ripened tomatoes, halved
2 tablespoons olive oil
2 tablespoons sherry vinegar
1 tablespoon soft brown sugar
4 sprigs lemon thyme

PARMESAN WAFERS

200 g (7 oz/2 cups) shredded parmesan cheese
1 tablespoon wholegrain mustard

BALSAMIC REDUCTION

250 ml (9 fl oz/1 cup) balsamic vinegar
1 tablespoon soft brown sugar
2 black peppercorns
1 clove
1 bay leaf

***

These individual cheese soufflés are served cold, with a whole slow-cooked tomato and a parmesan wafer and drizzled with a balsamic reduction — a classic favourite at Jimmy Watson's.

Preheat the oven to 200°C (400°F/Gas 6). Grease four 125 ml (4 fl oz/2 cup) ramekins with the truffle oil.

To make the soufflés, melt the butter in a small saucepan over medium heat, Add the flour and stir with a wooden spoon for 1 minute. Stirring continuously, slowly add the milk and combine well, then stir in the cheese and mustard and cook until the cheese melts. Remove from the heat, cool slightly, then beat in the egg yolks until well combined. Transfer to a large bowl.

Whisk the egg whites and a pinch of salt in a separate bowl until stiff peaks form. Add half of the beaten egg whites to the cheese mixture and fold in until nearly combined, then fold in the remaining egg whites. Divide the mixture among the greased ramekins, smooth the tops, and place in a deep roasting tin. Pour in enough hot water to come halfway up the sides of the ramekins. Bake in the oven for 20 minutes, or until the soufflés are puffed and golden. Remove from the oven, cool and then refrigerate for at least 2 hours.

Meanwhile, make the slow-cooked tomatoes. Reduce the oven temperature to 120°C (235°F/Gas ½). Place the tomatoes in a roasting tin, add the oil, vinegar, sugar and thyme, season with salt and freshly ground black pepper and toss to combine. Turn the tomatoes. cut side up, in the tin and bake for 1 hour, or until tender.

To make the parmesan wafers, combine the cheese and mustard in a bowl. Line a large oven tray with baking paper, then draw four 5 cm (2 inch) circles over the paper. Divide half the cheese mixture between the circles, using them as a guide. Bake for 20 minutes, or until golden and crisp. Repeat with the remaining mixture. Cool on wire racks, then store in an airtight container until ready to use.

To make the balsamic reduction, put all of the ingredients and 150 ml (5 fl oz) water into a small saucepan and bring to the boil. Reduce the heat and simmer for 35–40 minutes, or until the liquid has reduced by two-thirds. Strain the liquid through a fine sieve, discarding the solids.

Invert the soufflés onto serving plates and arrange a tomato, cut side up, beside each soufflé. Serve with a parmesan wafer and garnish with basil and a drizzle of the balsamic reduction.

White Balsamic Soused Sardines

Serves 6 as a starter

✳✳✳

16 butterflied sardine fillets
200 ml (7 fl oz) white balsamic or white wine vinegar

MARINADE

2 French shallots, finely chopped
200 ml (7 fl oz) olive oil
200 ml (7 fl oz) sherry vinegar or white wine vinegar
1 tablespoon finely chopped preserved lemon
30 g (1 oz/¼ cup) currants

CATALAN SAUCE

3 small overripe tomatoes, seeded and squeezed dry
3 garlic cloves, chopped
50 ml (1¾ fl oz) sherry vinegar
150 ml (5 fl oz) extra virgin olive oil

✳✳✳

These fresh sardines are a current feature on the fine-dining menu at Jimmy Watson's — testament to the great changes that have swept through the kitchen since it first started operating in the 1960s.

Lay the sardine fillets on a tray, flesh side up, and pour over the combined vinegar and 250 ml (9 fl oz/1 cup) water. Leave to pickle for 1 hour at room temperature. Drain off the pickling liquid and pat dry with paper towels. Place in a wide shallow heatproof container, flesh side up.

To make the marinade, place the French shallots, oil, vinegar, preserved lemon and currants in a small saucepan and simmer over medium heat for 5 minutes, skimming off any impurities that rise to the surface. Allow to cool for 1–2 minutes, then pour the marinade over the sardines. Cover with plastic wrap and refrigerate until needed.

To make the Catalan sauce, put the tomatoes, garlic and vinegar in a food processor and blend until smooth. With the motor still running, slowly add the oil to form a silky emulsion. Season with sea salt, to taste.

Place 4 sardines on each plate and pour over a little of the marinade. Scatter over the toasted pine nuts and serve with the Catalan sauce on the side.

There were few places on the planet not affected in some way by World War II and Lygon Street was no exception. There was the compulsory blacking out of windows, rationing and the sudden absence of many recognisable faces in the shops as people left their jobs and sometimes their businesses to go to war. (The only time David Campbell did not work at King & Godfree was 1941 to 1946, when he was with the armed services.) In an area like Carlton, with its sizeable visible Italian population, there were also arrests and hardships as many Italians were suddenly deemed enemy subjects under the National Security Act. This act was passed by the federal government, ostensibly to prevent foreign-born residents assisting Australia's enemies, but it was equally put in place to appease public opinion.

There had always been some hostility of the 'they're coming over here and taking our jobs' variety towards Italian immigrants, so when Italy declared war on Britain and France in 1940, there were not too many people protesting the internment of over twenty per cent of Australia's 40,000-strong Italian population. Most Italians who weren't interned had their freedom curtailed (many having to report weekly to the local police station), while others had vehicles and radios confiscated or were forced to close down their businesses and work at munitions factories to prove they were contributing to the war effort. It was difficult for Italians to gather in groups, and travel was forbidden except with official permission. Lygon Street hairdresser Ernesto Angerame was interned and others in the street had their movements and liberties curtailed. There was also a drop-off in business for many Italian shopkeepers as customers avoided buying from places that had the supposed taint of the enemy about them.

All this occurred despite the fact that many Italians had migrated to Australia in order to escape the rise of fascism. In fact, the most virulent anti-fascist group in Melbourne, the Matteotti Club (named after an Italian parliamentarian who had allegedly been murdered by Mussolini) had its headquarters opposite Trades Hall until 1932. Between meetings to decide how to deal with the growing numbers of local Italian fascist supporters (solution: physically intimidate them) there was also a courtyard where members could play bocce and smaller rooms where they could read international radical newspapers and play cards.

Just as it affected every other street and person who had to live through it, World War II also had an effect on Lygon Street. But it was really the years after the war, when waves of Italian and other immigrants flooded the area, that saw the street begin to alter in a way that even the wider community could not help but notice.

Again there was a mixture of migrants joining Lygon Street's melting pot, but they began to come in greater numbers. Jewish survivors of the holocaust arrived in Australia, but with increasingly established populations of Jews elsewhere in Melbourne, Carlton was no longer the only port of call. Those who did settle in Carlton — the ones writer Pinchas Goldhar described as having 'sad eyes and suffering faces', many with tattooed numbers on their wrists — came into a community that may have peaked a decade or so earlier but was still robust and supportive and provided comforting evidence for the new arrivals that Jewish culture had not been obliterated.

But the post-war period was really the time of the Italians. They were flooding into Carlton in greater numbers than any other group and as early as 1947 Lygon Street was being dubbed 'Little Italy' in newspapers such as *The Argus*. This label may have been a little premature as there were only about fifteen Italian-owned businesses along the street at the time — Angerame's hairdressers, Del Monaco tailors and Bosari's bicycle shop among them — but it was not long before the term 'Little Italy' was more than wishful thinking. It is estimated that at the end of World War II Carlton's Italian population numbered about 800, but within a decade and a half there were 7000 people of Italian origin living in the suburb, or about one-quarter of Carlton's total population.

The first Italian restaurants to appear on or near Lygon Street were not really restaurants at all but the dining rooms of boarding houses owned by Italian families. A sizeable number of the first waves of Italian immigrants were single men who filled the often dingy, pokey rooms that had been roughly fashioned from Carlton's numerous large and once-grand houses.

Some of these houses provided meals as well as rooms but many didn't and so the homesick and often poor young Italian men, missing their homes and the food they had always eaten, were left to find sustenance in a strange city that, to many of them, seemed to have an almost barbaric approach to food.

It is well documented that Italians have always been passionate about their food and a journey to the wilds of the southern hemisphere did nothing to dampen this passion (though it was surely tested at times). A good example is recalled by Nando (Fernando) Donnini who arrived in Australia after the war and was, like thousands of other European immigrants, taken to the Bonegilla Migrant Reception Centre, an old army camp near Wodonga in the north of Victoria. Nando, who would later become one of the owners of Lygon Street's University Café, remembers a time when tempers at the camp frayed over food:

At Bonegilla we had a riot one time and they had to send the tanks. It happened because there were 2000 Italians at the camp and in charge of the kitchen they put three Russian chefs and the Russians, they used to put sugar on the pasta. You can imagine what happened with us — we all got angry and then came the tanks and I thought: Oh no, they've come to kill us over the pasta!

Luckily, the stand-off ended peacefully but Nando's search for a decent meal was not over. When he and a friend made it to Melbourne in 1952, they went looking for something to eat:

The only thing you could get was steak and egg and bacon. We went into a place and we couldn't understand the menu but we saw spaghetti on it and so thought we would order some pasta. So we said spaghetti, please, and they sent us toast with spaghetti [the pre-made tinned variety] on top.

It is little wonder that word went around the Italian community that you could get home cooking in some of the Italian-run boarding houses. One of these boarding houses, about a block from Lygon Street at 82 Queensberry Street, was run by Attilio and Katerina Sartori. It became so well known in the community that it was simply referred to as 'Ottantadue' (Eighty-two). The Sartori's daughter, Silvana Mercogliano (who married one of the owners of Toto's Pizzeria, Salvatore Mercogliano), was about eight years old at the time and remembers clearly how her parents' boarding house operated:

Every day there were ten to twelve of these young Italian boys sleeping permanently at the house and my mother would clean and cook for them and so forth. And then every night we would have the rush at dinner time. We had two sessions every night. It would start at six o'clock. I would be at the door to open it when they knocked and I would let them in and they would come and sit down and have their meal with us because there were no restaurants in Lygon Street for the boys to go and have a home cooked meal for little money. This happened seven days a week. We weren't a restaurant, we were a boarding house, but it was where everybody ate. And it was all word of mouth. It was known that Ottantadue was the place to go. With two shillings they would have pasta and a main — minestrone or spaghetti — and then my father would cook some roast beef or something like that. It was almost like a sly grog place in a way, because the boys would come in and eat and play cards, but it wasn't about grog; it was about food.

The Sartori's would later go on to open a legitimate and popular restaurant — La Cacciatora — which is still operating on the corner of Drummond and Grattan Streets — but in the meantime, Lygon Street began responding to the culinary and social needs of the rapidly growing Italian community. It was the dawning of the age of the espresso bar.

There is some push and pull about who really opened the first espresso bar in Lygon Street but there can be little argument that the small shopfronts with espresso machines that began opening in the Street in the early 1950s helped pave the way for the café culture that the whole of Australia embraces so enthusiastically today. From the time that the *Herald* newspaper announced in March 1954, that 'Melbourne has an espresso coffee machine,

the first one in Australia' and named this sacred place as Mario Brunelli's grocery shop at 262 Lygon Street, things were set in place.

Even before the acknowledgment in the press, the little grocery store on the ground floor of a converted terrace was serving hundreds of coffees a day from its Faema machine — not just to Italians but to Europeans of all persuasions desperate for an espresso hit. The grocery side of the business was abandoned not long after. Mario Brunelli sold the business at the end of 1954 and the new owners — David Baccini and Maurice Bertocchi — cut the final grocery ties, renaming the business Café Sport.

✳✳✳

Around the same time that Brunelli's was being anointed there was another café at 272 Lygon Street that not only successfully caught the espresso bar wave but also began providing the sort of affordable homestyle Italian meals that the local migrant population was craving.

There had been a café operating at 272 Lygon Street since the 1930s. Until 1951, it was a fairly typical steak-and-eggs joint called the Mexican Café, but then the owner, John Allingham, took on recent immigrant Ero Milani as a manager. Ero bought the business in 1953 and the whole Milani family — Ero and his wife Eros, their son Gianni, daughters Gladis and Elena (known as Lena), and Lena's husband Nando Donnini — began working there, renaming it the University Café.

The changes wrought to the old Mexican Café by the Milani family were remarkable and were made almost entirely with an Italian clientele in mind. This made it different to most other restaurants operating in Melbourne that had to cater to the wider population. The University Café — like Café Sport and another café that opened on Lygon Street at around the same time, the Capri — not only saw itself as a place to provide food and coffee (and the occasional illegal glass of wine), but as a social hub where Italians could come together, exchange news from home, play cards and billiards, drink wine and reminisce about the Italy they had left behind.

According to Lena Donnini, there was not any awareness of them doing anything groundbreaking or revolutionary at the University Café. Certainly

Opposite: Elena (Lena) Donnini, daughter of Ero and Eros Milani who founded the University Café on Lygon Street. Lena married Fernando Donnini and continued working at the University until it was sold in the 1970s. Her presence is still felt on Lygon Street today, working occasionally in her grandson's restaurant, called Donnini's, which is located directly opposite the University Café (now known as the Universita).

they were creating a business that would cater to a gap in the market, but the Milani family simply set about creating the type of restaurant that they were familiar with; the sort of place that was something of a family tradition. Lena explains the birth of the University Café almost as if it was something that ran in the blood:

At the Mexican Café there was steak and eggs and bacon and it was a bit dirty when we went into partnership. When we opened in the 1950s we mostly opened to feed other Italians, mostly, yes. There were lots of single men living in Carlton who had no families with them and so places like this were like a home. We were just cooking the food that we cooked at home, that we learned from our mothers and our aunties and our nonnas.

I was from the north [of Italy] and so my mother and me started making what we were making at home. Everyone in Italy learned from their mama, from their family. My grandmother used to make tortellini with the broth and they would teach us how to do it. And all my grandchildren come here to learn and it is good to give them something that they can do, that they can make.

Tiberio Donnini, son of Nando and Lena, passionately believes that the birth of great Italian food in Melbourne started with the food cooked by people like his grandmother Eros Milani, and Nora Moar who was working at Café Sport:

One of the biggest people for food on this street was without a doubt my grandmother. Every bit of Italian food in Melbourne of any decency comes from my nonna. My grandmother was the first person in Australia to sell hand-made tortellini and ours was the first family to consider producing that sort of quality of food. Even the great Italian restaurants in town of that era, the Societies and the Florentinos and the Marios of the time, their menus were that Americanised, internationalised bistro-style food, you know, mixed grill and all of that. They just weren't serving the hand-made, home-style, regional dishes that my grandmother was producing.

***

Fresh Pasta

Serves 6–8 (makes about 1.25 kg/2 lb 12 oz)

* * *

**1 kg (2 lb 4 oz/8 cups) plain flour
8 eggs**

* * *

This pasta recipe is the basis for making all types of pasta at home. It is a staple at Donnini's Pasta Shop on Lygon Street, which was first opened by Tiberio Donnini (now owned by Gianni Omizzolo). This recipe is similar in style to the original pasta recipes that Tiberio's grandmother, Eros Milani, started making in the 1950s at the University Café.

Sift the flour onto a work surface to create a mound, then push your fist into the middle so it looks like a volcano.

Crack the whole eggs, one at a time, into the middle of the mound and add a pinch of salt. Use a fork to beat in the eggs and continue to beat in a circular motion, incorporating a bit more of the flour 'walls' as you go, until you have to discard the fork and use your hands.

Form the dough into a ball and knead it with the palm of your hands for about 10 minutes. If it feels a bit sticky, just sprinkle a bit of extra flour over the top and keep kneading — you will know when it is ready when you can push the tip of your finger into the dough and it comes out clean and the dough bounces back. Place the dough in a bowl, cover with plastic wrap and rest for about 20 minutes.

Clean and dry your work surface and dust with fresh flour to prevent sticking. Divide the dough into six equal portions — re-cover any portions that are not being worked on. Set your pasta machine at the widest opening. Flatten one portion of the dough with your hands so it roughly fits the pasta machine and pass it through the rollers. Fold the pasta into half or thirds as it starts to expand to fit it back through the rollers until the dough is even and smooth — as you work you will

need to reduce the setting to the required thickness. (Lasagne sheets will need to be thicker than other pastas.)

Lay your pasta sheet on clean tea towels to dry for about 20 minutes while you prepare the remaining dough portions — times will vary depending on the temperature and conditions of the room but the pasta should be transparent and retain its elasticity — turn a corner of the sheet over onto itself and if it does not stick it is ready. If you are making tortellini (see recipe page 118), then there is no need to dry the pasta — it should be a little sticky to help seal.

The pasta can be cut into any shape using a knife or pasta machine. You will need to use a knife to cut the pasta into lasagne sheets, although you may find it easier using the machine to cut taglietelle, spaghetti and angel hair pasta — follow the manufacturer's instructions. If the machine does not cut the pasta cleanly, then wait a little longer for it to dry and try again.

***

Stracciatella

Serves 6

✳✳✳

CHICKEN BRODO
1.5 kg (3 lb 5 oz) whole chicken
1 onion, unpeeled
2 sticks celery
2 carrots, peeled

4 eggs
a pinch of ground nutmeg
4 tablespoons freshly grated Parmigiano Reggiano cheese
2 teaspoons chopped flat-leaf parsley

✳✳✳

The name of this soup translates literally as 'torn eggs' and is a personal favourite of Tiberio Donnini.

Put the chicken and vegetables into a large stockpot with a lid. Pour in 3 litres (105 fl oz/12 cups) water to cover the chicken completely. Bring to the boil over high heat, then reduce the heat to as low as possible, cover and simmer for 1½ hours.

Remove the chicken and reserve for later use. Strain the broth through a fine sieve, discarding the vegetables. Strain again so that the liquid runs clear. Place the broth in a clean saucepan and bring to a rapid boil. (If you intend to freeze the broth for later use, first refrigerate it overnight, skimming off any fat that rises to the surface before freezing. The broth can be stored in the freezer for up to 3 months.)

In a bowl, mix together the eggs, nutmeg, Parmigiano Reggiano and parsley and season with freshly ground black pepper.

Stirring slowly, pour the egg mixture into the broth in a thin stream — be careful not to whisk in the eggs — the eggs will cook in the broth and form strands, giving the eggs their torn appearance — it should take about 3 minutes. Remove from the heat and serve immediately.

Tortellini

Serves 4

***

1 quantity of fresh pasta (see recipe page 114)

FILLING
1 tablespoon butter
50 g (1¾ oz) lean minced (ground) pork
50 g (1¾ oz) lean minced (ground) veal
50 g (1¾ oz) minced (ground) chicken
3 slices ham
3 slices prosciutto
3 slices mortadella
½ fresh nutmeg, grated
150 g (5½ oz/1½ cups) freshly grated Parmigiano Reggiano cheese
2 eggs

***

Tortellini are versatile and you can use almost any filling and sauce, although these are arguably best served in a broth (see recipe for chicken brodo, page 117). The filling is best prepared a day in advance of the pasta, to allow the flavours to develop.

To make the filling, heat the butter in a frying pan over high heat and fry the pork, veal and chicken until cooked through. Remove from the heat and allow to cool.

Transfer the meat and remaining ingredients to a food processor. Season with salt and freshly ground black pepper and blend to form a thick, smooth paste. Allow to cool, cover with plastic wrap and refrigerate, preferably overnight, until you are ready to make the tortellini.

Cut the rolled pasta sheets into rounds with a 5 cm (2 inch) biscuit cutter (if you do not have one of these cut it into 5 cm/2 inch squares instead). Place 1 teaspoon of the filling mixture into the centre of each round and fold over to make half-moon shapes, sealing the edges firmly together. Wrap each tortellini around your finger to cusp it in a ring and seal the two bottom edges together. After you have made each tortellini, set them aside on a tray and cover with a clean tea towel while you make the remaining tortellini.

Drop the tortellini in a saucepan of salted boiling water, return to the boil, then cook for 8–10 minutes. Drain and serve with your favourite sauce over the top. If you are making tortellini in brodo, drop the tortellini into a large saucepan of boiling broth and cook for 5 minutes, then divide the shells and broth between shallow bowls. You should allow for about 15 tortellini shells per person.

119

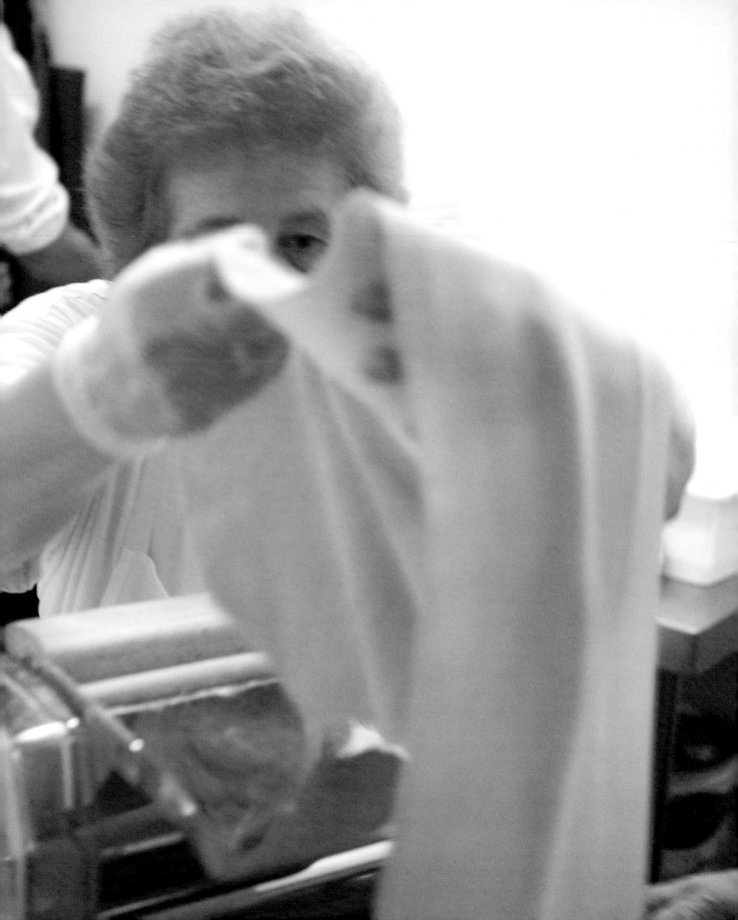

There is no doubt a million arguments about who did what when with Italian food in Melbourne, but there is a good case to be made that places like the University Café were the forerunners of the way we eat in restaurants today. The fashionable restaurants in Melbourne — and in the rest of Australia — particularly those in the city, stuck to the dominant restaurant paradigm of the era: you presented a printed menu and the kitchen produced the dishes on that menu, day in and day out, until the menu changed and was reprinted. Places like the University Café that were catering to a largely, if not exclusively, Italian working-class clientele did things differently. The kitchens, run by women who were cooking in the way they had learned at home, offered fewer dishes every day, but each day those dishes changed.

At the University there was a different soup every day, a different pasta every day, fish on Fridays and, without fail, the wonderfully nurturing and comforting hand-made veal tortellini in chicken brodo on Sundays. There might be *rigatoni alla matriciana* on Wednesdays and on Mondays risotto made with chicken hearts and mushrooms. Thursdays could see calves liver or tripe alongside the inevitable gnocchi and, on Saturdays, there would always be a roast, perhaps porcetta, perhaps beef. Consider that the University Café was, from 1954, pumping out gallons of coffee from its three-group Gaggia espresso machine (now on display in the front window) from six o'clock in the morning for the shift workers before they clocked on in the nearby factories and then in the afternoons when they clocked off again. There is little wonder that the Italian community was drawn to the place: it was a home away from home.

Not only was the Milani family's University Café a surrogate home to many, it also became something of a club. The upstairs residence housed Gianni Milani, who worked as a waiter in the family business. It was also home to three billiard tables in the front room overlooking Lygon Street, where many of the single men from the surrounding boarding houses would gather together. Though there was nothing actually illegal about billiards, they did have something of a seedy reputation, which tended to attract the attention of the police. Much attention was also given to the fact that wine was being illegally served on the premises, a big deal at the time of six o'clock closing and voracious vice squads. Italians were not big drinkers and so the threat of the gathered foreigners getting oiled and rampaging among respectable Aussie citizens was never going to eventuate. But the ruse (albeit a fairly obvious one) of serving wine to customers in Coca-Cola bottles and coffee cups to circumvent the law was like a red rag to a bull for the authorities, particularly at a time when southern European migrants in general were being looked on with some hostility.

Tales of police violence towards young Italian men are common among the Italians who lived in Carlton during this time. One man says he was bashed by the police after he 'said some words I was not supposed to say' and was then told not to go to the hospital if he knew what was good for him. Other tales from those who ran boarding houses tell of many of the young men afraid to go out at night, particularly if they didn't speak English, through fear of the police.

The University Café was raided on a regular basis and, sometimes, there was enough evidence found to drag one of the family down to the local cop shop and charge them. But mostly business went on as usual. There were plenty more strings to the University Café's bow than a bit of billiards and under-the-counter wine. Sport was an important one of these strings.

The University quickly gained a reputation among sports lovers as the place where the Italian boxers or jockeys visiting Australia to compete, would come to have dinner and meet the local Italian community. Nando Donnini was a boxing trainer and so many of the Italian boxers who came to Melbourne used to stay at the Donnini's house in North Carlton and would go to the University to eat. There were many Friday nights when the University was full to overflowing with excited male Italian boxing fans, eager to talk statistics and just as eager to hear news from home.

***

Tiberio Donnini recalls that the sight of all the Italians out on the street near the University Café always drew police attention:

On Friday nights when everybody would gather there would be a crowd outside the café and the police would come along and say: Move, move you can't stand here. There was a law at the time that said if there was more than three of you standing outside at the same time you were consorting. It was something none of the Italians could understand — that you weren't even allowed to stand on the footpath.

It is not that hard to understand that a crowd outside a café on Lygon Street at night time would draw attention to itself as there was so little else going on in the street at the time.

Nando Donnini recalls, 'Lygon Street was dead, there was nothing there, just the yellow light from the street lights, by 8 pm there was nothing.'

It is no wonder that these new cafés were so popular, particularly when they provided some life, noise and chatter away from the dark and silent street and the claustrophobic atmosphere of boarding house rooms. But beyond the warm and fuzzy nostalgia that these undoubtedly enjoyable scenes of home-style meals eaten among the noise of Italian being spoken and the hiss of the espresso machine evoke, it is easy to forget how limited a phenomenon this was in the 1950s, not only in Lygon Street but also in the rest of the country. It was also a phenomenon that was almost exclusively available to men.

Silvana Mercogliano, the daughter of the Sartoris who ran the Ottantadue boarding house, remembers Lygon Street at the time as not being particularly female friendly. She recalls her mother instructing her not to walk past the wine saloon at the southern end of the street where the drunks would spill out at six o'clock, many of them 'literally collapsing on the street and just lying there'. The Lygon Street espresso bars, too, were places she would never go, except on the odd occasion when her father would take her to have an espresso:

I can remember my father taking me to have an espresso in one of the first espresso bars that opened, the Mamba Coffee Lounge. It was in a terrace house that they had turned into a café and it had a pinball machine, a bar, a couple of tables, a jukebox and a coffee machine. I can remember it was all Italians, there were no Australians coming in at this stage.

If you went to those coffee bars in the 1950s it was all men, cigarette smoke, coffee and lots of chat. It was a place that the Italian men went to socialise without the wives but without going to the pub because the pub really wasn't an Italian thing. Lygon Street was a place that the men would go after dinner. They would have dinner at home and then would leave the wives at home and go and have a coffee or maybe a grappa and sit and chat to their mates about the soccer or politics. It was a place to be away from the women — very much a man's domain.

This idea of Lygon Street — and its growing number of espresso bars — catering to a fairly prescribed clientele was an impression that many people in the area had at the time.

Tom Lowenstein was a student at Melbourne University during the mid-1950s. His father, Joseph, owned Carlton Kosher Butcher at 338 Lygon Street, a place renowned for the quality of its smallgoods — 'frankfurts, salamis, liverwurst, a lot of sausages'. These were distributed throughout Australia and attracted both Jewish and non-Jewish customers in Melbourne to the Lygon Street store. Joseph Lowenstein had been a smallgoods maker in his native Czechoslovakia but the horrors of World War II — including his and his family's internment in concentration camps — led him to bring his family, including the teenaged Tom, to Australia.

The Lowensteins settled initially in East Brunswick, moving into a house just off Lygon Street. Joseph started working at the kosher butchers Batagol Brothers & Co. in Lygon Street. He saved enough money to buy Watkins Butchers, an existing kosher butcher business in Lygon Street, between Faraday and Elgin Streets. The family moved to Caulfield but, with the butcher shop and Tom's enrolment at Melbourne University, their ties with Carlton remained.

The block where Carlton Kosher Butcher plied its trade also included espresso bars, grocery stores, fruit shops and chemists owned by Italians, Jews and Anglo-Australians. There were also iconic businesses such as Jimmy Watson's Wine Bar and King & Godfree on this particular stretch and, less than a block away, places like the University Café. For Lygon Street in the 1950s, this was where much of the action was to be had. But for Tom Lowenstein, who began helping his father in the business some mornings, Lygon Street seemed more like a friendly sleepy neighbourhood shopping strip and 'wasn't really on the radar' as a place to go:

As soon as I had my licence and I could drive I used to go to the shop early on Thursday mornings to help pack the parcels that were going interstate and then drive them down to the railway station at Spencer Street to put them on the train to Sydney and so forth. That was when I started going regularly to Lygon Street. Very soon after I started working in the business there was an espresso bar that opened directly next to my father. I'd get up at three or four in the morning, hop in the car and drive to Lygon Street and the first thing I would do is hop in next door for a coffee.

What was interesting at that time was there was always a group of men in the espresso bar, migrants who had come out to Australia who had left their families in Italy and were sending money back home. So at five o'clock in the morning, there would be a dozen men in there and every night they were in there too. I remember they had a table soccer machine. In fact a lot of my friends whenever we were out in that direction, we would pop in for a couple of games of soccer. But normally if we went out we would go into the city, it was much more popular.

The main reason I would end up in Lygon Street was because my father was there. The espresso bars just had people sitting around at tables, drinking coffee — lonely men sitting around talking and playing cards. They weren't places where you would have a mixture of people. I don't think I ever saw a woman in there.

Lygon Street might not yet have registered on the radars of even the nearby uni students in the early- to mid-1950s, but as the decade moved into its second half there were signs in some of the businesses that new ingredients were being gradually added to the melting pot, most notably from the wider Anglo community.

At the University Café, on the crowded nights when visiting Italian sports people, most notably the boxers, would gather to eat and chat it became increasingly commonplace to see a small but noticeable number of Australian sports journalists mingling with the Italians, looking for the information and the stories that they could not get anywhere else. Tiberio Donnini believes that these sports writers were among the first to spread the word about Lygon Street and its Italian food.

✳✳✳

Just around the corner from Lygon Street on Faraday Street, next door to the Carlton Moviehouse that opened as the Carlton Picture Palace in 1924, was Genevieve's. This Italian café attracted an incredibly eclectic crowd of students, nurses and doctors from the nearby Royal Melbourne Hospital, musicians, shopkeepers, Greeks, Jews, Italians, Aussies, Lebanese, all drawn by the energy and the constant crowd, not to mention the quick, cheap food. As Tom Lowenstein says, 'We didn't really get as far as Lygon Street because we always reached Genevieve's first.'

And then of course there was Jimmy Watson's Wine Bar that continued to attract Europeans, Australian wine lovers and an ever-increasing trade from Melbourne University. According to Allan Watson, the place had always been popular with university academics but during the 1950s students were also drawn to Jimmy Watson's as a place that offered a slice of low-key European-style sophistication. Most people who went to Jimmy Watson's during the 1950s talk about the relief of finding somewhere to go and have a drink that wasn't a pub, in a crowd that was tolerant, no matter who you were.

Jimmy Watson's didn't serve food in the 1950s but there were always bowls of kabana from one of the local smallgoods makers or cheese from a nearby delicatessen to snack on at the bar. Watson's had no rule against people bringing their own food in to eat and so that is what a lot of people did.

Tom Lowenstein remembers coming down in the afternoon to Lygon Street with some mates from uni, grabbing a roll from one of the local delis and then going into his father's shop to get frankfurts. They would then take their hot dog over to Jimmy Watson's and eat it over a glass of wine in the garden out the back.

At one stage, Jimmy decided to provide a free lunch on Wednesdays, cooked by the chef from the reception centre the family owned and ran in Ascot Vale. There might be a goulash, cabbage rolls, curries, stuffed peppers or pasta, but when the word got out about the free food, the place began to fill with people who had never appeared before and who never came at any other time and so the free food experiment came to an abrupt halt.

A few years after this, Jimmy decided to put a barbecue in the courtyard out the back. He didn't supply any food to cook on the barbecue — that was up to the customers — but he provided plates, knives, forks and napkins free of charge. People would head across the road or up the street to grab a steak or some sausages or chops, some bread rolls from the deli, perhaps some salad vegetables from Victor Hecht's fruit shop just a couple of doors down, and then cook their own lunch. Allan Watson said that at one stage they were 'sending so many people up the road to Williams butcher that Mr Williams came down and offered to send some steaks down on a platter so people could buy them here'. Soon after, the nearby grocery store Moran and Cato's started making up salad platters for them and they sold those in the wine bar too.

So Jimmy's diverse crowd — workers and academics, students and businessmen, artists and defence force personnel, Europeans and Australians — all came together around the barbie, clutching glasses of wine and barbecue tongs. For many people who had grown up in Australia this was a different, and glamorous, mix of people, egalitarian but sophisticated. It was new and exciting and word started to spread about the culture that was brewing on Lygon Street.

LYGON STREET THE RIGHT INGREDIENTS

Of course, this sort of mingling was nothing new to the people who had businesses on Lygon Street. By the 1950s the street had 100 years of practice at accepting all comers, and it is one of the most frequent assertions you hear from the Lygon Street shop owners of the time about how friendly and village-like the street was — that everybody knew everybody and looked out for them.

This neighbourly culture was particularly advantageous at one point for Carlton Kosher Butcher. Tom Lowenstein says that there was an Italian chemist, Mr Montegano, directly opposite his father's butcher shop who called him over one time to ask him about what was going on with their deliveries of chickens:

He said to me one day: 'I'm just trying to work out what the hell is going on. I see a truck pulling up outside and the driver and his mate start bringing out these frozen chickens and taking them inside your shop. But then somebody in the shop starts throwing chickens back out through a window to the delivery driver and then he carries them back into the shop again. I can't figure out how that works.'

It was only later that it dawned that we had one bloke working for my father who had something going with the chook seller. They would deliver 100 chooks and 20 of those would go out the window and come back in and there would be the 120 that we had ordered and paid for. We didn't understand what was going on until the chemist talked to me about this.

Victor Hecht, who owned the fruit shop on the corner of Elgin Street and who had arrived in Australia in 1951, remembers Lygon Street as a very hospitable place:

People were very friendly to each other, not like now, with all the rush. The people in the street you knew by name and the people would come shopping every day, female or male. You knew everybody by name. It was not so sophisticated. You knew the whole street and it was always 'good morning' and 'buon giorno'. It was Italians and Jews and Australians. It was very nice.

This nice, friendly attitude that had developed in the street, the mostly civil interaction between different ethnic groups and the sense of being part of a community played a large part in Lygon Street's success. Throughout most of the 1950s, Lygon Street played its traditional role of catering to those who lived in Carlton, albeit now providing a few more things to do than shop for groceries or shoes. But the 1960s were approaching, the time when Lygon Street would be 'discovered' by many more people from beyond the borders of Carlton. While there were many factors that contributed to Lygon Street's increasing popularity, one of the most significant of these was the 1956 Melbourne Olympic Games.

Tiberio Donnini believes that it was the Olympic Games that really solidified Lygon Street's reputation as 'Little Italy' because it was the place where many of the Italian Olympic team and their support staff would go to eat. He says that they 'would finish off their day at Olympic Park or the MCG and because there was hardly any night venues then, they would come to the University Café to eat'.

Nando Donnini remembers that the Italian reporters would also come to the University Café:

I can remember during the Olympic Games there was one Italian journalist, a very good one, very famous, very important because he was in charge even of the soccer. And he comes at ten o'clock and knock on the door and says: 'Mr Donnini, please do something for me. I can't get a meal because everything is closed. I've finished my reportage on boxing and now nothing is open. What kind of country is this?' So we bring him in and make him some stracciatella chicken broth.

Silvana Mercogliano also remembers Lygon Street attracting the Italian team.

In 1956 with Olympics, we had a lot of Italian athletes coming out to Melbourne and where did they go to socialise? To Lygon Street, to the University Café, to Café Sport. A lot of the Italians didn't want to go and stay at the Olympic village, they wanted to stay with Italian families in

Carlton because the food they were serving out at the Olympic Village in Heidelberg was crap.

As well as the athletes and support staff, the Italian Olympic entourage also included a team of trained chefs, proving once again how passionate Italians are about their food. Some of these chefs, seeing the possibilities for a successful life in Australia decided to stay, adding their culinary expertise to the Melbourne pool. Among these was a young pastry chef called Giorgio Angele who later started a successful biscuit company and then in the late 1980s, bought the iconic Brunetti pastry shop from his long-time friend and fellow pastry chef Piero Brunetti.

There were other signs too, that Lygon Street was becoming the centre of all things Italian. The Valmorbida family who had bought Agostino's grocery store (later known as Lygon Street Food Store) in 1952 also bought the landmark King & Godfree grocery store in 1955 (a shop they still own today) and, though continuing with business as usual, put a definite Italian spin on the landmark store.

But the extent to which Lygon Street had truly become 'Little Italy' is most succinctly summed up in a 1964 study entitled 'Italians in the Carlton Area: The Growth of an Ethnic Concentration' written by F. Lancaster Jones. In it, Mr Jones writes:

In 1945 only fourteen shops in Lygon Street between Queensberry and Elgin streets had Italian proprietors, and most of these were the traditional Italian shopkeepers, the Italian fruiterer, the Italian grocer, the Italian tailor and the Italian cobbler. The 1960 Melbourne directory lists forty-seven Italian shops in the same area, including nine espresso bars, three hairdressers, three butchers, two electrical goods retailers, two photographers, two real estate owners, a chemist, a florist, a motor mechanic, a large emporium, and even an Italian hotel proprietor.

Alongside these there were businesses run by Greeks, Jews, Lebanese and Australians. The melting pot was through with simmering. It was coming to a boil.

133

***

WATT'S SHOE STORE

Quality
FOOTWEAR

Pollo alla Cacciatora

Serves 4

✳✳✳

2 tablespoons extra virgin olive oil
1.5 kg (3 lb 5 oz) whole chicken, cut into eight pieces (see note)
2 brown onions, chopped
2 garlic cloves, crushed
400 g (14 oz/1⅔ cups) tinned diced tomatoes
140 g (5 oz/½ cup) tomato paste
1 tablespoon chopped oregano or 1 teaspoon dried oregano
1 bay leaf
185 ml (6 fl oz/¾ cup) dry white wine, such as pinot grigio
185 ml (6 fl oz/¾ cup) chicken stock

✳✳✳

'Cacciatore' means 'hunter-style' — a simple but delicious method of cooking that was ideal, in the time it originated, for hunters in the forest when simple, hearty fare was needed. Chicken or rabbit is suitable for this robust dish of tomatoes, herbs and wine.

Heat the oil in a large frying pan over high heat. Add the chicken pieces and cook for 10–15 minutes, or until golden brown all over. Remove from the pan and set aside.

Reduce the heat, add the onion and garlic to the pan and cook for 3–4 minutes, or until the onion has softened. Add the tomatoes, tomato paste, oregano, bay leaf, wine and chicken stock. Season with salt and freshly ground black pepper, to taste, then bring the mixture to a boil, stirring often. Return the chicken pieces to the pan, reduce the heat to low, cover with a lid and simmer for 30–40 minutes, or until cooked.

Note: To joint the chicken, pull the legs from the body and cut at the thigh joints. Cut the legs in half through the thigh and drumstick joint. Cut through the base of the ribcage to separate the breast from the backbone. Cut the breast in half down the centre and then cut diagonally across each breast, leaving some meat attached to each wing.

Salsa Casalinga

Serves 6-8

***

1 kg (2 lb 4 oz) broccoli, cut into florets
4 tablespoons olive oil
1 brown onion, chopped
4 garlic cloves, finely chopped
800 g (1 lb 12 oz/3¼ cups) tinned diced tomatoes
¼ teaspoon allspice
2 tablespoons chopped flat-leaf parsley
2 tablespoons chopped oregano
2 tablespoons chopped basil leaves
400 g (14 oz) tinned borlotti beans, rinsed and drained
750 g (1 lb 10 oz) penne

***

This Casalinga-style broccoli sauce works well with penne, macaroni or any ribbed pasta, as this will hold the sauce and flavour — when cooked the smell calls you!

Put the broccoli in a large saucepan of salted boiling water and cook for 15 minutes, or until very tender — the broccoli will start to break up and when you squeeze the florets they should be spongy. Drain the broccoli and reserve the liquid for cooking the pasta.

Heat the oil in a heavy-based saucepan over medium heat. Add the onion and garlic and cook for 4–5 minutes, or until golden. Add the cooked broccoli, tomatoes, allspice and herbs, season with salt and freshly ground black pepper, and bring to the boil. Add the beans and 250 ml (9 fl oz/1 cup) of water and return to the boil, stirring occasionally, for 10–15 minutes, or until the liquid has evaporated and the sauce has thickened.

Meanwhile, cook the penne in a large saucepan of salted boiling water according to the manufacturer's instructions until *al dente*. Remove from the heat and drain well. Serve with the warm sauce spooned over the top.

139

Spaghetti alla Marinara

Serves 6

* * *

2 tablespoons extra virgin olive oil
3–4 garlic cloves, finely chopped
60 g (2¼ oz) butter
2 bird's eye chillies, seeded and thinly sliced
750 g (1 lb 10 oz) marinara mix, such as prawns, scallops, mussels
(whole shell), calamari and diced pieces of fresh fish fillet (you can
ask your fishmonger to clean your seafood for you)
lemon pepper, to taste (see note)
3 tablespoons dry white wine, such as pinot grigio
100 ml (3½ fl oz) fish stock
2 tablespoons chopped flat-leaf parsley
750 g (1 lb 10 oz) spaghetti or linguine

* * *

Marinara is a flexible dish and the fish may be varied according to the season. The name literally translates as 'sailors' pasta.

Heat the oil in a heavy-based saucepan over medium heat. Gently cook the garlic for 30 seconds, or until fragrant. Add the butter, then add the chilli and seafood and stir until almost all the seafood is opaque. Season with the lemon pepper and sea salt, to taste.

Add the wine and stock to the pan and simmer for 3 minutes, or until the sauce is slightly thickened. Add the parsley and stir to combine.

Meanwhile, cook the spaghetti in a large saucepan of salted boiling water according to the manufacturer's instructions until *al dente*. Remove from the heat and drain well.

To serve, remove the sauce from the heat and toss through the pasta.

Note: To make your own lemon pepper, combine 1 teaspoon freshly grated lemon zest with 1 teaspoon freshly ground black pepper. Alternatively, pre-made lemon pepper is available from most large supermarkets.

Fettucini alla Carbonara

Serves 6

***

2 tablespoons butter
2 garlic cloves, crushed
250 g (9 oz) pancetta or bacon, cut into small batons
300 ml (10½ fl oz) pouring (whipping) cream
750 g (1 lb 10 oz) dried fettucini pasta
3 egg yolks, beaten
125 g (4½ oz/1¼ cups) freshly grated parmesan cheese

***

This traditional Italian carbonara, with crisp pancetta in a cream and egg sauce, is a popular classic and has stood the test of time on many Lygon Street menus!

Heat 1 tablespoon of the butter in a frying pan over medium–high heat. Add the garlic and cook for 30 seconds, then add the pancetta and sauté for about 5 minutes, stirring with a wooden spoon, until the pancetta is golden. Add the cream and cook for 3–5 minutes, or until the cream has reduced.

Meanwhile, cook the fettucini in a large saucepan of salted boiling water according to the manufacturer's instructions until *al dente*. Remove from the heat and drain well.

Add the cooked fettucini to the cream mixture and carefully stir through until combined and heated through. Remove the pan from the heat, add the egg yolks, the remaining butter and the parmesan cheese and toss well to combine. Season, with freshly ground black pepper, to taste, and serve immediately.

Salsa di Fagiolini Verde per Pasta

Serves 8–10

***

750 g (1 lb 10 oz) green beans, trimmed and cut
into 2 cm (¾ inch) pieces
1 waxy potato, peeled and quartered
1 whole garlic clove, unpeeled, plus 2 cloves, finely chopped
125 ml (4 fl oz/½ cup) olive oil
1 small brown onion, chopped
250 g (9 oz) bacon slices, roughly chopped
1 bird's eye chilli, chopped
800 g (1 lb 12 oz/3¼ cups) tinned diced tomatoes
¼ teaspoon mixed spice
¼ teaspoon grated nutmeg
2 tablespoons chopped basil leaves
2 tablespoons chopped oregano
2 tablespoons chopped flat-leaf parsley

***

This green bean sauce makes a wonderful tomato-based topping for your favourite pasta.

Put the beans, potato, whole garlic clove and 2 teaspoons salt in a large saucepan of water. Bring to the boil over high heat and cook for 15 minutes, or until very tender. Remove from the heat. Strain the vegetables, discard the garlic and reserve the liquid for cooking the pasta.

In a separate saucepan, heat the oil over medium heat. Add the onion, bacon, chilli and chopped garlic and cook for 4–5 minutes, or until golden. Add the potato to the pan with the tomatoes, spices and herbs. Add 500 ml (17 fl oz/2 cups) of the reserved cooking liquid, partially cover with a lid, and boil for 30 minutes, stirring occasionally, or until the sauce has reduced and thickened. Add the beans and continue cooking until they are heated through, then cut the potato into small chunks if it has not already broekn up.

Remove from the heat, spoon the warm sauce over the freshly cooked pasta and serve immediately.

Osso Bucco

Serves 6

***

75 g (2½ oz/½ cup) plain flour
18 x 3 cm (1¼ inch) thick slices of veal shank
125 ml (4 fl oz/½ cup) olive oil
1 large brown onion, chopped
1 garlic clove, crushed
1 carrot, chopped
1 tablespoon chopped basil leaves
2 dried bay leaves
185 ml (6 fl oz/¾ cup) dry white wine, such as chardonnay
250 g (9 oz/1 cup) tomato paste
2 tablespoons chopped flat-leaf parsley
1 tablespoon finely grated lemon zest

***

A speciality of Milan, 'osso bucco' literally means 'hollow bones' in Italian, referring to the shin of veal, cut in steaks across the bone, that is used in this popular stew.

Season the flour with salt and pepper and use it to thoroughly cover the veal pieces until well coated.

Heat the oil in a large flameproof casserole dish over high heat and cook the veal for 5 minutes, turning to brown on all sides. Remove the veal from the dish and set aside until needed.

Add the onion, garlic and carrot to the pan and gently sauté for 2 minutes, or until the onion is translucent. Add the basil, bay leaves, wine, tomato paste and 250 ml (9 fl oz/1 cup) water. Stir well and bring to the boil. Return the veal to the dish, reduce the heat to low, cover and simmer for 1½ hours, or until the veal is tender. Remove the lid 10 minutes before the end of cooking and increase the heat — this will thicken the sauce slightly before serving.

Remove from the heat, adjust the seasoning if necessary and sprinkle with the parsley and lemon zest. Serve immediately.

149

chapter 04 Coming to a boil

Coming to a boil

The 1960s saw change come to Lygon Street in many different guises and from many different directions. Changes blew into the street from the legendary social upheavals occurring elsewhere in the world, but they also arrived in a specifically local form. This was a decade when Lygon Street's ethnic mix began to shift once again, when restaurants, cafés and food stores emerged as one of the street's defining features and when artists, bohemians, academics and disciples of the counter-culture started to appear in noticeable numbers and forcefully stake their claim to this part of Lygon Street's history.

It was also a time when the street faced government-sanctioned obliteration as developers hovered in the wings with plans to raze Lygon Street — along with a sizeable portion of the suburb around it — and transform it into a valley of high-rises. In many ways it was this threat of imposed urban renewal that really increased the heat under the melting pot. Potential destruction made it clear to many people that Lygon Street represented something more to them than just a collection of shops. It also made them understand that the only way they would be able to stop the destruction was to band together.

It may seem unbelievable, even ludicrous, in the current climate of stringent heritage overlays that can protect historic toilet blocks and electricity substations from demolition, that whole swathes of a suburb like Carlton could be earmarked as wrecking-ball fodder. But, while there may have been a growing appreciation in some quarters for the unique atmosphere found on and around Lygon Street at the beginning of the 1960s, there was still an entrenched perception in the wider community that the area was little more than a slum full of unkempt buildings well past their use-by date that were populated by insular groups of foreigners and riddled with crime and immoral behaviour.

These attitudes and preconceptions didn't escape the people who were living in the area at the time and were part of the reason why many immigrants aspired to move out of Carlton as soon as they had saved the money. The noticeable decline in the number of Jewish businesses in Lygon Street in the 1960s seems to prove that many immigrants thought leaving Carlton was, as writer Arnold Zable puts it, the 'first step on the Australian escalator'.

Silvana Mercogliano, the daughter of the Sartoris who opened La Cacciatora restaurant a block off Lygon Street in 1960, distinctly remembers Carlton's bad reputation.

I can remember when I was younger and people would ask me where I lived, I used to be embarrassed to say Carlton because if you said that, you were basically telling them you were living in the slums. It was pretty run-down in some parts but it wasn't dangerous at all. I can even remember that when we opened the restaurant my dad would put the milk bottles and the money out at night and the money would still be there when the milkman came in the morning.

Long-time Carlton resident and active member of the Carlton Association, Chris Lee moved into Carlton in the mid-1950s to study Arts at Melbourne University. She liked the area and so when she landed a job teaching at Princes Hill High School, she and her husband decided to settle in Carlton.

153

All my husband's relatives said, 'You can't live in Carlton, it's a slum.' It was acceptable to be here as a student but not to settle here. My mum was a farmer's wife and she wasn't snobbish in any way, but she thought of it as a place where Squizzy Taylor was likely to shoot you, or the painters and dockers might throw a bomb. I can remember going into the city and trying to cash a cheque. If you said you lived in Carlton nobody would cash it ... When we went to get our first bank loan, we couldn't borrow

Top: Aldo Tasca (right) and Johnny Bogotto at work behind the counter of the Varrenti Grocery Shop on Lygon Street. Norina 'Mamma' Varrenti opened the 'High Class Continental and Australian Grocery and Delicatessen' in 1952 and sold mostly imported Italian food products, such as chocolates, cheeses, tinned foods and olive oils, to newly arrived immigrants. Johnny Bogotto went on to own the popular Lygon Food Store. **Bottom:** The Borsari Emporium was opened on Lygon Street (on the corner of Grattan Street) in 1941 by Nino Borsari. It stocked bicycles, household goods, jewellery, and imported Italian magazines and newspapers. It was extended in 1961 to include a sports and bicycle section. Nino and his wife, Fanny, ran the shop until 1992.

money because Carlton was thought of as a slum and people thought it was all going to be razed.

The constant, lurid reporting of crime in the area by the city's newspapers did not help ease these perceptions of Carlton as a hotbed of slum-bred crime. The Italian espresso bars that were proliferating along Lygon Street were the specific target of repeated stories and speculation during the early 1960s insisting they were centres of gambling, illegal drinking, prostitution rackets and the all-round bad behaviour that was threatening to shred Melbourne's social fabric. These types of stories were given the most oxygen in *The Truth*, a notorious scandal sheet that had been launched in Melbourne in 1902 as 'a fearless exposer of folly vice and crime', but was more commonly recognised as a 'wretched little paper reeking of filth'. A story in *The Truth* in January 1961 about 'Jill' aka 'The Espresso Bar Girl' who had supposedly been a victim of a teenage prostitution racket run by European immigrants (but who later was found out to be a hoax) was the type of story that helped set many minds against espresso bars and the streets on which they plied their trade.

Most of the activities that were making newspaper readers in leafier suburbs shudder in horror seem laughably harmless when put into a current context. There were the stashes of wine poured into coke bottles and coffee cups so that people could have a drink with their dinner. And then there was the illegal gambling in the form of card games that ran late into the night in back rooms up and down the street. One of the most well known (to those in the know) of these was held on a Monday night out the back of the University Café. Tiberio Donnini remembers watching the games as a child.

We used to run a Manilla game out the back that was pretty big on a Monday and all the Italians and all the 'hoods' of the era would congregate and we would have a pretty good card game. It started at one or two in the afternoon and it would go for 16 or 18 hours. With a game like Manilla,

155

it was just a churn of players that would keep on coming. Fresh money would turn up at eleven at night and then someone would turn up at one in the morning, somebody else at two. I'd end up asleep on the billiard table. The vice squad in that era started to get a bit pissed off with us and they would bust us every six months.

Obviously there was some truth to some of the rumours about illegal behaviour but there was little happening in Lygon Street that could not be found elsewhere in the city. But it was the presence of so many Italians gathered in one place that gave the stories an added dark menace and allure. Even the newspaper stories about Lygon Street that began appearing in the late 1950s and early 1960s that accentuated the positive, mainly food-related upside of the surge in the Italian population tended to write about Lygon Street and Carlton as if they were sending missives back from some strange foreign land.

In an article in *The Age* newspaper on 12 November 1960, entitled 'Melbourne's Carlton Was A One-Time Suburb of Distinction', writer Mary Holyoake discusses the changes that were occurring in the area:

The most striking change in present day Carlton is the strong Italian influence everywhere; the Italian owned espresso bars, the bistros, the sight of washing hanging up on a line strung across the front balcony of the terraced houses, the sight, during summer particularly, of Italians sitting on the kerb, peeling their vegetables and doing odd jobs while they watch the passers by.

Another landmark in Carlton, but not to be confused with any Italian or 'foreign' influence is Jimmy Watson's, where you can cook yourself a huge steak, drink the best wine the country produces and meet all your cronies … With its rich mixture of dinkum Aussies, cosmopolitans, students and dons, Carlton is a true reflection of the changing life of our old city.

A few years earlier, in 1956 John Monks, writing in *The Herald* noted that 'it mightn't help rapid assimilation into the Australian way of life, but for the next few generations at least we must get used to the idea of Carlton being Little Italy'. Later in the article he writes:

'Yes, Little Italy is there to stay until someone shows the Italians how to live as Australians — and it will be all to the good if the Italians pass us a few hints on the art of living at the same time.'

Even among the more informed commentators of the time, there was a perception that it might take a while but, eventually, the Italians — and the Greeks and other immigrants — would eventually drop their strange foreign ways and weird food and become more like Australians. The changes that were happening on Lygon Street, however, seemed to show that assimilation was going to be a two-way street. As more immigrants opened successful businesses — in particular the cafés, bistros and grocery stores — more Australians found themselves drawn to the shabby but cosmopolitan charm of Lygon Street, attracted to a style of eating, a kind of food and the sort of atmosphere that they couldn't find anywhere else; a place that gave them a taste of an older, wider world.

Stephanie Alexander, who would later open her first business, Jamaica House, on Lygon Street towards the end of the 1960s, was a student at Melbourne University at the end of the 1950s and remembers the street 'before it went bohemian':

This was a time when it was more real, when it was a Jewish and Italian shopping strip. I remember a beautiful cake shop down where Jimmy Watson's is that used to sell very European cakes. We used to pig out on them when we were in the middle of writing an essay. Lygon Street was real in the sense that some of the very first of what we now call 'gourmet food stores' like Agostino's, which was the precursor to the Lygon Food Store were there. I can remember Mr Caputi had a lovely shop that always used to smell of salt cod and other things and I found it absolutely fascinating. They were real shops catering to a real Italian population.

***

John Portelli, who now owns Enoteca Sileno in Lygon Street, Carlton North, also recalls some of the delicious smells that were emanating from shopfronts along Lygon Street at this time. One in particular was Mrs Varrenti's grocery store.

Mrs Varrenti was the real classic old deli operator. Her shop was very clean but she didn't have the variety. Johnny Bogotto [who would later own the Lygon Food Store] worked for Mrs Varrenti. He told me she used to grate parmigiano down to the crust where you can't grate it any more. Then she would put all the crusts aside and accumulate them. All the bread that was left over she would also accumulate it and bake that. And with the ends of the mortadella and salami, she would peel off the skin and mince them up. Then she would get some fresh meat from the butcher and with the parmesan crusts and the breadcrumbs and the salami she would make this incredible mixture and make meatballs. So while she was in the shop she had the stove nearby and she would be cooking up this slow-cooked tomato sugo that she would serve with the meatballs. So you can imagine walking into a delicatessen, smelling the tomato sugo with these meatballs, which had cost her nothing to put together and people just couldn't resist. She used to sell these amazing meatballs that people would take home for dinner. It was like fast food but fifty years ago.

***

It was little wonder then that more Australians were being drawn to the street. Beverly Caprioli was one who heard the siren song of Lygon Street's cosmopolitan attractions. As an eighteen-year-old, she was looking for part-time work and heard of a job going at an espresso bar on Lygon Street called Don Basilio. Part of the reason she took the job was that she needed a job outside of normal working hours but she also admits that she was seeking to broaden her horizons. Lygon Street seemed an excellent place to start, although her mother was not at all happy about the new job.

My mother was horrified that I even came to Lygon Street. She said to me, 'Why does a nice girl like you want to go to Lygon Street?' It had a bad name because there were foreigners and all these stories about prostitution, about girls of the night who would frequent the place and pick up single blokes. Australians were pretty narrow-minded back then and I would always be arguing with people and saying: what's the matter with them, they're alright. And then I'd be saying to the Italians when they criticised Australians: Well why don't you go back to Italy then. I had it coming from both sides but you soon get used to it.

Don Basilio's was more a man's venue with a slot machine, pinball machine and a billiard cellar on the side. There was no cooking, but you could get panini. It was very much male dominated, not the place for women. If you worked there it was alright because you had your place, but if you walked past an espresso bar, you'd feel intimidated because all the men would ogle all the girls going past, and you'd never think about going in. But I always felt safe when I was behind the counter.

Not long after she started working at Don Basilio in 1960, Beverly met her future husband Giancarlo Caprioli, recently arrived from Rome and working at Café Sport, making coffee and washing dishes. Within a year, Giancarlo had saved enough money to buy a half share in Café Sport (for 300 pounds), which the Caprioli's ran until 1965.

After she became engaged and before her marriage, Beverly moved in with the Milani family who owned the University Café 'to learn how to cook and how to be a good Italian wife'. It seems somehow prescient that Beverly was taught how to cook at the University Café because she and Giancarlo own it today, having bought it from Tiberio Donnini (grandson of the original Milani owners) in the 1970s.

I went through something like an apprenticeship with Mrs (Eros) Milani and so the way I cook now is very traditional. Her family was originally from Modena which is famous for pasta and so I learned how to make pasta by hand because that was the way she made it.

Marriage between Australians and Italians was not common at the time and found that there was a fair bit of suspicion, if not hostility, coming from both sides of the divide. Working on Lygon Street with its multicultural mix of businesses might have smoothed the path somewhat but it still took some time for her to feel as if her marriage had been accepted:

It took a while for me to be accepted into the community because the Italians were very jealous of their own young men marrying Australian girls and also our Aussie families didn't like their girls marrying the Italians, so you had all these things in the way. But once the Italians saw you were fair dinkum about being interested in their culture, they would give you an overload of information. They would come along to tell you how things should be done and with all the different regions doing things differently you would get all these conflicting stories about how things should be, how you should cook things a certain way. One region does it this way, while the other does it that way and they were all adamant that theirs was the right way to do it. And then there were all the old wives tales about why you did or didn't do things a particular way or at a particular time so it was a big learning curve for me and then I had to learn the language. All the horizons opened up for me and I became very passionately involved with the Italian community.

∗∗∗

ERSITY

CAFE

Pasta e Fagioli

Serves 4–6

✳✳✳

1 kg (2 lb 4 oz/5 cups) dried borlotti beans
400 g (14 oz) piece prosciutto with skin on, roughly chopped
2 tablespoons olive oil
1 brown onion, finely chopped
1 garlic clove, finely chopped
200 g (7 oz/¾ cup) tinned diced tomatoes
200 g (7 oz) small pasta shells
extra virgin olive oil, to serve

✳✳✳

This Tuscan bean soup with pasta, from the Universita menu, is best prepared two days before you wish to serve it.

Put the borlotti beans in a large bowl, cover with cold water and soak overnight. Drain the beans in a colander, rinse well, then drain again.

Place the beans in a large saucepan and cover with enough water to come 5 cm (2 inches) above the beans. Bring to the boil over high heat, then reduce the heat to low and simmer for 30 minutes. Add the prosciutto and simmer for a further 30 minutes. Add salt, to taste, and continue simmering for 1 hour, or until the beans are tender. (It is important not to salt the beans until they have been cooking for 1 hour as the salt will cause the skin on the beans to toughen.)

Meanwhile, start preparing the tomato and onion sauce, called the soffritto (see note). Heat the oil in a frying pan over medium heat and add the onion and garlic. Cook for 3–5 minutes, or until the onion has softened. Add the tomatoes, season with salt and freshly ground black pepper, and continue to cook for 10 minutes, or until thickened. Add the soffritto to the bean soup and simmer for a further 30 minutes to marry all the flavours. Remove from the heat, cool, then cover with plastic wrap and refrigerate overnight to allow the flavours to develop further.

To serve, bring the soup to a boil over medium heat. Add the pasta and cook for about 8 minutes, or until *al dente*. Season to taste, then ladle the soup into bowls and drizzle with extra virgin olive oil. Serve with crusty bread on the side.

Note: Soffritto is the Ligurian word for the base of the sauce, the ingredients of which give a dish its traditional identity.

Spaghetti Universita

Serves 4

***

375 g (13 oz) spaghetti
4 tablespoons extra virgin olive oil
3–4 garlic cloves, finely chopped
3 red bird's eye chillies, seeded and finely sliced
1 large handful flat-leaf parsley, finely chopped
400 g (14 oz) button mushrooms, finely sliced
1 tablespoon dry white wine, such as pinot grigio or chardonnay
grated Parmigiano Reggiano cheese, to serve

***

In 1978, Beverly Caprioli introduced this pasta dish with mushrooms. At the time, mushrooms were not readily available in the way they are today, so this dish was considered a delicacy.

Bring a large saucepan of salted water to the boil. Pasta water needs to be well salted, so add a generous handful. Add the spaghetti to the boiling water and cook according to the manufacturer's instruction until *al dente*, stirring well to separate the strands.

Meanwhile, heat the oil in a large frying pan over high heat. Add the garlic and chilli and cook for 1 minute, or until the chilli just changes colour. Toss in the parsley, then add the mushrooms and toss until just tender and coated with oil. Add the wine, cook for 30 seconds, then season with salt and freshly ground black pepper, to taste.

Drain the pasta thoroughly, then add to the pan with the mushrooms. Toss to combine and serve with the grated cheese sprinkled on top.

Penne all'Amatriciana

Serves 4

***

2 tablespoons olive oil
250 g (9 oz) piece mild pancetta, skinned and finely diced
2 garlic cloves, finely chopped
2 red bird's eye chillies, seeded and finely sliced
400 g (14 oz/1²/₃ cups) tinned diced tomatoes
500 g (9 oz/5½ cups) penne rigate
grated pecorino cheese, to serve

***

This short tube pasta with pancetta, chilli and tomato sauce is a popular favourite among regulars at the Universita.

Heat the olive oil in a large frying pan over high heat. Add the pancetta and sauté for 1–2 minutes. Add the garlic and cook for 30 seconds, or until fragrant. Add the chilli and tomato and season to taste with salt and freshly ground black pepper. (Take care not to use too much salt as the pancetta can be quite salty.) Continue to cook over high heat for about 10 minutes, or until the sauce thickens slightly, stirring occasionally to prevent the sauce from catching.

Meanwhile, bring a large saucepan of salted water to the boil. Pasta water needs to be well salted, so add a generous handful. Add the penne to the boiling water and cook according to the manufacturer's instruction until *al dente*, stirring occasionally to keep the pasta separated.

Drain the pasta and add it to the pan with the sauce. Give it a good toss and serve in individual bowls with the grated pecorino cheese.

Saltimbocca alla Romana

Serves 6

✳✳✳

12 even-sized pieces veal scallopine (about 65 g/2½ oz each),
pounded thinly (see note)
12 sage leaves
12 thin slices prosciutto
plain flour, for dusting
2 tablespoons olive oil
1 tablespoon butter
125 ml (4 fl oz/½ cup) dry white wine
2 tablespoons freshly squeezed lemon juice

✳✳✳

This is a traditional Roman dish of simplicity and succulent flavours —
the name translates to 'Roman jump in the mouth'.

Lay the veal escalopes on a clean work surface, place a sage leaf on top of each one and season with freshly ground black pepper. Place a slice of prosciutto over the top of each escalope and press down firmly with the heel of your hand to help adhere. Lightly dust the escalopes with flour and carefully shake off any excess.

Heat half of the oil and butter in a large frying pan over high heat. Add half the escalopes, prosciutto side down, and cook for 1 minute, or until lightly golden. Turn and cook the other side for a further 1 minute, then transfer to a serving platter. Heat the remaining oil and butter in the pan, cook the remaining escalopes, then add to the serving platter and keep warm.

Add the wine to the pan and cook, scraping the base of the pan to remove any residue, and simmer until slightly thickened. Stir in the lemon juice, season to taste and pour over the warm escalopes, to serve.

Note: Veal scallopine is cut across the grain from the top round. It should be a solid slice of meat, so avoid slices with any muscle separation as they will cook differently.

171

Beverly's learning curve may have been steeper than that of the average Aussie Melburnian at the time, most of whom were still only glancing with narrow-eyed suspicion in the direction of Carlton. But as more and more non-Italians began to take notice of and venture into the wilds of Lygon Street, culinary horizons were being widened, palates were being educated and preconceptions overturned. More restaurants and cafés opened serving traditional Italian dishes using ingredients that many Australians still thought were good only for pet food or fish bait.

One of these pioneering new restaurants was the Sartori's restaurant, La Cacciatora, that was a block from Lygon Street, on Drummond Street. Attilio Sartori had bought two adjacent buildings in 1956 and opened the restaurant in 1960. The family moved in upstairs. His wife Katerina continued to run Ottantadue, their boarding house in Queensberry Street, for another year because, according to daughter Silvana who worked in the restaurant from age fourteen, 'We didn't have the clientele for us to just rely on the restaurant at first.'

Silvana and her family were never trying to achieve anything fancy or trendy at La Cacciatora. They just wanted to serve honest, traditional food that had been cooked by their family and in their region of Italy for as long as they can remember. It is an the attitude they still take today. Much of La Cacciatora's longevity can be attributed to this straightforward approach that was able to come into being in simpler and admirably under-legislated times.

When my father opened here, he didn't have to get permission or worry too much about permits. He just decided that he was going to open a restaurant in the two properties that we had bought on the corner and so he knocked some walls down and put in a kitchen. Then we put in some chairs and tables and Mum made the tablecloths and that was it. We were open for business. I think we were one of the first to introduce game to the menu. My dad was a hunter and he would go out and hunt and kill the quail and so on himself and he would bring them back to the restaurant and Mum would peel the quail and cook them. We'd serve them to the customers and they would be spitting out the pellets from where dad had shot them. If you did that nowadays, can you imagine? They'd close you down in a second.

The food we served then is the same as we serve now — the authentic Italian cuisine where you leave with your tummy full. There might be two slices of polenta, some pheasant and veggies and we would also have pasta like spaghetti bologna and then scaloppine, minestrone, pasta fagioli. And then we would have the game — rabbit or quail or pheasant or whatever was going. We would also do crumbed brains and things like that, but we didn't do much seafood. That was more of a southern thing and we came from the north.

We had a mixed clientele, very Italian to start with, but then we started to get a lot of the lecturers from the university. We didn't get the students, but at lunch during the week it was mostly university professors. On the weekends we would get the Italian families who had small businesses that would close on the weekend and so they would come out to eat at La Cacciatora.

We also used to do a lot of weddings out the back for when the Italian boys would get married and we would give them half a chicken and some roast potatoes and so on. We had to do the weddings, particularly in the early days because in those days we weren't getting too many people just walking in off the street.

***

173

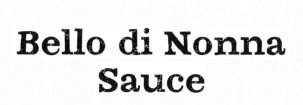

Bello di Nonna Sauce

Serves 4

***

3 tablespoons olive oil
3 garlic cloves, finely chopped
1 kg (2 lb 4 oz) fresh roma tomatoes, peeled, seeded and chopped, or
800 g (1 lb 12 oz/3¼ cups) tinned diced tomatoes, drained
a pinch of sugar
1 handful basil leaves

***

Beatrice, mother of Salvatore Mercogliano who runs La Cacciatora in Carlton, was a passionate cook from San Paolo Bel Sito, Napoli. Known as 'Nonna Bibi' to her grandchildren, her Napoli sauce has gained quite a reputation over the years, stirring a great fondness for her and her cooking! Serve this sauce with your favourite pasta.

Heat the oil in a large heavy-based saucepan over medium heat. Add the garlic and cook for 30 seconds, or until lightly golden. Add the tomatoes and sugar and season with salt and freshly ground black pepper, to taste. Reduce the heat and simmer, stirring occasionally, for 15–20 minutes, or until thickened — the oil will rise to the surface.

Tear the basil leaves and stir into the sauce halfway through cooking. Serve the sauce spooned over your favourite fresh pasta (see recipe, page 114).

Margherita Pizzas

**Makes 2 x 20 cm (8 inch) thick-crust pizzas or
4 x 20 cm (8 inch) thin-crust pizzas**

✳✳✳

PIZZA DOUGH

**30 g (1 oz) fresh yeast or 15 g (½ oz/1 tablespoon) dried yeast
500 g (1 lb 2 oz/3⅓ cups) strong flour or plain flour
1 tablespoon olive oil**

TOMATO SAUCE

**400 g (14 oz/1⅔ cups) tinned diced tomatoes
2 garlic cloves, finely chopped
2 tablespoons chopped basil leaves
2 tablespoons chopped oregano or 1 teaspoon dried oregano**

TOPPING

**250 g (9 oz) mozzarella cheese, thinly sliced
16 basil leaves**

✳✳✳

Salvatore Mercogliano, one of the co-owners of Toto's Pizza House in 1966, made this pizza margherita many times. He is still a chef working in Carlton, alongside his wife, Silvana, whose family owns another iconic restaurant, La Cacciatora.

To make the pizza dough, dissolve the yeast in 375ml (13 fl oz/1½ cups) tepid water and stand for 5 minutes. If using dried yeast you will need to stir to dissolve the yeast in the water; if using fresh yeast, crumble the yeast into the water.

Place the flour and salt in a mixing bowl and make a well in the centre. Pour the yeast mixture into the well and add the oil, stirring to form a dough. Turn the dough out onto a lightly floured surface and knead for 5–8 minutes, or until the dough is smooth and elastic.

Return the dough to the bowl, cover with plastic wrap or a clean tea towel. Leave in a warm place for approximately 1 hour, or until the dough has doubled in size.

Meanwhile, make the tomato sauce. Put the tomatoes in a food processor and blend until smooth. Transfer to a bowl, add the garlic and herbs and stir to combine. Season with sea salt and freshly ground black pepper, to taste.

Preheat the oven to 220°C (425°F/Gas 7). Lightly grease the pizza trays; you will need four 20 cm (8 inch) trays if rolling out a thin crust, or two 20 cm (8 inch) trays if you prefer a thick crust.

Turn the dough out onto a lightly floured surface and divide into two or four even-sized portions, depending which style of crust you prefer. Knead each portion again briefly, then roll or push the dough out to line the base of each pizza tray. Spread the tomato sauce over the surface of each pizza base leaving a ½ cm (¼ inch) border around the edge. Place some basil leaves on each pizza, roughly 1 leaf to each quarter. Arrange the cheese slices evenly on top and bake the pizzas in the oven for about 15 minutes each, or until the base is golden brown.

Alternative: For a lighter pizza dough, add 50 g (1¾ oz/¼ cup) mashed potato to the flour when mixing the dough.

Anatra Marostichana

Serves 2

***

2 tablespoons olive oil
1.7 kg (3 lb 12 oz) whole duck
125 ml (4 fl oz/½ cup) dry white wine
100 g (3½ oz) piece pancetta, roughly chopped
1 brown onion, chopped
1 carrot, chopped
2 celery sticks, chopped
1 rosemary sprig
4–5 sage leaves

SAUCE
1 tablespoon butter
125 ml (4 fl oz/½ cup) red wine
200 g (7 oz/1 cup) tinned pitted black cherries in juice
2 tablespoons brandy or cognac

***

Preheat the oven to 200°C (400°F/Gas 6). Lightly grease the base and sides of a large baking dish with the olive oil.

Place the duck in the centre of the dish and pour in the wine. Scatter the pancetta, onion, carrot, celery, rosemary and sage over and around the sides of the duck. Roast in the oven for 30 minutes, then turn the duck and continue cooking for a further 40 minutes, or until golden all over.

Remove the dish from the oven and transfer the duck to a chopping board, reserving 1 cup of the cooking juices to make the sauce and discarding the vegetables.

To make the sauce, melt the butter in a large frying pan over medium heat. Add the red wine and reserved cooking juices from the duck and bring to the boil. Add the cherries and juice and cook over high heat for 10–15 minutes, or until the liquid has reduced by two-thirds and has thickened. Add the brandy or coganc and stir to combine.

Using a large knife, cut the duck in half lengthways and remove the ribcage bones. Place the duck in the frying pan with the sauce, skin side up, and spoon the sauce over to coat. Simmer for 5–6 minutes, or until the duck is heated through. Serve with mashed potatoes on the side.

Around the corner at the University Café, they were still packing in a mostly Italian crowd though, as the 1960s wore on, there was a small but noticeable increase in the number of Anglo-Aussie faces in the crowd. Sports writers, eager for scoops on the Italian jockeys and boxers who used to frequent the University Café, were the thin end of the Anglo wedge but as the 1960s wore on, non-Italian customers began to arrive from much closer by.

Tiberio Donnini recalls that it 'started with the university professors — they were the first ones to break out — and then the students came because they could come and just have some minestrone and get free bread'. Tiberio says that there are numerous leaders of industry who still frequent the University Café, loyal to the place that helped feed them in their poverty-stricken student days.

The academics and students and, later, the artists and actors who began frequenting Lygon Street's Italian cafés were, as Tiberio says 'the first to open their minds'. And they would have to have been fairly broad-minded because places like the University were not in the business of catering to Australian tastes.

The University (and other places like Café Sport) started using ingredients like calamari, that, in Australia, had been sold cheap at the markets as bait, or fresh sardines that had traditionally ended up as cat food. Tiberio can remember going to the Victoria Market with his father and, when they ordered twenty pounds of squid, the fishmonger would always say, 'You do a lot of fishing, you blokes'. And though it was difficult to get at the time, the University Café always used real parmesan cheese, bought from one of Lygon Street's Italian grocery stores like Varrenti's or King & Godfree (which by this time had been bought by the Valmorbida family) that were importing the cheese from Italy.

Elsie Valmorbida, whose husband Carlo had bought King & Godfree in the mid-1950s, remembers how difficult it was not only to find parmesan cheese locally, but also to convince others to buy it.

There was no parmesan when we first had the shop and so Carlo started importing it. When it arrived, he would take it around to the other grocery shops but people wouldn't buy it. They didn't think any of their customers would buy it or they didn't know what it was. He would come home and say, 'I've left them a piece and said try it and if you don't like it don't pay me for it.' And that was the way he got parmesan out there because people tried it and liked it.

It is these seemingly small touches that made Lygon Street so influential in terms of Italian food, not just in Melbourne but throughout Australia. The concentration of so many Italians in a relatively small area meant that cafés, restaurants and grocery stores that opened along Lygon Street and in the area around it, could offer traditional Italian food and ingredients and still keep their businesses afloat. In other areas of the country where the population of Italians was not so concentrated, it was too precarious for Italian restaurant owners to offer only traditional cooking to a culinarily wary population that loved its steak and eggs, its mixed grill and its French-tinged American international cuisine. In these areas, traditional menus were 'modified' in the interests of assimilation and economic sustainability.

Once non-Italians began to venture into the Lygon Street cafés and restaurants, however, they were being exposed to authentic Italian food, not the assimilated versions that modified dishes and ingredients to suit local tastes (as was — and mostly continues to be — the case with Chinese cooking in Australia). Subsequently, it is no coincidence that Melbourne has the best and most widespread Italian food culture in Australia because much of the current Italian food scene was built on the simple, authentic home-style cooking of these first restaurants on Lygon Street. Australians on their Italian-food training wheels were being exposed to the real thing from the beginning and so it was the authentic that they came to expect.

***

Italians were certainly visible in Lygon Street at this time but alongside the ascendant Italian flavour there continued to be plenty of non-Italian influence shaping the street. Anglo-Australians who started frequenting the street in the 1960s almost always recall a distinct Jewish presence, despite the fact that Lygon Street and Carlton were long past their peak as a centre of Melbourne Jewish life. In fact, the Kadimah, the Jewish cultural centre built on Lygon Street and once the scene of world-renowned Yiddish theatre, pulled up stumps in 1968 and headed south of the river. But there were businesses on the street — Carlton Kosher Butcher, Mirsky's drapers and Victor Hecht's fruit shop among them — that kept the memories of Jewish Carlton alive.

There was also a Greek presence on Lygon Street around this time. It may not have been as pervasive as the Italian influence but Greek-run businesses like the Sevdalis Brothers fishmongers were well established, having been trading at 390 Lygon Street since the 1940s. Another long-standing Greek business at the time was Grenos Café, one of the first cafés on Lygon Street that probably owed much of its remarkable longevity (it also opened in the late 1940s) to having adapted to the steak and eggs café culture. The Grenos is remembered as a shadowy place with a series of wooden booths, like an American diner without the flash and chrome, with a menu that ran the gamut from grilled steak and lamb to grilled sausages, usually served with a 'salad that included tinned beetroot slices and orange pieces'. It lasted into the 1970s, a sure sign that it was doing something right.

Lygon Street also had a Greek milk bar — one of many that sprouted up around Carlton at the time. It was run by the Ageri family and stocked all the usual cigarette and lolly suspects but also supplied olives, feta cheese, halva and loukoumia. Just near the milk bar was Peter's Cordials, run by Peter Evangelos.

Lygon Street was also home to a Greek Church and there was a Greek family living on the street that sponsored young Greek men and women to Australia, provided board when they arrived, organised employment and arranged marriages for the new immigrants. It was an important touchstone for young Greek immigrants and one that ensured Lygon Street is also remembered by the Greeks as being part of their history in Melbourne.

Lygon Street contributed to many histories of many different ethnicities that had been able to coexist for decades, but it was during the 1960s when the many disparate pieces first began to swirl together in what was to become a recognisable style. Elsie Valmorbida remembers the scene in King & Godfree at the time.

We had people of all nationalities coming in. It was Spanish, Italian, Greek, Anglo-Australians, lots of different people, men and women. We had a roaring trade with the university, from all the colleges that would ring up and we would deliver their orders to them. We had wonderful times in the business. We had lots of young people working with us, it was like a family, and there was an excitement about building something and bringing all this new food in that people hadn't seen before or hadn't seen since they'd been in Australia.

It is interesting to note that despite the constantly changing mix of ethnicities on Lygon Street, the phenomenon of the street operating like a village where people looked out for each other remained pretty much intact. One of the most poignant examples of how the Lygon Street community operated occurred on the day of Jimmy Watson's funeral in February 1962.

News of Jimmy Watson's death was announced on national radio and in the local newspapers and more than 600 people attended his funeral. He was a much-loved person, not just for the way he approached and embraced wine and the wine culture, but because he was a genuinely affable host — egalitarian, witty and enthusiastically knowledgeable. His qualities as a host are still remarked on by people who had shops along Lygon Street at the time and so it seems fitting that many of the shop owners on Lygon Street closed their businesses on the day of Jimmy's funeral. Some attended the funeral while others joined the crowd that lined Lygon Street, paying their respects to an elder of the village by watching his funeral procession. On the day of the funeral, the cortege moved down Lygon Street before stopping outside Jimmy Watson's Wine Bar. It stayed there for a minute or two and there was silence on the street as the crowd farewelled and paid respect to one of their own.

187

Allan Watson says that in many ways his father's funeral was 'almost like a state funeral'. But of the respect paid to his father by fellow Lygon Street traders he says, 'It was more intimate then and so the loss of anybody had a devastating effect on the whole street.'

Allan took over the running of the wine bar after his father's death and continued with some changes that he and Jimmy had been discussing since 1960. There had been talk of changes being made to Victoria's liquor laws that would make it compulsory for any place that served booze to also serve food (the changes came into force in 1962) and so the Watsons started thinking about how they would incorporate the new laws — and a new kitchen — into the running of the wine bar. Jimmy's initial thought was to build an entirely new restaurant and wine bar on the site of his existing three Lygon Street shops. He engaged the prestigious architectural firm Grounds, Romberg and Boyd (recent winners of the commission to design the National Gallery of Victoria and the Victorian Arts Centre) to draw up the plans that included a kitchen. After seeing Roy Grounds' initial plans, Jimmy rethought his decision and realised it was renovation rather than demolition he was after. He wanted a building that would retain the atmosphere of the old, much-loved wine bar, while creating something that also embraced the new.

Robin Boyd finished the plans for the renovation in late 1962, less than a year after Jimmy's death. Boyd had a dream client in Allan Watson who agreed to almost everything that was suggested, including removing most of the first floor in the centre shop to create a greater sense of space but excluding the use of louvre windows on the Lygon Street frontage.

Boyd's austerely beautiful whitewashed, Mediterranean-style shopfront was in stark and modern contrast to anything else on the street. It ruffled some feathers but mostly the design was enthusiastically embraced, not just by the architecture fraternity and the uni crowd, but with the majority of its customers and most of the Lygon Street traders.

Leo Donati is the owner of Donati's Fine Meats, which is directly opposite Jimmy Watson's and the only butcher shop left on Lygon Street, the one holding the flame for the many Italian (and Jewish and Aussie) butchers that preceded Leo on the street. Famous for its cotechino, veal and pork meatloaf and quality offal, Donati's is perhaps equally famed for the presence of Leo himself who remains a well-known figure in the neighbourhood. When Jimmy Watson's was being renovated, Leo was yet to own his own business but was working as a butcher in the area at the time and kept an eye on what was going on in the neighbourhood when he was out making deliveries. He can recall being immediately enthusiastic about Boyd's design for the wine bar and remembers the excitement of seeing something new that seemed to show that the area was finally moving with the times.

'It was just shopfronts before and then all of a sudden you have this great design. It looked good then and it looks good now and it's still going to look good in fifty years time. Good design lasts forever.'

***

It was an interesting time for Watson's to be making a modern and dramatic architectural statement on Lygon Street. It was an attention-grabbing move that signalled a commitment to the street's future and viability at a time when Lygon Street was under a serious government-backed cloud.

There had been talk of 'slum clearance' in Carlton since the 1930s but in the late 1950s moves were made to add some action to all the talk. The image created by decades of newspaper stories about the vice, squalor and slums of Carlton had created widespread approval for the idea that the southern part of the suburb should be pretty much flattened and rebuilt. Widespread, that is, except within the suburb itself where there was little consultation with anybody who actually lived or did business there.

The most radical part of the slum clearance plan came from the Housing Commission of Victoria's (HCV) commissioned Perrott Report. This report was based on the notorious 'windscreen survey' of 1960 that involved a couple of HCV bigwigs driving through the area, noting down the areas that they thought were uninhabitable and in need of demolition, without ever actually getting out of, or even stopping, the car.

189

191

Poussin with Sage

Serves 4

***

**4 x 400–500 g (14 oz–1 lb 2 oz) poussin (baby chickens), halved
(ask your butcher to do this)
2 garlic cloves, crushed
1 bunch fresh sage, leaves torn
4 red bird's eye chillies, seeded and finely sliced
1 lemon, thinly sliced
2 tablespoons extra virgin olive oil**

***

This dish is one of Leo Donati's favourites. The poussin, or small chickens, are halved and slow-cooked with garlic, lemon, sage and chilli. The result is a delicious and subtly flavoured roast chicken dish that you can enjoy without the hassle of carving.

Preheat the oven to 220°C (425°F/Gas 7). Lightly grease a large roasting tin.

Season the poussin with salt and freshly ground black pepper, then rub all over with the garlic. Place the poussin, skin side up, in the roasting tin, scatter over the sage and chillies then tuck the lemon slices between the poussin halves. Drizzle over the olive oil and cook for 45 minutes, or until the poussin is golden and just cooked through.

Transfer the poussin, sage and lemon slices to warm plates. Serve with a potato and parsnip mash with green beans on the side.

Roast Beef Fillet with Green Peppercorn Sauce

Serves 6

***

1 tablespoon extra virgin olive oil
2 kg (4 lb 8 oz) beef fillet in one piece, trimmed of fat and sinew
185 g (6½ oz/¾ cup) Dijon mustard
55 g (2 oz) tinned green peppercorns in brine, drained
125 ml (4 fl oz/½ cup) brandy
125ml (4 fl oz/½ cup) pouring cream

***

This recipe was developed by Leo Donati and influenced by his mother, who often used brandy in her veal roasts. The beef is coated in a mustard crust and studded with green peppercorns, then both are added to the pan juices with some brandy and cream to create a delicious sauce.

Preheat the oven to 220°C (425°F/Gas 7). Lightly grease the base of a deep roasting tin with the olive oil.

Tuck the thin end of the fillet underneath to ensure it is an even thickness all over and secure with kitchen string.

Spread the mustard all over the beef fillet and place in the roasting tin, then scatter with the peppercorns. Roast in the oven for 20 minutes for a rare result, or 30 minutes for medium. Remove the tin from the oven and pour 80 ml (2½ fl oz/⅓ cup) brandy over the top. Using the blunt side of a knife or a spatula, gently scrape some of the peppercorns and mustard from the beef and into the roasting tin. Remove the fillet from the dish and place on a serving plate. Cover with foil to keep warm and rest for 10 minutes.

Meanwhile, place the roasting tin over medium–high heat and bring to the boil, scraping the bottom of the tin to remove any residue. Stir in the remaining brandy and any juices from the resting meat. Bring to the boil, add the cream and season to taste with salt and freshly ground black pepper. Cook for 1–2 minutes, or until the sauce has thickened slightly.

Carve the beef into thick slices and spoon the sauce over the top. Serve with boiled new potatoes and steamed broccolini.

BUTCHERS' SERVICE
ENGINEERING Co.
424 RACECOURSE RD.
FF 1062   NEWMARKET.

"Clean Cut"

MEAT SAW

JUNIOR MODEL

The Perrott Report that resulted from the slum clearance plan was released in 1964. It put in black and white all the worst fears of the area's traders and residences — that a rabid, non-consultative government department was out to get them. The report contained recommendations that a huge 160-hectare slab of Carlton — an area bound by Grattan, Swanston and Nicholson Streets and up to Melbourne General Cemetery, through which the main commercial stretch of Lygon Street ran — be completely cleared and rebuilt. Multi-storey towers would replace terraces, shops would be tucked away beneath the towers and wide, straight Lygon Street would act as one of the major conduits by which cars would enter the CBD. Sniffing the desire from the majority outside of Carlton to do something, anything, about the city's 'slums', the HCV proceeded with a confidence (some would say arrogance) of a body moving to fulfil a foregone conclusion. What the HCV had not bargained on, however, was the collective force of will of the Lygon Street traders.

The Carlton Business & Property Owners' Association (CBPOA) was formed to fight the redevelopment and there were many long-standing and well-known Lygon Street businesses taking key roles — Ridgeway hardware, Williams butcher and Del Monaco tailors among them. They formed the association not just because of the personal economic threat, but because a way of life that they really appreciated was under threat and some hard-working people's dreams of stability — both economic and physical — were in danger of being trashed.

Michael (Mick) Del Monaco was an inaugural member of the CBPOA. He had owned his tailor shop on Lygon Street since 1938 and so was obviously angered by the HCV threat to take both his business and his property. But it was more than personal motives that drove him into the traders' association.

For many years, Del Monaco was not only known for the quality of its tailoring, but also as a place where Italian immigrants could come and get legal documents and letters written in English translated into Italian. This had always been something of a small sideline for the shop but in the early 1960s, Del Monaco began to see more and more distraught Italians clutching eviction notices that they could not read or understand.

The HCV had started implementing its slum clearance plans by the late 1950s and there was enforced reclamation of people's homes. People would come home to find Housing Commission orders pasted on their front door informing them that their house had been declared unfit for human habitation, had to be vacated immediately and demolished at the owners' expense. Insultingly small compensation was offered and immigrant homeowners who had put everything they had saved into their houses were the hardest hit. In fact, around half of the Carlton residents turfed out of their homes during this period were foreign-born, more than a quarter of them Italian.

The suffering and heartbreak of the local residents alongside their own potential loss of both business and property drew the Lygon Street traders together. They commissioned and widely distributed a booklet entitled *Hands Off Carlton*, that was both critical of the arbitrary and high-handed way the HCV was behaving and very persuasive about the unique architectural and cultural charms of the suburb. Using the wave of support that swelled in the wake of the booklet, the CBPOA then went on to successfully lobby the state government and had the Perrott Report shelved. Houses continued to be lost and there were Housing Commission towers built along a stretch of Lygon Street (between Elgin and Princes Streets) later in the 1960s, but a brake had been applied to the wholesale destruction of Carlton. Lygon Street had been saved.

This group of traders were the forefathers of the many associations and residents groups that were formed over the following decades to secure the integrity and interests of Carlton, as developers and government housing and planning departments hovered about. They were also the first, in the form of the *Hands Off Carlton* booklet, to recognise and make official the suburb's idea of community, that there was more to it than bricks and mortar. Carlton — and Lygon Street with it — had suddenly become as much a philosophy as it was a postcode. As Giancarlo Giusti, the founder of Grinders Coffee puts it, 'If Carlton didn't exist we would have had to invent it.'

Giancarlo came to live in Carlton, just off Lygon Street in 1962, having arrived in Australia in 1960. He worked at several different jobs, including one as a sales rep for the Valmorbida family and for Moccopan coffee company. While working for Moccopan, he realised that coffee had great potential as a business opportunity in Melbourne and that Carlton would make a good coffee-selling base. Giancarlo and his friend Rino Benassi each put up 1000 pounds (Giancarlo borrowing the money from some Australian friends) and opened Grinders Coffee House at 277 Lygon Street at the end of 1962.

I chose Lygon Street because through my coffee round I had seen that Lygon Street and Footscray at the time were the best areas for coffee because of all the Europeans. In Carlton there was the Italians and the Jewish community, in Footscray there were Italian, Greek and other Europeans but I decided on Carlton because I was living there, just 50 metres from the shop. It was very easy in those days. People would just come in and ask for coffee — there was not the choice or the knowledge around then. I didn't roast coffee until 1969. Until then we just bought coffee that was already roasted and we sold coffee-making equipment and machinery, all of it imported from Italy.

A speciality coffee retailer on Lygon Street was not the only sign of the changes occurring in 1960s Lygon Street. The word that was first being whispered by places like the University Café, the Capri, Café Sport and Genevieve's was now being spoken louder as other parts of the street started sprouting restaurants that upped the anti in terms of décor and prices, and were obviously casting their net beyond the local Italian community. These Italian bistros and cafés on Lygon Street may not have been as upmarket, expensive and fashionable as places like the Florentino, Mario's and the Society in the city, but they were doing something that appeared to be more authentically cosmopolitan, even bohemian, and it was catching an increasing amount of attention.

***

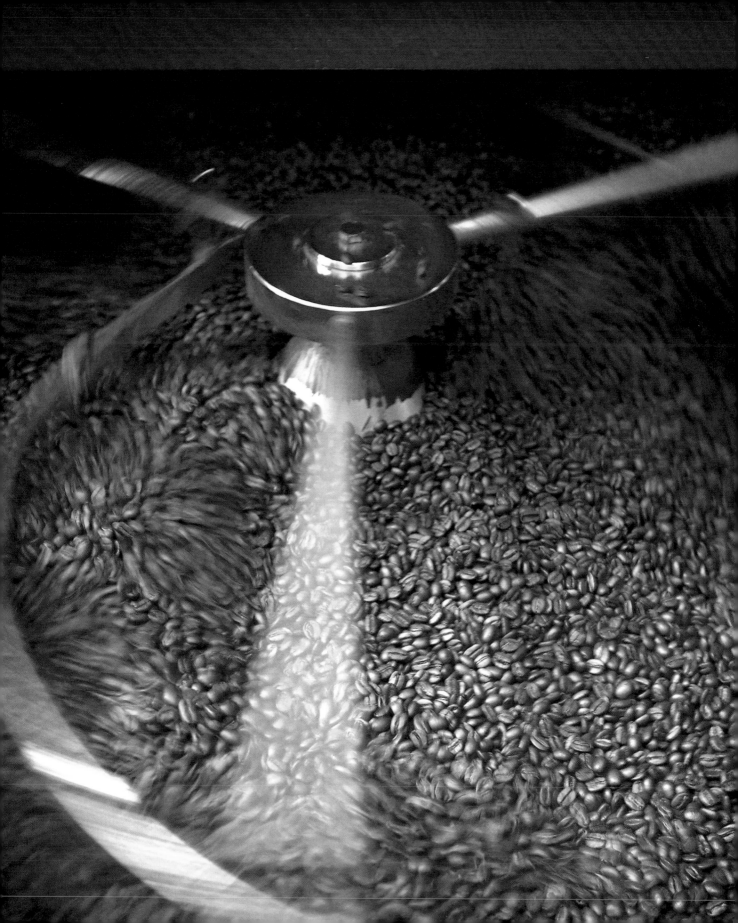

Biscotti

Makes 60 biscuits

***

500 g (9 oz/4 cups) plain flour
500 g (9 oz/2¼ cups) caster sugar, plus extra,
for sprinkling
2½ teaspoons baking powder
1 tablespoon finely grated lemon zest
100 g (3½ oz/1 cup) flaked almonds
100 g (3½ oz/¾ cup) hazelnuts
150 g (5½ oz/1 cup) unsalted macadamia nuts
150 g (5½ oz/1 cup) pistachio nuts
100 g (3½ oz/¾ cup) sultanas
100 g (3½ oz/½ cup) mixed candied peel
150 g (5½ oz/¾ cup) dried figs, quartered
150 g (5½ oz/¾ cup) dried apricots, halved
5 large eggs

***

Biscotti is a crisp Italian biscuit that is ideal to serve with coffee. The combination of nuts and fragrant citrus results in a delicately flavoured and moreish biscuit.

In the bowl of an electric mixer with a paddle attachment, combine the flour, sugar, baking powder and lemon zest. Add the nuts and dried fruits and combine well. Add the eggs in two stages, stirring to combine. You may need to bring the dough together with a 'wet hand'. Cover with plastic wrap and allow to rest for 30 minutes.

Preheat the oven to 160°C (315°F/Gas 2–3). Line two baking trays with baking paper. Divide the dough into three even-sized portions and roll each portion out into an 18 x 8 cm (7 x 3¼ inch) log. Lightly sprinkle a sheet of baking paper with some extra sugar. Lay a log on the paper and roll the log to coat it in sugar. Repeat with a little more sugar and the remaining logs. Place the logs on the prepared trays, allowing room for them to expand. Refrigerate for 30 minutes, to firm up the dough.

Bake the logs for 30 minutes each, or until cooked — the logs should feel firm when pressed. Remove from the oven and allow to cool. Reduce the oven temperature to 150°C (300°F/Gas 2).

Place the logs on a board and cut diagonally into thin slices, approximately 5 mm (¼ inch) thick. Return the biscotti to the lined trays and bake in the oven for a further 25 minutes, turning the biscotti halfway through cooking; the biscotti should be dry and crisp with minimal colour. Cool on the tray and store the cooled biscotti in an airtight container for a few weeks. The cooked loaf can be stored for 1 week in the refrigerator, then sliced and dried in the oven. Alternatively, you can individually wrap the cooled baked loaves in plastic wrap and place in the freezer for up to 3 months. You will need to defrost the log for 1 hour at room temperature before slicing and drying in a low oven.

203

Gina's was one of the first Italian-style bistros on Lygon Street, a place run by Franz Denk, a one-time member of the Vienna Boys Choir, and his wife Gina.

Gina's father was the chef. Opened in the late 1950s, Gina's was a rare beast, a bistro with a licence to sell alcohol. Giancarlo Caprioli who later went on to own the University Café, worked as a waiter at Gina's for a period and, according to his wife , Gina's was where he 'learned about wine and the finer arts of service'. Later in the decade Gina's expanded into a second shopfront and included a dance floor (which many one-time fans believed killed the atmosphere and, eventually, the business) but when it first opened, the small shopfront with its raffia-covered Chianti bottles and rustic wooden features exemplified a certain bohemian chic.

Heymie Wald, who grew up in North Carlton, remembers Gina's as an important venue in the courtship of his wife.

When I was courting my wife Frida, we would come to Lygon Street for meals. I saw coming here was part of the sophistication I thought I had at the time. We often went to a restaurant called Gina's and it was like nothing else at the time. There were checked tablecloths and the Chianti bottles with the candles in them and the wax dripping down — Chianti bottles all over the place. We would be tasting and eating Italian food that we'd never had before and would eat it over a bottle of red and then have to help each other out of the restaurant. It was just beautiful. There was nothing else like it in Melbourne. It felt like going to Rome without buying an air ticket.

Another fondly recalled bistro of this time was around the corner from Lygon Street, in Elgin Street. It was called Ferdi's and was run by Fernando (Nando) Varrenti, the son of the formidable Norina 'Mamma' Varrenti who had owned an Italian grocery store at 305 Lygon Street for many years. Ferdi's had started out in life as an espresso bar with one of the first espresso machines in the country but, in the mid-1960s it went for a change of pace, gained a licence and transformed itself into a bistro that became, as playwright Jack Hibberd puts it 'the haunt of gay dogs, hussies and Stalinists'.

Tiberio Donnini remembers it as 'one of the first bistro restaurants with waiters dressed to the hilt, an area to have a drink in, the whole thing, just like the Society in the city'.

Butcher Leo Donati also remembers Ferdi's.

I used to go to Ferdi's to deliver meat and they had a bar, you could serve wine at the table and this was the first bistro in the area, not a restaurant. It was like the beginning for me. It seemed suddenly that we were in the big world and had at last come out of this dark age. We had a bistro! You could finally say things like that.

Revolutionary stuff indeed, but there was more revolution to come on Lygon Street. And it came in the form of pizza.

✱✱✱

Salvatore Della Bruna had tried to start a pizza business in Canberra as far back as 1952 but an unsuccessful attempt there and in Sydney saw him make his way to Melbourne and to Lygon Street. He opened Australia's first commercial pizza house, Toto's, in 1966. In an interview in *The Age* in 1988, Salvatore, whose family owned a pizzeria near Naples, said that it was almost inevitable that he would end up with his own pizzeria.

Did I come here to make pizza? No. I would have stayed in Italy if I wanted to make pizza and spaghetti because my family had the business from my great grandfather. My father told me, 'You can go to Australia. You can go to America. You will end up with a pizza in your hand because that's the only thing you can do!'

Though it was on the more neglected, quieter southern reaches of Lygon Street, Toto's was an immediate success. Salvatore, in partnership firstly with Franco Fera and then, in 1968 with Silvio Tuli and Salvatore Mercogliano, had definitely opened in the right place at the right time. It was the period when

more and more Melburnians were discovering Lygon Street, and Toto's pizzas — cheap, tasty, adaptable and non-threatening — were able to attract an appreciative Aussie crowd. For many, it was their first exposure to the street and to reasonably authentic Italian home-style food.

Silvana Mercogliano, wife of one-time Toto's co-owner Salvatore Mercogliano, believes that Toto's was largely responsible for fuelling the rapid change in Lygon Street from the slightly shady, foreigner-tinged shopping strip of the early 1960s to one of Melbourne's first fully fledged eating destinations by the end of the decade.

To start with it was just one little shop with maybe thirty chairs. It had a licence to open until midnight and it was cheap and so of course all the uni students came. It was mainly Australians that came, these uni students, not so much the Italians because they already had this food at home. It was the novelty of the pizza that brought them in. The uni students were living all over Melbourne and so when they went to Toto's they brought the attention of all those suburbs — Toorak, Camberwell, Kew — to Lygon Street. The wider community suddenly started to notice what was going on here.

Toto's was justifiably famous for its pizzas and spawned countless imitators (the first was on Lygon Street and opened about six months after Toto's) but its influence went beyond the Neapolitan pie. Toto's was also famed for its self-serve buffet table where the ravenous student crowd were introduced to delights such as arancini, wilted spinach served with lemon juice, stuffed mushrooms, grilled calamari and *cotoletta* (crumbed veal cutlets). It was the sort of food Italians had been eating in their homes for years but that Australians had very little exposure to. As Bianca Mercogliano, daughter of Salvatore and Silvana says:

The buffet was so popular in the 1960s because at the time the Australian food, the veggies particularly, were all over-cooked and the Australians didn't realise that mushrooms and all the other veggies could taste that good. You have to remember that this was a time when eggplant and zucchini were exotic.

209

Just like the dishes being cooked in Italian homes, the Toto's versions were being prepared by women. As the male pizza makers at the front of the restaurant entertained rapt and fascinated crowds by tossing and twirling pizza dough, a fleet of home cooks were working out the back replenishing the buffet table. It was these women, working a few nights a week to supplement their husband's income so they could save more quickly to buy a house, that people like Silvana Mercogliano believe were responsible for a 'golden era' of Italian food in Lygon Street during this period.

It was a meeting of circumstances that saw Lygon Street have this golden era. There were more places opening up like Toto's and Quo Vadis (where Copperwood is now) and the Black Pearl (now Tiamo's) and other places and they needed cooks. Then there were all these women coming out from Italy who were good cooks. Their husbands usually worked two jobs in order to save money for a house and these women wanted to help too. They wanted to earn some extra money but they also wanted to go to work to get out of the house. See, the men had their work and the cafés, the espresso bars, but the women had nowhere to go but the house and many of them spoke very little English and so life could get very lonely. So they needed the money and they wanted to work.

If you had spoken to them in Italy none of them would have dreamed that they would be working in a restaurant in Australia. But because they didn't speak English and cooking was the only skill they had, that's where they went – to the restaurants on Lygon Street. The restaurant owners loved it. Salvatore always said that he'd rather have one woman in the kitchen than three chefs because she would cook better and then clean up after herself. So that was how this came about that all these places were serving plates of really good food, just like what was being cooked in the Italian homes. It was why people kept coming.

And people did keep coming, not just from Carlton and the university, but from suburbs across Melbourne and even from interstate and overseas, many drawn by newspaper and magazine articles that had begun to anoint cosmopolitan, bohemian Lygon Street as one of Melbourne's fashionable destinations. Within a year of Toto's opening, other cheap student-friendly places had opened on the street, marking the beginning of a swell that would completely transform the way people used and viewed Lygon Street.

By the end of the 1960s the street may no longer have been the simple, shopping street of a decade or so before, but it still continued to serve as the main shopping strip for many locals. Despite the attention-grabbing presence of all the cafés and restaurants, Lygon Street still supported a thriving colony of butchers, fruit shops, grocery stores, tailors, banks, dry-cleaners, hairdressers and chemists.

It was the presence of these types of businesses that allowed Lygon Street to hang onto the 'authenticity' that so many people lamented the loss of when the street shifted up a gear and then another in the next couple of decades. It was not just that these businesses existed on Lygon Street, but that they had existed for many years and gave the street a feeling of organic solidity. They made it feel 'real'.

Old troopers like King & Godfree had been around since 1886, Watt's Family Shoe Store and Jimmy Watson's since the 1930s and the Holdsworth Funeral Parlour across the road from Watson's since 1908. There was even a local saying that had grown up around Jimmy's wine bar and the Holdsworth family's funeral parlour that had faced each other across the expanse of Lygon Street for so many years: *Ashes to ashes, dust to dust, if Watson's doesn't get you, then Holdsworth's must.*

There were other long-standing businesses around this time that have since disappeared and have slipped from many memories. Lesley's Ham and Beef, an Australian deli that was a favourite not just with Aussie locals but many of the immigrants because it was known for having the best bacon on the street and had cheeses like gouda, Wensleydale and tasty, that were not being stocked by the Italian delis. There was Papaleo tailor shop, famous for its carefully arranged window displays, Lucchini's cake shop, the original pasticceria on Lygon Street and the Angerame barbers, started in 1938 by Ernest Angerame (known as 'Deadly Ernest'), that became one of the most famous haircutters in town, clipping and shaving everybody from Governors General (Sir Zelman Cowen) to football players (as the official barber of the Carlton Football Club for many years).

213

BORSARI'S
CORNER

EX-OLYMPIC

CHAMPION

RISTORANTE

BORSARI

BORSARI RISTORANTE
BYO & LICENSED   LUNCH & DINNER   7 DAYS   9349 1444

BORSARI
RISTORANTE

PH: 349 1444
BYO   LICENSEE: SANDHURST BAY PTY LTD   FULLY
ON PREMISIS LICENCE   LICENSED

NOMINEE   LIZA MAGNO

These places, owned by people from a variety of ethnic backgrounds, combined to give Lygon Street the unique multicultural village atmosphere that was instrumental in attracting a crowd aware of the winds of social change blowing in from overseas and increasingly eager to try it out on their own turf. Artists, writers and actors flocked to the area, joining the locals, the academics and the students and forcing an upsurge in Lygon Street's cultural and artistic life that had been simmering quietly away for decades.

Another ingredient was being added to the Lygon Street melting pot within the Italian community itself. Just as many Australians were being educated in the flavours of Italy through the restaurants and cafés that were appearing on the street, the Italians who immigrated to Australia and settled in Carlton were also getting a culinary education. Silvana Mercogliano believes that this was what helped make Lygon Street attractive to the Italians as well.

In some ways it was as much an education for the Italians as it was for the Aussies. Italians before the war used to eat very regionally and so would never have tried the food that was being cooked in other regions. Before the war my father had never even heard of a pizza. So there were all these different cuisines coming into Carlton from all over Italy and blending. Where I come from in Italy is inland and so we never had a lot of seafood traditionally, whereas in Naples it is all calamari, fish, seafood. Italians were seeing things and trying things that they never had before.

Lygon Street had become a place to try new things in an atmosphere of solid, visible connections with the past. By the end of the 1960s, the Italian population of Carlton had started to decline and the new wave of 'immigrants' swept more students, academics, artists and bohemians into the mix. It was a time when many walks of life mingled together in a remarkably harmonious way. There was a blend of old and new, migrant and local, shop owner and artist, all pulled together by Lygon Street's atmosphere. The melting pot, it seems, had hit its ideal heat, able to embrace anything that was added to the mix. It was the perfect incubator for the social changes the new decade was to bring.

***

The Mayor
of Little Italy

Artists and counter-culturalists may have been poised to claim Carlton as their own in the late 1960s, but Lygon Street's main identity was still overwhelmingly that of Little Italy. When Italian President Giuseppe Saragat paid a visit to the street in 1967, he not only gave Lygon Street its first ostensibly official recognition but also paid tribute to one of the street's favourite and best-known sons, Nino Borsari.

On the day of the visit, President Saragat's motorcade made its way up Lygon Street before stopping outside of Nino's shop, Borsari's Emporium, where a large crowd of Italians had gathered to greet the President. Borsari's was decked out with Italian flags and green, white and red bunting and the speech the President made in front of the shop was widely covered in the local media and televised in Italy.

In Lygon Street in 1967, there could not have been a more fitting place for President Saragat to stop and make his speech. Nino Borsari was one of the Lygon Street village's most prominent elders and had been dubbed the 'unofficial Mayor of Little Italy' by the newspapers.

Anyone who has seen the famous Borsari neon sign on the corner of Lygon and Grattan Streets will be aware that Nino Borsari was an Olympic medallist, having won gold in cycling at the 1932 Los Angeles Olympic Games. Following this success he was invited to Australia to compete in Victoria's Centenary Bike Race in 1934, which he won. During a second cycling tour of Australia in 1939, he became stranded by the outbreak of World War II and was classed as an enemy alien though his sporting fame saved him from being interred. Instead, with the help of some benefactors, he opened a bicycle repair shop on Lygon Street in 1941. The business expanded and began selling everything from jewellery and bonbonniere to espresso machines, radios and kitchenware. The neon sign, installed in 1948, is one of the oldest in Australia.

Nino was a forceful presence on Lygon Street and his shop became one of the main social centres of the Italian community at the time. Nino was known for his generosity towards new immigrants, finding them work,

Below: Socialising upstairs at the University Café in 1957 are Ero Milani (left), owner of the University café, Nino Borsari (centre) and an unidentified man (right). Nino was a popular and much-loved member of the Italian community on Lygon Street.

organising places for them to stay and providing financial help. Borsari's was a place where immigrants could gather and speak of home, buy Italian newspapers and magazines and feel part of the Italian community. Nino was honoured by the Italian government for his services to the Italian community and also played a prominent role as a delegate for Australia in Melbourne's successful bid for the 1956 Olympic Games.

The Borsari name remains on Lygon Street to this day though Nino is no longer with us. Borsari's Restaurant operates in the former Borsari Emporium and Borsari Cycles, a few doors down, still continues the bicycle trade though Nino's family aren't involved in the business.

It was places like Borsari's that fostered the sense of community in Lygon Street. Not only did Nino run his business but he also participated in the life of the street, using it as his village. He shopped in King & Godfree and regularly met friends at Jimmy Watson's for a glass of wine. It was this intermingling, the sense of belonging, that Lygon Street engendered. It made it one of the first multicultural success stories that Australia produced. A true melting pot.

***

The summer of love

chapter 05

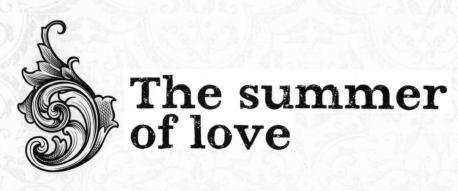

The summer
of love

On 26 September 1973, the *Melbourne Times* newspaper carried a centre supplement entitled 'The Lowdown On Lygon Street'. This is how it began:

Saturday morning in Lygon Street — cars triple-parked, footpaths overflowing with people carrying anything from a bunch of violets to the most ornate Victorian bedstead imaginable; hairy students clutch brown paper bags filled with nutmeat pies and macrobiotic rice; black-clad Mediterranean ladies laden with string bags and surrounded by neatly bow-tied children; south of the river tourists slum it up with the locals. The Range Rover set arrives after the long, hard haul up Lygon Street and totter into Watson's for a reviving glass of champagne before loading up with a camembert and a bottle or two of red to see the afternoon out; fancy dogs prance after their owners or trendies abound, what's it all about?

The stretch between Elgin and Grattan Streets is the place to be, being seen and seeing your friends seems to take precedence over the actual business of shopping. Although there are a few dogged shoppers staggering about under piles of cartons, and we saw an elegant Italian girl coping with the problem of shopping baskets and a tribe of kids by deftly balancing a whole sack of oranges on her head, most people keep their hands free for waving to their friends.

…Opinion varies among the shopkeepers as to how these changes have affected business. The shops have certainly changed a lot. King and Godfree's is a smart self-service with a roaring trade and no longer smells of sawdust and coffee beans; there is no pawn shop in Lygon Street now and not even a real junk shop. Bright colours and smart window displays are the thing and food shops stocked with tantalising delicacies.

Lygon Street was in the papers a lot in the 1970s and, for the first time in decades, the stories were not all about slums, crime and migrant ghettoes.

Instead, the new interest in Lygon Street was all about restaurants and food shops, theatre, music, alternative culture, wine and the apparently unbelievable sight of people from many cultures and all walks of life commingling peacefully, even harmoniously, along Carlton's main commercial artery. The smoke-filled Italian espresso bars and cafés with their mostly male clientele, shadowy backrooms and clandestine card games were no longer the cause for moral panic but a sign of how sophisticated, bohemian and multi-layered the city had become. Disused factories and warehouses that had once added to the area's reputation as a slum and helped fuel the desire to level the entire suburb were now hosting avant-garde theatre and idealistic film co-operatives. The street was even being name checked in pop songs. Skyhooks' song penned by Greg Macainsh, called 'Carlton (Lygon Street Limbo)', had a whole generation of pop fans visiting the street, humming 'Do the Lygon Street Limbo/How low can you go-go'. In an era where hotels in California and highways numbered 66 or 41 were all the rage, Lygon Street had suddenly become a space that previously had only been accessible by buying a ticket on a plane.

But even in the early 1970s, when Lygon Street bohemia was still a relatively new 'discovery', the mostly glowing newspaper stories commonly tended to single out for slightly supercilious treatment the 'trendies' who were now flocking to the street. The main gist of the comment about this maligned group (that would be known in future decades as yuppies or chardonnay socialists) was that they were only there because the street had become fashionable and were invading the area, ruining the tone of the place and taking up the room that could be better used by those who truly understood Lygon Street's unique bohemian charms.

This attitude perhaps more than anything else that was happening at the time represents the changes that were taking place on Lygon Street during the 1970s. Suddenly, it was no longer just a shabby but bustling shopping street that had always happily made room for all comers, but it had become a desirable and fashionable destination. And once something becomes fashionable, there will always be people who suddenly want to claim it as their own, as if they had discovered it and had sole say over its future. History was ignored and the present was the only acceptable place to dwell.

As the following years proved, any perception of Lygon Street actually closing its doors against the invading trendy barbarians was not only inaccurate but misguided, despite some people wanting to seal the borders and freeze it in time. Lygon Street continued to change as it always had, responding to the crowds that had begun arriving in greater numbers and from further afield than any time since the street's last fashionable heyday at the end of the previous century.

But among all the de rigueur cynicism of the early 1970s about trendies and Lygon Street becoming a bit too cool for its own good, there was also an underlying and slightly baffled sense of joy in all of the commentary, as if people couldn't quite work out how stodgy old Melbourne had suddenly and successfully sprouted this unique and cosmopolitan mojo.

This sense of slightly bewildered excitement was not limited to the press. People who had been wary of Carlton in the past, experiencing it mainly from having driven through it, were also surprised and delighted at how Lygon Street and the current rage for bohemia had coincided so perfectly. How could they not have seen it before?

John Dunham, who later in the 1970s owned landmark vegetarian restaurant Shakahari with his partner Beh Kim Un, had been working and studying in Europe for several years before arriving in Carlton in 1970 to take up a position at Melbourne University. Originally from Sydney, John had memories of visiting Lygon Street on trips to Melbourne as a teenager and of being singularly unimpressed with what he saw. The changes, both in his own perceptions and in Lygon Street, came as something of a delightful surprise.

223

Melbourne had always seemed very weird to me in comparison to Sydney. It seemed very 'woggy', I guess. I can remember coming down from Sydney when I was younger and coming to Lygon Street and seeing all these bloody verandas sticking up everywhere on the street. In Sydney we'd got rid of all of those a long time ago, but Lygon Street was full of them. I remember as a teenager thinking, my God, it's all so backward here, when are they going to catch up. And then when I came back here after being in Europe for a couple of years I immediately thought, thank God it is all still here.

I had been studying in university towns in Holland and so when I came back it seemed to me that Carlton was very much like one of those European university towns. What a wonderful thing it was. The atmosphere of the place made you feel as if you were in a very cosmopolitan, international kind of place with a strong Italian base. It was funny because it still felt 'woggy' but woggy had gone from being a negative to being a plus.

So had Lygon Street really changed so dramatically in just a few years or was it just that the wider community was finally taking notice of the street that made it appear to have transformed? The answer, as these things usually do, lies somewhere between the two.

On the one hand, the changes that were happening in Lygon Street in the late 1960s and early 1970s — one ethnic group started to move out, another began to move in; artists and musicians mingled with working families and students; businesses started opening that were specifically catering to the latest influx — were just a continuation of the constant state of flux the street had been in since its very earliest days. Those same changes could be applied at many stages of Lygon Street's past.

But it could also be argued that in this particular period, the changes in Lygon Street were more rapid, numerous and visible than at any time in the past. It may be that Carlton was caught up in the currents of change that were sweeping much of the Western world, for certainly the rise of the counterculture with its hippies, protests, drug experimentation and disdain for social conventions had found fertile home ground and an appreciative audience in Lygon Street. But whether the changes came from outside or were home grown, there is little doubt that Lygon Street's shabby bohemian look suited the mood and the spirit of the students and artists who had begun to gather.

Businesses started opening on Lygon Street that had little or nothing to do with the street's status as 'Little Italy'. Obviously there were still many Italian businesses along the street but in the late 1960s, the new businesses that were opening were aimed more at a bohemian market than an Italian one.

Stephanie Alexander opened her first restaurant, Jamaica House, in Lygon Street in 1966. She had been living in London for several years where she met her first husband, a Jamaican-born man known to everybody as Monty. Stephanie and Monty had resolved that when they returned to Melbourne they would open a coffee shop (or 'coffee lounge' as they were known back then), through which they would showcase Jamaican food products that Monty was going to import. When thinking about a location for Jamaica House, Stephanie says that there was no doubt in her mind that Lygon Street was the only place for it.

Lygon Street wasn't dramatically different to what it had been like when I was a student back in the late 1950s. It still was a mixed shopping strip with all the normal shops — you could buy fruit and veggies, you could buy meat and fish. Really you could buy everything in Lygon Street except glamour clothes.

By that stage there were a couple more restaurants. Gina's was right next door to where we opened Jamaica House. Gina's was very sophisticated, I can remember having my first Tournado Rossini there which I thought was pretty special. I saw Lygon Street as a lovely place to be and I saw that it had a special character and so for me it was the only place to go.

With spectacularly bad timing, Jamaica House opened three weeks after Stephanie had given birth to her first daughter, Lisa. With bills to be paid and very little money around, delaying the opening was not an option, so Stephanie and Monty opened the doors to their tiny terrazzo-floored shopfront with its Anna Rubbo-designed entrance at the front and 'very ordinary little domestic kitchen out the back'.

Jamaica House was successful from the day we opened. We were run off our feet. We had everybody coming in really, the general public and a lot of the local traders who used to come in every Saturday after they'd closed their shops at midday. People like Pat Knox (owner of the Poppy Shop) and Sigmund Jorgensen (from the Eltham artist colony, Montsalvat) had a long tradition of coming for lunch on a Saturday.

In the very first days that it opened we had no idea what we were doing. I was running the kitchen with my friend Kristin Green as she was

225

then — she is now Kristin Williamson, David Williamson's wife. She had a child that was six weeks old so we had these two babies and we thought we could run a café at the same time and it was a bit of a mess. It was open at night too, so it was not a happy time to look back on in any way really. It was just one foot in front of the other, keep going, keep going because you couldn't possibly afford to stop.

Despite the apparent chaos, both commercial and personal (Stephanie's marriage to Monty ended with this first incarnation of Jamaica House, in 1969), Jamaica House continued to pack them in. With its exotic food, charming Jamaican owner out the front and zeitgeist-channelling bohemian scruffy décor, this was one of the new businesses that were signalling that Lygon Street was not just about Italian restaurants and espresso bars any more.

I devised the menu with the initial concept in mind that it was supposed to be a way of promoting products which Monty wished to import from the West Indies and sell wholesale. The café was meant to be like a showroom and a showcase for the products, but it became very obvious very quickly that the real appeal was the food and so the importing of food became a secondary thing and we ended up importing the food in order to sell it in the café.

The big thing in Jamaica is ackee (a pear-shaped fruit that is said to have the taste of scrambled eggs), as in 'ackee rice salt fish at night' that Harry Belafonte sings about. The ackee was imported in tins and we used to turn that into a dish like the traditional Jamaican one, combining salt fish, which we were able to get from the Italian delis on the street with the ackee we were importing. So we did that and very simple toasted sandwiches with things like tamarind jelly that we got from Jamaica. But then the demand was such that we had to do something else so I devised an extraordinarily simple curry and a very simple deep-fried chicken with breadfruit segments that also came from a tin and away we went. I also made a very simple chocolate rum cake that was very popular.

***

Deep-fried Chicken

Makes 8 pieces

***

LIGHT CHICKEN STOCK
1 chicken carcass, chopped
1 brown onion, halved
1 carrot, sliced
1 celery stick, sliced
4 cm (1½ inch) strip lemon zest
6 whole black peppercorns
2 flat-leaf parsley sprigs

4 chicken marylands
vegetable oil, for deep-frying
½ teaspoon cayenne pepper
240 g (8½ oz/3 cups) fresh breadcrumbs
75 g (2¾ oz/½ cup) plain flour
2 eggs, lightly beaten

***

This deep-fried chicken dish was developed by Stephanie Alexander at Jamaica House when she needed something more substantial than the lamb and guava jelly sandwiches they were serving at the time. They became quite a novelty and were served in a basket with deep-fried chunks of breadfruit (imported from Jamaica in tins). The breadfruit was later replaced by sweet potatoes and sometimes even fried banana!

To make the chicken stock, put the chicken carcass in a large stockpot with 1.5 litres (52 fl oz/6 cups) water. Bring to the boil over high heat and skim the surface to remove any scum that rises to the top. Add the onion, carrot, celery, lemon zest, peppercorns and parsley, reduce the heat, and simmer gently for 1 hour 30 minutes. Strain the stock, discarding the vegetables and bones, and return the strained stock to the warm pan over low heat — you should have about 1 litre (35 fl oz/4 cups) of stock.

Rinse the chicken pieces and pat dry with paper towels. Place the chicken in a large deep-sided frying pan and pour over the warm stock. Cover with a tight-fitting lid and bring to the boil, then reduce the heat and simmer for 30 minutes, or until cooked through and tender. Remove from the heat and allow the chicken to cool in the stock for 30 minutes. Remove the chicken from the stock, pat dry with paper towels and cut each maryland into two pieces.

Heat the oil in a deep-fryer or large heavy-based saucepan to 180°C (350°F), or until a cube of bread dropped into the oil browns in 15 seconds. Toss the cayenne pepper through the breadcrumbs. Working quickly, dust each chicken piece in the flour to coat, then dip into the egg, followed by the breadcrumbs, shaking off any excess. Deep-fry the chicken pieces, in batches, for about 4 minutes each, or until a rich golden brown. Drain on paper towels and repeat until all the chicken is cooked. Serve immediately.

229

Beef Curry

Serves 6

***

400 g (14 oz/1⅔ cups) tinned chopped tomatoes
3 tablespoons olive oil
2 brown onions, diced
4 garlic cloves, chopped
2 tablespoons finely chopped fresh ginger
3–4 tablespoons hot curry powder
1.5 kg (3 lb 5 oz) chuck or blade steak, cut into 3 cm (1¼ inch) cubes
60 g (2¼ oz) plain flour
1 teaspoon allspice berries, coarsely ground
2 whole small dried red chillies

***

This curry was always made in great quantities at Jamaica House, using Bolst's curry powder, and was served with an assortment of condiments, such as chopped chillies with cucumber and yoghurt, and a dish of green beans fried with turmeric and cashews.

Preheat the oven to 150°C (300°F/Gas 2). Blend the tomatoes in a food processor and set aside until needed.

Heat the olive oil in a heavy-based flameproof casserole dish over low heat. Add the onion, garlic, ginger and curry powder and cook for 6–8 minutes, stirring constantly, until the onions have softened.

Meanwhile, toss the steak cubes in a bowl with the combined flour and allspice until well coated. Add to the casserole and stir to combine, then add the puréed tomatoes, chillies, 2 teaspoons salt and 185 ml (6 fk oz/¾ cup) water. Cover with a lid, transfer the dish to the oven, and cook for 2 hours 30 minutes, or until the meat is tender and the sauce has thickened to a coating consistency. Adjust the seasoning, to taste, and serve.

After the demise of the first Jamaica House, Stephanie left both Lygon Street and the food industry (for the moment) and took a job as librarian at Princes Hill High School. Monty, however, kept the Jamaica House's fire burning and opened a second version of the restaurant on the first floor of a shop further down Lygon Street. The chef he had working for him at the beginning of 'Jammy House' Mach II, was Tony Bilson.

Tony was Melbourne-born but had been living in Sydney for a few years training to be a chef. On his return to Melbourne he was doing some landscaping work in the city's other bohemian hotspot, Eltham, when he heard that Stephanie and Monty were looking for someone to work in Jamaica House.

I worked at Jamaica House for about a year. It was a very exciting time — the restaurant was busy and I can remember that the West Indian cricket team came in to eat when they were in town. We were doing salt fish and goat curries, when we could get the goat — it was hard to get a lot of goat in those days. I also did a stew of pigs' tails and beans. There wasn't a lot of information about Jamaican food around and so I made up some dishes. I remember we did a whole snapper with lemon and mango curry which was a dish I invented, my own Jamaican dish. That was really good fun.

There wasn't a lot happening on Lygon Street in terms of food in those days. It certainly wasn't a restaurant strip, just Watson's and a few Italian places. But I was very aware of Lygon Street as a place where all the bohemians would go. I was pretty bohemian in those days. I used to go to an old beatnik pub down near Russell Street that was quite famous for musicians and poets. Lygon Street was really the hub of intellectual café life in Melbourne and that was really what distinguished it. Watson's had this great mixture of commercial people and academic people mixing in a sort of bohemian way, which didn't really happen in Sydney. Sydney was very different. There was the Push in Sydney which was libertarian and more philosophically orientated, whereas Melbourne was arts orientated, more literary, with a really exciting theatre scene.

Talk to anybody who was associated with Lygon Street at this time and you can still get a sense of the excitement that being in the midst of an artistic revolution brought to the area. Though Lygon Street had had its share of musicians, writers and actors from the very earliest days, the late 1960s was when artists began to define Carlton as much as the Italians and Jews had defined it in previous eras. As Bob Watts, owner of Watts Corner Shoe Store, comments, 'Lygon Street had always been a little bit arty below the surface and now it was arty above the surface too.' The cafés, restaurants, espresso bars and pubs of Lygon Street became the meeting places, where people discussed new works, argued philosophical points, penned their plays and novels and watched each other for hints on how to live the bohemian life.

The most significant factor that led to Carlton's reputation at this time as Australia's home of alternative theatre was the establishment of La Mama theatre by Betty Burstall.

***

In the mid-1960s, Betty had returned to Melbourne from New York where she had become enamoured with the coffee houses that were putting on theatrical performances that punters could sit and watch for the price of a cup of coffee. It was something that she thought should be happening in Australia — cheap accessible theatre that was immediate, exciting, challenging and, most importantly, reflected Australian experiences and Australian voices. She decided that Carlton, 'a lively tatty area with an Italian atmosphere and plenty of students', was the perfect place for her to try the experiment.

Behind the Del Monaco tailor shop on the corner of Lygon and Drummond Streets there was a small, two-storey building that had been around since 1883 and was now owned by the Del Monaco family. The building had been used as a printers' workshop, a boot and shoe factory, an electrical engineering workshop and a silk underwear factory over the years but in 1967, it was vacant and up for rent. Betty Burstall decided to

rent it and opened La Mama as a coffee house and a place to stage poetry and play readings. The first play it staged was Jack Hibberd's *Three Old Friends* and La Mama soon became the epicentre of the Carlton theatre scene with an alumni that includes David Williamson, Louis Nowra, Jane Clifton, Evelyn Krape, Graeme Blundell and Barry Dickens. Still operating, La Mama is acknowledged as one of the most important small theatres in Australia.

Opening when it did, La Mama was like a lightning rod for artists in the area and soon there were offshoots and breakaway groups, two of the most influential being the Australian Performing Group which operated out of the Pram Factory in Drummond Street (where the car park entrance to the Lygon Court development now is) and the Melbourne Filmmakers Co-Operative which had its base in the Holdsworth Building on Lygon Street. This was the time of Helen Garner's groundbreaking novel *Monkey Grip*, that was set among the alternative culture of the suburb and names Lygon Street and places like the University Café in its pages. There were poetry readings in Lygon Street at businesses like Café Paradiso and the walls of cafés like Tamani where the bohemian crowd hung out were plastered with a constantly changing collage of posters advertising performances, happenings, casting calls and demonstrations.

***

In the book *Carlton, A History*, Bill Garner, an actor and playwright who was immersed in the Carlton theatre scene at the time, describes what it was like to be among it.

Chalked footpaths advertised shows 'tonight!' and every night there was a show, for although Carlton had barely a single theatre building, every space was a potential performance space: factories, pubs, streets, lanes, parks ... Photographers rose like trout to snap at the action as poets jumped on tables and actors did handsprings on the street ... This was not theatre

237

as a profession or even as an art form; this was theatre as a life. A whole community of theatricals had miraculously appeared and for a few years Carlton was Melbourne's demimonde.

As tempting as it may be to dismiss some of these memories as romanticised delusions of golden days fuelled by free love, cheap booze and a fairly hefty swag of joints and mescaline, the energy and enthusiasm of the artist/bohemian crowd did not simply remain with them to mythologise. The excitement bled into Lygon Street as a whole and people who had been living and working in the area for years were also swept along with the artistic tide. Lygon Street once again proved itself to be a unique, village-like place capable of reflecting the aspirations of all the people who lived on and around it.

Silvana Mercogliano from La Cacciatora who had grown up in Carlton remembers this period well.

For me, Lygon Street was at its peak in the late1960s. It was a very fun place to be. Where Lygon Court is now there was the pram factory that was turned into a theatre and there were all sorts of performances going on there all the time. Across the road here we had David Williamson living and you would see all sorts of well-known people walking along Lygon Street. We had all these intellectuals living on our doorstep. It was very hippy, it was great fun and it made Lygon Street a very exciting place to be.

Tiberio Donnini, who was a young teenager when the social revolution hit his neighbourhood, has other fond memories.

I went through the 1960s here as a teenager which was just the best. There was a place on the corner of Faraday and Drummond Streets that was called the Love In, and it was the first genuine hippy café around. Everybody used to wear felt hats, and the girls had no bras and so we'd hang around as twelve- and thirteen-year-old kids who were just starting to think about what we wanted to do with that. The Love In actually burnt down a few years later and it remained a burnt-out shell for a lot of years.

Butcher, Leo Donati, says that the arrival of the bohemian and artistic crowd to Lygon Street did not seem so much a revolution as just another extension of the community spirit that was in Carlton at the time. To his way of thinking, the Lygon Street community took the latest changes in its stride.

We all participated in it but not in any conscious way. You might go and have a couple of beers at the Albion for instance which was where the artistic crowd was, but you didn't go there because it was an institution or anything, you went there because that was where you went to have a beer. You know, you went to the Pram Factory sometimes because someone who came in here might have been in a play or you lent them an apron for a play. You were around and so you were involved indirectly, or directly, but you just heard about what was going on. I just thought it was a community and if you were in the community you were part of what was going on.

It seems that if you wanted to know and be amongst what was going on, the Albion Hotel on the corner of Lygon and Faraday Streets on a Friday or Saturday night was the place to be. Depending on who you speak to — and whether you drank in the front or the back bar — the Albion was either a rough and dangerous watering hole frequented by petty criminals and the scene of at least one murder, or the gloriously seedy backdrop against which all the day's leading writers and artists gathered to drink, smoke, argue, pick up and check out who else was and wasn't in the room that night. Whichever way you viewed the Albion, to miss a Friday or Saturday night in the pub was to risk social death.

Mark Rubbo, who now owns Readings Bookstore and in 1972 ran a record shop on Lygon Street called Professor Longhair's Music Shop, remembers that the Albion's front bar was 'really rough but the back bar was all about the literati, the journalists, the writers, the publishers. There was never any literary events or poetry readings or anything, that was not what the Albion was about. You went there because everybody else went there and you went there to drink.'

Leo Donati never considered the Albion a particularly rough place.

The Albion wasn't rough. Sure there were fights there and someone got shot but that doesn't make it rough. You may not have seen a brawl the entire time you were going there and then one night, say when the Festa was on there's a thousand people and they're all drunk so what do you think is going to happen? It might have had a reputation for being rough but where are the bodies?

Writing in *The Age* in 2000, Jack Hibberd remembered that Friday nights at the Albion were 'packed and feral'.

The Albion attracted customers from La Mama (across the road), the Pram Factory, as well as minor crooks. Many remember barred and padlocked toilet cisterns. The gullible thought these measures were to prevent them from being flogged, not for the curtailment of drug drops.

Tony Knox, one of the founders of the *Melbourne Times* newspaper, remembers the Albion fondly as a pub that everybody went to before pubs were gentrified. It was, he says 'grubby but good' and he particularly remembers the 'huge ra ra ra' that happened when Tony Bilson started cooking, although, as he remembers, it may not have been all about the food.

It was really just simple straightforward cooking. It wasn't elaborately presented restaurant food or anything. There were things like veal shank on the menu. But if you put it into context of other pub food at the time it was outstanding. Add the fact that Tony had an absolute genius for getting a social scene going and it was no wonder the place was so popular.

Tony Bilson had left Monty and Jamaica House in 1970 to start his own restaurant — La Pomme d'Or in conservative leafy Camberwell. The restaurant was a critical success but failed to attract a crowd and so in 1971, Tony was back on Lygon Street. He set up 'a basic kitchen with a decent bain-marie' in the grotty Albion Hotel and turned the back room into a dining room serving Elizabeth David-inspired French provincial food like pot au feu of veal shanks and noisettes of pork with apricot and dijon mustard. The era of the gentrified pub was still some years off so, for many, cooking edible, let alone French, food in a hotel was highly unusual. Tony didn't see it that way.

I never found doing food like that in a pub odd because it was simply part of the tradition of French bohemia that had been around for years. My inspiration was always the Belle Époque and people like Toulouse Lautrec, because the books I read about that period were the first books that had sex in them and so that was the inspiration for what we were doing at the Albion, the sort of artists' café thing.

The Albion was at the centre of a very libertarian, bohemian scene at the time. There were a lot of loose women around, thank God, and a lot of very randy men. That's not a joke. It was a time of new liberation. It was pre-Aids and all that sort of stuff so it was incredibly open. Our generation was enjoying the new economics of prosperity that was around and the new intellectual liberation of the times. It was that pre-Whitlam era and our generation was really trying to create our own culture.

Tony believes that he and his sous chef at the time, Jules Lavareck (later to become head chef at Mietta's), were doing some of the best food on Lygon Street at the time, but that their sense of décor left something to be desired. 'I think the dining room at the Albion was distinguished most likely by the brown Arabia Ware plates we were using and the tie-dyed tablecloths we had. It was hideous beyond belief but so hip and cool at the time.'

The Bilson era at the Albion was to be short-lived. Tony says that the dining room became so popular that the publicans were having trouble getting people into the bar and so they came to a parting of ways. Tony had recently come into some money and had bought a troublesome convertible Porsche. He had also recently fallen in love with a woman called Gay Morris who later became Gay Bilson. As Tony Knox puts it, 'Tony and Gay set off for Sydney in the Porsche one day and they never came back.'

Veal Pot au Feu

Serves 4–6

***

1.8–2 kg (4 lb–4 lb 8 oz) loin of veal, boned and rolled
(ask your butcher to do this)
80 g (2¾ oz) butter
1 small carrot, peeled, cut into 1 cm (½ inch) dice
½ brown onion, cut into 1 cm (½ inch) dice
1 small celery stick, cut into 1 cm (½ inch) dice
bouquet garni (see note)
500 ml (17 fl oz/2 cups) riesling or chardonnay
2 egg whites, lightly beaten
3 leeks, white part only, cut into 5 cm (2 inch) lengths
6 all-purpose potatoes, each cut into 4 thick slices
14 baby carrots, peeled
Dijon mustard, to serve
horseradish, to serve

***

Tony Bilson's veal pot au feu was very popular during his days at the Albion Hotel. It is a simple savoury recipe requiring long, slow cooking and a great recipe to serve on special occasions. Ideally it should be prepared in the morning and reheated to serve in the evening.

Preheat the oven to 120°C (235°F/Gas ½). Season the rolled loin of veal with salt and freshly ground pepper.

Heat the butter in an flameproof casserole dish with a lid over medium heat and add the veal. Cook for 8 minutes, or until brown all over. Remove the veal to a plate, add the diced vegetables to the pan and cook for about 10 minutes, or until light golden. Return the veal to the dish, spreading some of the vegetables over the veal.

Add the bouquet garni, wine and 500 ml (17 fl oz/2 cups) water and bring to the boil, skimming off any froth that rises to the surface. Cover with a lid, transfer to the oven and cook for 2½–3 hours, or until the veal is very tender.

Remove from the oven and transfer the veal to a large plate using a pair of tongs or a slotted spoon; set aside. Strain and reserve the liquid from the dish, discarding the vegetables. Allow the liquid to cool and refrigerate. When the liquid is cold, skim any fat from the surface.

Return the liquid to a saucepan over medium heat and whisk in the egg whites. Bring to the boil, then reduce the heat and simmer for 3 minutes. Strain through a square of muslin (cheesecloth) into the cleaned casserole dish. Season with salt.

Return the veal to the clarified consommé and add the leeks, potatoes and baby carrots. Gently bring to the boil and simmer for about 30 minutes, or until the vegetables are cooked and the veal is heated through. Remove from the heat and slice the veal. Serve with the vegetables, mustard and horseradish.

Note: A bouquet garni is a bundle of herbs tied with string or wrapped in cheesecloth (muslin) or a blanched leek leaf and is used for flavouring sauces, stews and soups. It usually consists of thyme, parsley stalks, celery leaves, bay leaf and possibly peppercorns. If using dried herbs or peppercorns, wrap them in muslin and tie with string.

243

Top right: Inside Mondo Music Store which was opened by Ugo Ceresoli in the late 1960s at 304 Lygon Street. Pictured behind the counter are Ugo Ceresoli and Jo Muhrer. Bottom right: Pat Knox in the Poppy Shop on Lygon Street in 2008. Pat bought the shop in 1967; it now trades as a toy and gift shop.

The Albion Hotel continued to be as popular as ever. Pat Knox, who owns the Poppy Shop on Lygon Street (which she bought with then-husband Tony Knox), remembers the hotel firing for the next few years.

The Albion, particularly when the Pram Factory was really going, was the watering hole where everybody went. On a Friday night if you weren't at the Albion you were no one. I mean it would take you half an hour to get a drink because it was so crowded. But it was like a who's who of the Melbourne arts scene with all the hangers-on and the other people from around the traps. It was amazing fun. If you wanted to get in touch with somebody you would go to the Albion on a Friday night. It used to be very rough but the people who moved in cleaned it up a little bit. It was just one of those places that any time you went in for a drink there would be people you knew in there. It was just a regular pub, nothing special about it except the people who went in to drink. Tony Bilson was cooking there for a while but really, it was simply a place — like Jimmy Watson's — to go and have a drink.

Pat Knox has been running the Poppy Shop on Lygon Street since 1967 and many people in the area remark on Pat's genius for helping them choose exactly the right gift. The business had already been operating as the Poppy Shop before she and her then-husband Tony Knox bought it from the owner, Judy Davis who used to sell hand made rag dolls and 'some second hand stuff'.

We met Judy at dinner one night. I was a teacher at the time but in those days they threw you out when you were five months pregnant so I was looking for something to do. Judy was wanting to get out of the shop and so over dinner we sort of acquired it. I ran the shop while Tony did his photography upstairs before he and Ann Polis started the Carlton News, *which began as a news sheet put out by some of the traders.*

We used to deal in a lot more second-hand stuff. Tony would go to the auctions and buy furniture and all sorts of things and we would sell them in the shop. We used to have armchairs out on the street. We were buying a bit of new stuff too, Danish design and that sort of thing. When Tony and I split up, I kept going to auctions for a while but then I had to pay for delivery and the prices at auction went up so I went more into gift lines. Then one day somebody came in who had a toyshop and they wanted to get out and asked me if I wanted to buy the toys, which I did, and so that was when I started to do the toys. Before that it was more gifts and candles, nicky-nacky sort of stuff.

Not one to lament the changes in Lygon Street, Pat nonetheless remembers the quieter, more village-like street she first experienced and the excitement as bohemia took hold.

Lygon Street was very Italian and there was still a Jewish influence. I remember that when I first started working in the shop when I was pregnant a lot of the Italian guys who owned businesses on the street would come in and give me baby clothes that their wives had sent in. It was very sweet. I also remember Mrs Varrenti's grocery store where I used to go after I had children. Mrs Varrenti would always say to me, 'I don't understand, your children are so beautiful and you and your husband are so plain.' I wouldn't mind if she'd said it once but I think she must have said it about a thousand times, every time she saw me with the children. I was quite pleased when she left really.

There was more variety in the shops back then, though many of them were run down, particularly further down the other end where there was quite a few run down shops with lots of flies in the window, uncared for. When we started there was the best shoe shop in the world just near us. It was owned by two sisters and a brother and it had a skylight and cedar counters and I reckon they had shoes dating back to the 1930s. It was the most wonderful shop and when they retired it became a second-hand place called the Carlton Bazaar, where people used to rent out spaces. They still had the skylight then, but then they closed it all off and renovated which was a real pity because it was such a lovely shop.

The hippy thing started in the late 1960s, when we came in. La Mama opened in October or November that year and introduced a whole new wave of people coming here. Carlton became very trendy. It became the place to be.

We used to go to La Mama when my daughter was a baby and we would back our old VW into a corner out the front while she was asleep in the back and we'd go in and see plays. We'd go out and check her every now and again. Nowadays you'd be put in gaol for that. Betty used to do this wonderful Friday night thing where she'd cook a meal for everybody. She had an open fire and she would make a big casserole, it was a great time. We'd go there on Friday to eat and drink and then the theatre would be on Saturday and Sunday, if I can remember right.

They used to do a pantomime for the kids every year at the Pram Factory and I always used to take my kids. There were always two levels operating, childlike and very adult. I used to see millions of shows and they used to have parties there. It was a great, great time. When the Pram [Factory] went it all fragmented a bit, that whole scene, but it was a very exciting time to be here while it lasted.

***

Poppy Shop was not the only long-lasting business that started in this period of Lygon Street's history. One of the street's major drawcards today, Readings Bookstore, was opened by Ross and Dorothy (Dot) Reading and Peter Reed at 366 Lygon Street in 1969. An advertisement for Readings in a 1973 issue of the *Melbourne Times* trumpeted its 'wide selection of paperbacks' and claimed that it was 'particularly strong in the arts, sociology and environmental works'. The bookstore was initially kept afloat by Dorothy's teaching wage and it was not unheard of after a busy day's trading for Ross and Dot to temporarily restock the shelves from their bookshelves at home.

Current owner Mark Rubbo bought Readings with a couple of partners in 1976 after Ross and Dot — beating the trend by about thirty years — opted for a tree change in central Victoria. Mark had owned Professor Longhair's Music Shop a few doors down since 1972. The music at Professor Longhair's was an eclectic mix. According to a 1979 *National Times* article by Virginia Duigan:

… you will find ethnic music, punk magazines and an exhaustive collection of feminist records which, they claim is as good as you will find anywhere in the world. Alix Dobkin: 'Living with Lesbians', 'Wake Up Sister', 'Young and Female', 'Jazz Women', 'A retrospective'.

Readings was also mentioned in the same article:

Again, the windows are plastered with scrawled notices: rooms to let, pub poetry, rock concerts, continental films, gay dances. And the odd collector's item: kind lesbian homes wanted for happy healthy ginger and white kittens. Ah yes, this is Lygon Street. This is living in the seventies.

There were plenty more signs of living in the 1970s than just the presence of lesbian-owned kittens. There was the Small Planet food store that stocked fresh bean curd, free-range eggs, goats' yoghurt, rennet-free cheese and featured jars of herbs like burdock root, angelica, wild carrot and coltsfoot. There was Rosie's, a shop that stocked everything from Japanese kimonos and Iranian carpets to silver jewellery and batik scarves, and another store called Pumpkin that specialised in leather bags, sandals, pottery and Indian clothes. The counter-culture was definitely flying the commercial flag.

The most enduring (and, many would argue, endearing) of the hippy/counter-culture businesses on Lygon Street is the vegetarian restaurant Shakahari. Owned since 1980 by Beh Kim Un (Kim) and John Dunham, Shakahari opened in 1972, across the lane from Jimmy Watson's (it now operates from a couple of single-storey terrace houses just around the corner in Faraday Street).

In its original Lygon Street location it was a vegetarian café of its time, serious, committed, ideological and decorated on the smell of an oily rag. Hessian bags hung in the front window and were stapled to the inside walls and painted. Upstairs, silver insulation foil with tar backing decorated the ceiling and colourful flags hung about. It was, as Kim (who started working at Shakahari in 1978) says, 'very theatrical'. 'People liked it because it was one of the original hippy hangouts. They would come upstairs and say, wow, a silver ceiling, that is so spaced out.'

Kim had started working at Shakahari after he had returned from a stint in England. He was attracted to the alternative lifestyle that Carlton offered and the moment he walked into Shakahari he decided he was going to work there.

It was a time when everyone who was here was looking for a break from normal life. Back then you had options, you didn't have to achieve anything if you didn't want to. Living in an alternative way was considered an achievement. Our focus was to be alternative — that was your profession. When I walked into Shakahari, I said, 'I love this shop'. It was all very spiritual and alternative and very strong and I thought I would do anything in this restaurant and if I can't get a job I'll go back and be a chemist. Then they said we don't have anything but a dishwasher [position] and so I said, 'I'll take it'. I had only been working there for a short time when they asked me if I knew how to cook. I said I would try, even though I was not a vegetarian.

We didn't have any dairy, we used only wholemeal unbleached flour and organic food, and whatever veggies we could source, which were always from someone's farm. We didn't have a coolroom and so we would use whatever someone brought to the door that day. When I started here, they didn't have an idea about the science of balancing food and so they would have blanched veggies and raw nuts on the menu. I thought we could do it better. We wanted to attract meat eaters as well as vegetarians. And so we introduced the idea of the four balances in our cooking — everything we created had to have carbohydrate, protein, mineral and texture. I started using all the Asian ingredients and elements of cooking, but using original Western fusion and multicultural concepts, combining the two ways of doing things.

251

Vegetarian Lasagne

Serves 6–8

***

FRESH TOMATO SAUCE

1 kg (2 lb 4 oz) roma (plum) tomatoes
2 tablespoons olive oil
1 brown onion, chopped
1 garlic clove, chopped
1 teaspoon grated palm sugar
2 teaspoons oregano or 1 teaspoon dried oregano

PUMPKIN AND SWEET CORN PURÉE

1 kg (2 lb 4 oz) Jap pumpkin, peeled, seeded and
cut into ½ cm (¼ inch) slices
a pinch of ground allspice
2 tablespoons olive oil
4 corn cobs, kernels removed
2 garlic cloves, crushed
1 tablespoon chopped rosemary

BLACK OLIVE ALMOND PESTO

1 tablespoon olive oil
1 brown onion, chopped
250 g (9 oz/2 cups) slivered almonds, lightly toasted
125 g (4½ oz/1 cup) pitted black olives
1 tablespoon oregano

SPINACH AND TOFU

250 g (9 oz) English spinach leaves
1 tablespoon olive oil
350 g (12 oz) firm tofu, cut into 2 cm (¾ inch) cubes

8 fresh or 24 dry lasagne sheets
250 g (9 oz) soy mozzarella cheese or bocconcini, thinly sliced

***

This delicious Shakahari vegetarian lasagne is served with a fresh tomato sauce on the side. A special saffron lasagne sheet is prepared for the restaurant to use for this dish, but for the home cook it will work just as well with fresh or dry lasagne sheets.

To make the tomato sauce, score a cross in the base of the tomatoes. Place in a heatproof bowl and cover with boiling water. Leave for 30 seconds, refresh in iced water, then peel and chop the tomatoes.

Heat the olive oil in a frying pan over medium heat and cook the onion and garlic for 6 minutes, or until the onions have softened. Add the tomatoes and cook for 30 minutes, or until thickened, then add the palm sugar and oregano. Remove from the heat, season to taste and set aside. (You will need to gently reheat the sauce before serving.)

Preheat the oven to 180°C (350°F/Gas 4). Lightly grease a baking dish. To make the pumpkin and corn purée, put the pumpkin slices into the baking dish and sprinkle with the salt and allspice. Cover with foil and bake for 25–30 minutes, or until soft. Drain off any liquid from the cooked pumpkin and reserve. Heat the olive oil in a frying pan and add the corn kernels, garlic and any leftover juices from the pumpkin. Toss for 2–3 minutes, then add the rosemary. Remove from the heat, set aside, and allow to cool. Place in a food processor with the pumpkin and process to combine — it should still be have quite a bit of texture.

To make the pesto, heat the oil in a saucepan over medium–high heat. Add the onion and cook for 6–8 minutes, or until the onion is golden, but not browned. Add the almonds, olives and oregano, then remove from the heat and transfer to a food processor to blend to a coarse paste. Set aside until needed.

To make the spinach and tofu, bring a saucepan of water to the boil over high heat and blanch the spinach for 30 seconds, or until wilted. Drain and squeeze as much excess liquid from the spinach as possible. Finely chop the spinach. Heat the olive oil in a frying pan over medium heat and cook the cubed tofu for about 10 minutes, or until golden and crispy. Remove from the heat, transfer the tofu to a bowl and mash using a potato masher. Combine with the chopped spinach.

Preheat the oven to 190°C (375°F/Gas 5). Lightly grease the base and sides of a deep 34 x 22 cm (13½ x 8½ inch) baking dish.

To assemble the lasagne, line the base of the dish with a layer of cooked fresh lasagne sheets (or dry lasagne sheets). Spoon the pumpkin and sweet corn purée evenly over the top, followed by another layer of lasagne sheets. Spread with the pesto, followed by a layer of lasagne sheets. Spread the spinach and tofu mixture evenly over the top and finish with a layer of lasagne sheets. Scatter the cheese over the top.

Cover the dish with foil and bake for 45 minutes, then remove the foil and cook until the cheese is melted. Serve with warm fresh tomato sauce on the side.

255

Shakahari has served 'a whole book-full of famous people', including the likes of Barry Humphries ('referred to us by a Japanese medical person'), kd Lang, David Bowie and Helen Garner ('she used to write in Shakahari — a lot of people did for inspiration'). The hessian bags and silver ceiling may have gone with the move around the corner to Drummond Street, but not the conviction held by John and Kim that Shakahari was the first restaurant to be offering serious east–west fusion food. This 'first in the world' crown is also claimed by California (Alice Waters) and Adelaide (Philip Searle and Cheong Liew), but John believes that Kim's dishes, such as an Asian-leaning vegetarian lasagne with tofu, spinach and nuts, made the restaurant a pioneer that scored another first for Lygon Street.

It was never a token, fad thing. It was a seriously intellectual exercise to see if we could survive doing this type of food. It was an era of fad diets and so on, but we wanted to do something that was new and would last. We didn't do what the recipe books or magazines said because we had easy access to all these new Asian ingredients and treated them in a serious way. It was a period of great openness and people responded to it. It took the critics a while — we confused them because they didn't know whether we were a cheap-eats place or a serious restaurant. They had a thing about white tablecloths back then. Some called us radical but now we're part of the old guard.

It is sometimes difficult to see past all the tofu lasagne, clouds of incense, hand-tooled sandals, Indian clothing and theatrical happenings of 1970s Lygon Street to observe what the other less counter-culturally inclined businesses on the street were doing. During the 1970s, the old-school Italian restaurants and food stores were joined not just by vegetarian and health food businesses but by Chinese restaurants (The August Moon being the best known), a couple of Lebanese places (King Hiram and Green Cedars) and an Indonesian restaurant called Bali. But there was no coasting along on the 'Little Italy' wave for the Italian businesses on Lygon Street, particularly those that wanted to survive. Many of the old grocery stores

— Mr Caputi and Mrs Varrenti among them — and many of the old-time shoe stores, chemists and pawn shops disappeared around this time as a new crowd, disinterested in daily staples, started shopping on the street. Rents started to climb and businesses started to change their focus to suit the incoming crowd.

Chandler Ridgeway, the traditional hardware shop that had been on the corner of Faraday and Lygon Streets since the 1930s began to stock lines of cookware, French casserole dishes and black cast-iron pots, while at Grinders, Giancarlo Giusti had gone from simply serving 'coffee' to offering a large variety of blends and beans from Indonesia, New Guinea, Brazil, Turkey and Kenya, among others. A sign in the front window of Grinders spoke volumes about the Lygon Street mix at the time: 'Never mind if you don't speak Italian, we speak a good broken English.'

King & Godfree was also responding to the change in the street. The Faraday Street frontage (next to the building from which Radio Station 3XY broadcast) had been turned into a shiny supermarket that took advantage of new laws and opened extended hours, while the original grocery section of the shop was given over to wine and spirits with a deli section at the front that stocked a wide range of cheeses and meats. The cellar at King & Godfree was also refurbished at this time, a project instigated by Carlo Valmorbida, that saw the bluestone walls stripped of their whitewash, new racking built and an atmospheric space, marked by some impressive iron gates at the top of the stairs, created for wine tastings, launches and the occasional function.

David Campbell, who celebrated his fortieth year with King & Godfree in 1978, remembers that John Valmorbida, the son of Carlo and Elsie, organised an artists market with stalls running along the lane behind the store. As David recalls, it was a fairly counter-culture sort of event, with lots of craft, pottery and candles sold, and it also produced, in the weeks that followed, a small crop of marijuana plants that sprouted from the cracks in the cobblestones from where seeds had been inadvertently dropped on the day. For a few months in the early 1970s, King & Godfree also arranged for the intersection of Lygon and Faraday Streets to be closed to traffic on Saturday mornings, and tables and chairs were set up in the street for shoppers to sit and drink coffee and watch the passing 1970s parade.

Perhaps the business that best read and responded to the changing demographic was the one at 263 Lygon Street, the Lygon Food Store. Originally known as Agostino's before the Valmorbida family (who also owned another Agostino's in Swanston Street) bought it in 1952, the Lygon Food Store soon became well known as a good source of quality Italian produce, particularly pasta and parmesan cheese. Johnny Bogotto who had been working in the city store was appointed to run the new Lygon Street shop, having had previous experience in Lygon Street, working at Mrs Varrenti's grocery store. In the 1960s, the Valmorbida family sold the business to Johnny and under his ownership it was to arguably become the best deli in the country.

John Portelli, the owner of Enoteca Sileno, started working part-time at the Lygon Food Store in 1970 and two years later, at the age of sixteen, he started full-time work. It was, he says, 'the best apprenticeship anybody could have ever had in his or her lifetime'. His obvious enthusiasm for the store and what it achieved remains intact to this day, more than twenty years after he left to work with his father-in-law, Gino Di Santo at Enoteca Sileno.

Lygon Food Store was the most important delicatessen store that Australia had at that time. It had a reputation Australia-wide and journos from interstate would ring me for info all the time, as people were becoming more and more aware about the Italian foods.

We were pioneers in the specialised Italian and delicatessen food. We had all the specialties from France, what was available from Spain and Italy as well as all the smallgoods. One of the things that made us unique was that we had a lot of cheeses that nobody else ever had. In those days we used to airfreight cheeses fresh from overseas. We had a very large component of raw milk cheeses that were allowed in at the time — raw Brie de Meaux, raw goats' milk cheeses, raw camembert, rocquefort.

We had all those products freely and liberally available. To put the cheese away on a Saturday afternoon would take three hours. We used to cut a wheel of Parmigiano a day with an almond knife, six days a week. We would sell eighty prosciutto crudi every week. Hotels like the Hilton and the Regent would call us up and order three or four thousand slices of prosciutto at a time. That was what the volume of business we were doing was like. We would have nine people behind the counter in a shop at busy times. This was in a shop that was barely four metres wide and no more than seven metres long. When it was busy, people would come in the front door and would leave out the back door once they had been served. There was no room for people to turn around.

When we ordered Parmigiano we would order forty wheels at a time. We had eighty kilogram wheels of Emmenthal and aged them, 250 kilogram logs of provolone that we would age for three years. They aged in the store and we had a block and tackle to move them. We used to age a lot of cheese in the front window. The shop itself had a blind for when the sun shone in the morning and we installed a really large coolroom refrigeration unit. So this cooling unit would cool down the whole shop, literally like a large coolroom. It was not like an air conditioner because it didn't dry the product. Coolrooms maintain the moisture.

You could smell it when you walked past and with all this cheese in the window, people would always stop and look and then they would come in. It wasn't just Italians shopping at this stage, we had Spanish people, Greeks, Jews and Australians coming in too. People came because we had products that no one else had. We were still in touch with that new generation of migrants, the people who had migrated in the 1950s, the 1960s who wanted the real products. The Women's Hospital had a lot of migrant workers behind the scenes so they would pass by and all the pregnant women would pass by and stop off for their cheese fixes and so on. As Lygon Street became more of a tourist precinct and because we used to get a massive amount of media coverage we'd get lots of people coming here from the country and interstate.

I can remember Johnny had ordered a display fridge that was 20 feet long — maybe the only 20-foot fridge in Australia. When they delivered it they had to take the front window out of the shop and get it in that way. It was an amazing exercise, but what was even more amazing was that we continued to serve customers while all this was going on.

The Lygon Food Store introduced many products that had never been seen before, everything from fresh hand-made and hand-knotted bocconcini and raw milk fontina to balsamic vinegar and, in the 1980s, extra virgin olive oil. But it was not the only shop on Lygon Street to offer something new.

In 1973 an Italian pastry chef called Ottorino Pace set up a pasticceria-gelateria in the Carlton Continental Cake Shop at 374 Lygon Street. He was the first to bring gelati to the area and started something of an avalanche over the next couple of decades. Ottorino and his wife Joanna (who owned the Pancake Place next door to Ottorino's new shop) still own a gelati shop on Lygon Street called Casa Del Gelato, but the original pasticceria-gelateria was later sold to Pierro Brunetti. Renamed Brunetti's, it became one of Lygon Street's defining businesses, even when it moved around the corner into Faraday Street.

***

261

Olive Regionali

Serves 8–10

***

2 teaspoons extra virgin olive oil
1 garlic clove, finely sliced
1 red bird's eye chilli, sliced
1 rosemary sprig
200 g (7 oz/2 cups) small black Ligurian olives
100 g (3½ oz/½ cup) large green olives

***

The happy tradition of eating regional olives with a glass of wine is not limited to the eastern Mediterranean or tapas of Spain. The Italians also enjoy spending an evening grazing on small plates of food, usually served in casual bars. These dishes are known as assaggini, cichetti, spuntini or stuzzichini, depending on where you are. These olives go particularly well with some *carciofi alla romana* (globe artichokes preserved with stem on) which are wrapped in the best *prosciutto di parma* you can find.

Heat the olive oil in a frying pan over medium heat. Add the garlic, chilli, rosemary sprig and olives and cook for 2–3 minutes, tossing to combine, until fragrant. When the olives are warmed through transfer to a bowl with the oil, garlic and chilli and serve immediately.

Olive all'Ascolane

Makes about 60 stuffed olives

***

500 g (1 lb 2 oz) pitted cerignola olives, or other large green olives
with a mild flavour
70 g (2½ oz/½ cup) plain flour
1 egg, lightly beaten
50 g (1¾ oz/½ cup) dry breadcrumbs
olive oil, for deep-frying

MEAT FILLING

1 tablespoon peppery extra virgin olive oil
2 tablespoons finely diced brown onion
2 tablespoons finely diced carrot
2 tablespoons finely diced celery
½ garlic clove, finely chopped
1 teaspoon tomato paste
50 g (1¾ oz) minced (ground) beef
50 g (1¾ oz) minced (ground) pork
50 g (1¾ oz) minced (ground) veal
2 tablespoons white wine
a pinch of nutmeg
½ teaspoon finely grated lemon zest

FISH FILLING

1 tablespoons peppery extra virgin olive oil
2 tablespoons finely diced brown onion
½ garlic clove, finely chopped
2 tablespoons finely diced carrot
2 tablespoons finely diced celery
1 tablespoon finely diced red bird's eye chilli
125 g (4½ oz) skinless and boneless firm white fish fillets, diced
2 tablespoons dry white wine
½ teaspoon finely grated lemon zest
1 small handful flat-leaf parsley, finely chopped

***

These Enoteca Sileno stuffed olives are coated in breadcrumbs and deep-fried. You can stuff them with either the meat or fish fillings — both of which work well on a shared table or as an appetiser.

Make a spiral cut from one end of the olive to the other to allow for expansion. Using a piping bag with a 5 mm (¼ inch) nozzle fill the olives with the meat or fish filling (see methods below).

Roll an olive in the flour to coat, then dip into the egg and finally roll in the breadcrumbs, shaking off any excess. Leave to rest a moment, so the crust can set a little. Repeat the crumbing with the remaining olives.

Fill a deep heavy-based saucepan one-third full of oil and heat to 180°C (350°F), or until a cube of bread dropped into the oil browns in 15 seconds. Lower the olives, a few at a time, into the oil and fry for about 2 minutes, or until golden and crunchy. (Be careful not to overcrowd the pan.) Drain on paper towels and serve immediately.

Meat filling

Heat the oil in a frying pan over medium heat. Add the onion, carrot and celery and cook for 5 minutes, or until soft. Add the garlic and tomato paste and cook for another 2–3 minutes, stirring to combine. Crumble the ground meats into the pan; continue to stir with a spoon to break up any lumps. Cook for 7 minutes, or until the meat has browned. Add the wine, then reduce the heat to low and simmer for 3 minutes, or until most of the liquid has cooked off. Stir through the nutmeg and lemon zest and season with salt and freshly ground black pepper, to taste. Remove from the heat.

Allow to cool slightly before transferring to a food processor and processing to form a chunky paste. Use the filling to stuff the olives as directed.

Fish filling

Heat the oil in a frying pan over medium heat. Add the onion and cook for 5 minutes, or until soft. Add the garlic, carrot, celery and chilli and cook for 5 minutes, or until the vegetables are tender. Add the fish pieces and white wine and continue to cook for 2 minutes, or until the wine has evaporated. Stir through the lemon zest, parsley and season with salt and freshly ground black pepper, to taste. Remove from the heat.

Allow to cool slightly, before transferring to a food processor and blending to a smooth paste (it should still have a bit of texture). Use the filling to stuff the olives as directed.

Gnocchi
with Porcini

Serves 4

***

GNOCCHI
1 kg (2 lb 4 oz) large all-purpose potatoes, such as desiree, unpeeled
1 egg, lightly beaten
350 g (12 oz/2⅓ cups) plain flour

120 g (4¼ oz) butter, diced
3 garlic cloves, thinly sliced
15 g (½ oz) dried porcini mushrooms, soaked in 125 ml (4 fl oz/½ cup)
water (reserve the liquid)
200 g (7 oz) assorted mushrooms, such as field and King brown, sliced
250 ml (9 fl oz/1 cup) dry white wine, such as pinot grigio
50 g (1¾ oz/½ cup) grated Parmigiano Reggiano cheese
1 large handful of flat-leaf parsley, chopped

***

The secret to good gnocchi is lightness of texture — it should be delicate when cooked. This gnocchi recipe from Enoteca Sileno tastes superb tossed through a sauce of wild porcini mushrooms.

To make the gnocchi, place the potatoes in a large saucepan of cold water and cover with a lid. Bring to the boil over high heat, then lower the heat and simmer for 50 minutes, or until they are tender (a skewer or sharp knife should pierce the flesh through to the centre without resistance). Drain the potatoes and peel off the skins while they are still warm.

Using either a potato masher or a sieve, purée the potatoes and allow to cool a little. Working on a clean work surface, place the potato purée in a mound and make a well in the middle. Add the egg, a pinch of salt and about three-quarters of the flour and use your hands to gently knead into a soft dough with a smooth, silky texture, adding more flour if the mixture is too moist. Do not over-knead — you should only just combine the potato and flour; kneading the dough too much will yield a glue-like consistency.

Flatten the dough with the palm of your hand until it is about 1.5 cm (⅝ inch) thick all over and then slice into 1.5 cm (⅝ inch) wide strips. Gently roll each strip into a log and slice the log into 1.5 cm (⅝ inch) long gnocchi pieces. Place on a tray lined with a tea towel, cover and refrigerate until ready to cook.

To make the porcini sauce, heat the butter in a large frying pan over medium heat. Add the garlic and cook for 30 seconds, or until fragrant. Add the porcini and other mushrooms and cook for 5 minutes to stew in the butter. Pour in the wine and the reserved soaking liquid and continue to simmer for 2 minutes, or until the liquid has reduced by half and the sauce has thickened and become glossy. Keep warm until ready to serve.

Meanwhile, bring a large saucepan of salted water to the boil and add the gnocchi. Cook for 2 minutes, or until the gnocchi rise to the surface. Remove the gnocchi with a slotted spoon and place in the pan with the warm porcini sauce. Add the cheese and parsley, season to taste, and toss gently to combine. Spoon into bowls and serve.

269

Note: After they have been cut, the gnocchi can be frozen. Lay the pieces out on baking paper and freeze until solid, then transfer to an airtight container and freeze for up to 1 month.

Risotto Con Triglie, Taggiasche e Broccolini in Salsa di Cacciucco

Serves 6

***

1 kg (2 lb 4 oz) red mullet, filleted (bones reserved for stock)
80 g (2¾ oz/½ cup) plain flour, for dusting

CACCIUCCO BROTH

2 tablespoons olive oil
1 small white onion, chopped
2 garlic cloves, finely sliced
1 large carrot, chopped
1 celery stick, chopped
2 red bird's eye chillies, seeded and sliced
100 ml (3½ fl oz) white wine, such as pinot grigio
650 g (1 lb 7 oz/2⅔ cups) tinned diced tomatoes
1 litre (35 fl oz/4 cups) fish stock

RISOTTO

100 ml (3½ fl oz) extra virgin olive oil
1 white onion, finely chopped
400 g (14 oz/1¾ cups) carnaroli rice (see note)
2 thyme sprigs
1 fresh bay leaf
100 ml (3½ fl oz) dry white wine
500 g (1 lb 2 oz) broccolini, florets broken off and stems discarded
120 g (4¼ oz) pitted small black olives, such as taggiasche

***

From Liverno, on the north Tuscan coast, cacciucco is a fish stew flavoured with wine and chilli. Featuring the fish from the day's catch, it usually includes shellfish, crustaceans and squid. In this recipe the fresh and robust flavours of the cacciucco broth are adapted to make this wonderful risotto with red mullet, taggiasche olives and broccolini. If you have the opportunity, try making it with a Tuscan olive oil, which are renowned for their peppery pungency and perfect for this dish.

To make the cacciucco broth, heat the olive oil in a large saucepan over medium heat. Add the onion, garlic, carrot, celery and chilli and cook for 5 minutes, or until the onion is soft. Add the red mullet fish bones and cook, stirring, for about 3 minutes. Add the wine and cook until almost evaporated, then add the tomatoes and fish stock. Reduce the heat, and simmer gently for 35–40 minutes. Remove from the heat, strain through a fine sieve and discard the solids. Return the broth to a clean pan and keep at a gentle simmer.

To make the risotto, heat 1 tablespoon of the extra virgin olive oil in a large heavy-based saucepan over medium heat. Cook the onion for 5 minutes, or until soft, then add the rice and stir well to coat each grain with oil. Add the thyme, bay leaf and wine and stir for 3 minutes until most of the wine has been absorbed. Add several ladlefuls of cacciucco broth and stir through. When the rice has absorbed most of the liquid, add another ladle of cacciucco. Continue in this manner until the rice is *al dente* — you may not need to use all of the broth.

Towards the end of cooking, add the broccolini florets, half of the red mullet fillets and half of the olives and cook for 2 minutes, stirring through gently. Turn off the heat and cover with a lid. Leave to rest for 5 minutes, then stir through 2 tablespoons of the extra virgin olive oil.

Meanwhile, lightly coat the remaining mullet fillets in flour that has been seasoned with salt and pepper. Heat the remaining oil in a frying pan over high heat. Cook the mullet for 1 minute, or until crisp. Turn the fish over and cook the other side for 30 seconds, or until just firm. Remove from the pan and drain on paper towels.

Ladle the risotto into serving bowls, topping each with a fish fillet and scatter with the remaining olives.

273

Note: Carnaroli is a 'superfino' grade of risotto rice, grown in the Veneto region of Italy. It has a longer grain than arborio and softer starches that make the dish creamier. It is ideal for use in any seafood risotto, however, if you cannot source it, use arborio rice as a substitute.

Cannoli alla Ricotta

Makes 24

✳✳✳

CANNOLI

500 g (1 lb 2 oz) Doppio or '00' flour (see note)
4 egg yolks
200 ml (7 fl oz) olive oil
100 ml (3½ fl oz) marsala
1 egg white, for sealing
vegetable oil, for deep-frying

600 g (1 lb 5 oz/2½ cups) ricotta cheese
140 g (5 oz/⅔ cup) caster sugar
200 g (7 oz/1¼ cups) diced candied orange peel
220 g (7¾ oz/1 cup) mascarpone cheese
45 ml (1½ fl oz) orange-flavoured brandy, Cointreau or Grand Marnier
icing sugar, for dusting

✳✳✳

These ricotta cannoli are best eaten on the day you make them. To prepare the cannoli you will need to buy proper cannoli moulds from a kitchenware store or, if you are short on time, purchase pre-cooked cannoli shells from your local pasticceria or Italian delicatessen.

Mix together the flour, egg yolks and olive oil in a bowl. Add just enough wine to form a firm dough. Shape the dough into a disc, cover with plastic wrap and refrigerate for 30 minutes.

Roll the pastry out using a pasta machine or rolling pin until it is about 2 mm ($\frac{1}{16}$ inch) thick. Working on a lightly floured surface, cut the dough into twelve 10 cm (4 inch) squares and roll around the cannoli moulds, corner over corner, then seal the edges with the lightly beaten egg whites.

Heat a large heavy-based saucepan one-third full of oil and heat to 150°C (300°F), or until a cube of bread dropped into the oil browns in 40 seconds. Deep-fry the cannoli, two or three at a time, for about 2 minutes each, or until lightly golden and crisp. Drain on paper towels, cool, then remove from the moulds.

To make the ricotta filling, beat the ricotta and sugar together until smooth. Add the remaining ingredients and combine well. Pipe the filling into the cannoli shells using a piping nozzle — it is best to fill half the cannoli from one end, starting in the middle, before filling the other side. Dust with icing sugar to serve.

Note: In Italy, flour is classified either as '1', '0', or '00', and refers to how finely ground the flour is. The most highly refined is '00'. If you cannot source '00' flour, then plain flour is the best substitute.

The Lygon Street Festa

There are many versions of who first came up with the idea for a street festival on Lygon Street. Allan Watson, son of Jimmy Watson, believes the first version of it started in the 1960s.

Jack Ridgeway, the bank manager and myself started thinking that we should do something for Lygon Street, so we came up with an idea for an art festival. We asked everybody who had shops to put a painting in the window — I don't know who we got to do the painting but we organised it — and then we organised Allan McCulloch the art critic, Keith Dunstan and Twiggy, who was out here at the time, and so the three of them were the judges and that was the festival. Then the young bloods decided to do something else.

Tony Knox believes that he and Hec Pedutti, one of the managers at King & Godfree came up with the idea of a street festival 'three or four years before the festa happened', but could not convince people to have it in the street rather than a park. In 1978, however, the idea of a street party like the ones that were common in Italy was given full support by a group of Lygon Street traders (including Ottorino and Joanna Pace) and the Lygon Street Festa was born.

It was an instant success with attractions like a greasy pole competition, fencing competition and waiters race, attracting 250,000 people in the first year. Joanna Pace says that even the traders who had been planning for the Festa for months were slightly overwhelmed.

One of the things that was very worrying for us in the beginning was whether or not we would be able to manage the crowd, to feed them all, because there were so many. There were much fewer restaurants in those days and there really were a lot of people. At the first one I think everybody was running out of everything by the end of the first day. I know we were out of coffee and I knew what was coming; I expected it to be big. The second year everybody was much better prepared and we also invited all the Italian clubs and they set up sausage sizzles which was great, because their ladies used to make all their own sausages.

Beverly Caprioli echoes a common thread among the traders who witnessed the Lygon Street Festa when she says that 'the first two were the best'.

It went on a downhill run after that until they were flogging a dead horse. There was a better feeling at the first Festas. A few of the Italian regions would bring out flag throwers and different acts and there were stages for singers. I didn't get around much because we were too busy. We set up gelato stalls out the front of the University. My kids had bruised arms with the amount of ice cream we sold. The greasy pole was situated in front of our place and that was a big drawcard on a Sunday afternoon about three o'clock. You could not move in the street, it was just jam-packed with people and different teams from a lot of the different Italian clubs around town would come and compete in the greasy pole to win a prosciutto or whatever was hanging from the top of it. It was always busy and all sorts of people used to come. It was a melting pot really.

***

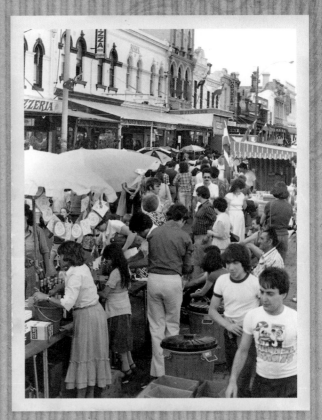

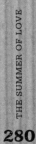

Despite the changes happening on the street, the old-style Italian atmosphere had not disappeared or lost its edge. The 1970s seemed to be a time in Lygon Street where all of the elements worked together. There may have been a more obvious hippy and bohemian presence up and down the street, but there were still a few espresso bars and late night card games that the Italians had been running since the 1950s.

The University Café continued to run its Monday night card game into the 1970s, but a place known as Black Joe's, run by Joe Prinzi, that was located upstairs above a shop (later to become the notorious 24-hour hangout L'Alba) had a card game going every night. It was also one of the few places in Melbourne that had a kitchen running into the small hours of the morning. But this was not a business that anybody could walk into. It was more like a club and, though there were other nationalities there from time to time, it was overwhelmingly Italian.

Joanna Pace often headed to Black Joe's after she had finished work at the Pancake Place.

I used to come up late at night with Otto because they used to have their own chef. I felt quite privileged at this stage to be allowed to come because it was mainly Italians that were there. I can remember watching the card games while we were eating our pasta and seeing all the money that was piling up on the table. It was a very big card school and there was a lot of money going through it. The entrance to Black Joe's was an unmarked door that you would have to knock on to let them know you were there. It really was like a private club.

Tiberio Donnini was also a regular at Black Joe's where he would go after finishing work at the University Café to 'hang around and watch all the really good card players that came from all over Melbourne'. Tiberio had been working at the University Café since the early 1970s (though he had been hanging around the café for a lot longer than that) and when his mother and father decided they were going back to Italy to live he took over the running of the University himself, the third generation of his family to do so. But when he too decided to move to Italy, the decision was made to sell the University.

281

In 1977, twenty-five years since the family had bought it as the Mexican Café, the University Café was sold to Giancarlo and Beverly Caprioli. The Donnini name was not absent from the area for long. Tiberio returned from Italy and opened, to widespread acclaim, Donnini's in Drummond Street in 1979.

***

Restaurant goers were probably not particularly aware of the ownership changes. The University Café continued to draw a crowd of academics, politicians, trade union officials, artists and students who came to eat the home-style Italian food that Beverly Caprioli was cooking, which she based on the recipes she had been taught by Tiberio's grandmother.

Across the road, the upstairs restaurant at Café Sport was continuing to pack them in, attracting hordes of students and artists who made the trek through the espresso bar with its wall-mounted TV and smoking, watchful Italian men, to the dining room where traditional Italian food — suckling pig, tripe, home-made pasta — was being served.

Up and down Lygon Street more restaurants plied their trade — Il Gambero, Papa Gino's, Tiamo, Copperwood — though there was more space between them than there would be less than a decade later. This was also the era when Café Notturno, the first 24-hour café to appear on Lygon Street, opened. It was a godsend to shift-workers at the nearby hospital and to local night owls. In the beginning, Notturno was half café and half amusement parlour, full of pinball machines and the like, but gradually the café side of the business took over the entire space.

It seems obvious that Lygon Street in the 1970s was very much in the business of attracting a crowd. Good food, excellent food stores, eclectic shops, a cosmopolitan/bohemian atmosphere, 24-hour cafés and a slight sense of dangerous illegal allure was an irresistible combination. And then in 1978, just to draw a little more attention to its charms, came the Lygon Street Festa, the first street festival in Australia.

***

The image of hundreds of thousands of people from all over Melbourne crammed into Lygon Street to experience an Italian-flavoured festival probably says everything that needs to be said about where the street found itself at the end of the 1970s. Many who experienced the street at this time believe that this was the end of a golden era for Lygon Street. Certainly, the next two decades saw immense changes in the street that included the threat of large developments, the decline of retail shopping and the rise of a nasty reputation for being a hoon and gangster magnet. The upward trajectory that had been Lygon Street's lot since the 1950s began to develop an unmistakable wobble. Lygon Street was changing again, as it always had. But this time the changes were fuelled more by its own success than by changing demographics. Whether these new changes would be for the better remained to be seen.

***

Gelato al' Limone

Makes 1 litre (35 fl oz/4 cups)

***

400 g (14 oz/1¾ cups) caster sugar
200 ml (7 fl oz) freshly squeezed lemon juice
finely grated zest of 1 lemon
1 egg white

***

This lemon gelato is the most classic and popular flavour at Casa del Gelato on Lygon Street — it tastes best when it is made with perfectly ripe lemons.

Combine the sugar, lemon juice, lemon zest and 800 ml (28 fl oz) cold water in a jug or bowl and leave to stand for 10 minutes, stirring occasionally to dissolve the sugar.

Strain the mixture, then transfer to an ice-cream machine and churn according to the manufacturer's instructions.

Whisk the egg white in a small bowl until stiff peaks form, then add to the ice-cream machine 5 minutes before you finish churning and churn to combine — this lightens the texture of the gelato.

Freeze the gelato according to the manufacturer's instructions. Alternatively, transfer to a shallow metal tray and freeze, whisking every couple of hours, until frozen and smooth. Freeze for at least 5 hours or preferably overnight.

Variation: You can replace the lemon juice with lime juice to make a lime gelato, or replace the water with 800 ml (28 fl oz) freshly-squeezed orange juice and decrease the amount of sugar to 350 g (12 oz/1½ cups) to make an orange gelato.

Bombolone

Makes 36

***

1½ tablespoons dried yeast
3 eggs
1 kg (2 lb 4 oz/8 cups) '00' or plain flour
(see note page 277)
100 g (3½ oz/½ cup) caster sugar, plus extra, for dusting
200 g (7 oz) unsalted butter, chopped
safflower oil, for deep-frying

***

This doughnut recipe is the original from Otto Pace, who owned the Continental Cake Shop on Lygon Street for many years, which later became Brunetti. He is now owner of Casa Del Gelato.

Put the yeast in a small bowl and add 3 tablespoons of warm water, stirring to dissolve the yeast. Allow to rest for 5 minutes, then add the eggs and beat with a fork to combine well.

Put the flour, sugar and a pinch of salt into the bowl of an electric mixer. Mix on low speed, then add the chopped butter and beat on medium speed until combined. Add the yeast mixture and then, with the motor running, gradually add 435 ml (15¼ fl oz/1¾ cups) warm water. Beat for 5–8 minutes on medium speed, or until the dough is smooth and elastic. Cover with plastic wrap and set aside for 1–2 hours, or until the dough doubles in size.

Knock the dough back in the bowl to expel the air and cover for a further 10 minutes. Transfer to a lightly floured surface and knead lightly for 2–3 minutes, or until the dough is elastic to the touch. Divide the dough into two equal portions and roll each portion out to 2 cm (¾ inch) thickness on a lightly floured surface.

Using a round 6 cm (2½ inch) biscuit cutter, cut rounds and place each on baking trays lined with baking paper, uncovered, for about 30 minutes, or until doubled in size and a crust has formed — you should make about 36 in total.

Heat the oil in a large heavy-based saucepan to 150°C (300°F), or until a cube of bread dropped into the oil browns in 25 seconds. Lower the doughnuts into the oil, in batches, crust side down, and cook for 3 minutes each, then turn and cook the other side until golden and crisp. Drain the doughnuts on paper towels and roll in the extra sugar while still warm.

Tiramisu

Serves 6–8

✳✳✳

300 ml (10½ fl oz) marsala
5 egg yolks
200 g (7 oz) caster sugar
300 ml (10½ fl oz) pouring cream
100 g (3½ oz/½ cup) mascarpone cheese
250 g (9 oz) Italian savoiardi (sponge finger) biscuits
300 ml (10½ fl oz) black unsweetened espresso coffee, cooled
unsweetened cocoa powder, for dusting

✳✳✳

Gently heat the marsala in a small saucepan over low heat.

Place the egg yolks and sugar in a heatproof bowl and sit over a saucepan of simmering water. Using hand-held electric beaters on medium speed, beat the yolks and sugar together until combined, then gradually beat in the warmed marsala. Continue beating for 8–10 minutes, or until the mixture is thick and creamy and has doubled in volume. Remove from the heat, cool slightly, then cover and refrigerate until cold.

Whisk the cream until soft peaks form, then add the mascarpone cheese and gently mix until just combined. Fold the chilled marsala custard into the cream and whisk for about 5 minutes, or until the mixture has thickened.

Pour the coffee into a shallow container, then dip half of the sponge fingers, one at a time, into the coffee, turning to coat, then arrange in a single layer in the base of a 20 cm (8 inch) square dish. Pour half the marsala custard over the sponge fingers, then repeat with the remaining coffee, sponge fingers and custard. Cover the bowl with plastic wrap and refrigerate overnight.

Dust generously with cocoa powder just before serving.

The heart and soul

chapter 06

The heart
and soul

If the newspaper articles about Lygon Street in the 1970s were all about its bohemian cosmopolitan groove, then the stories that appeared from the 1980s onwards were evenly divided between its fall from grace and its imminent demise. Though neither of those fates actually eventuated, there was an overriding sense at the time that a peak had been reached, a threshold crossed, and that nothing would ever be the same again. Many people believed that something had been lost when the big crowds and big parties arrived and that Lygon Street had become a victim of its own success. But the street had already shown itself capable of surviving more threatening challenges than an excess of success and so it was to prove again that it was more than capable of staring this one down too.

As in troubled times in its past, Lygon Street received little help from the media. Headlines like 'All Change: will Lygon be bygone?', 'Development Gloom in Lygon Street', 'Has Lygon Street Lost It?' and 'Lygon In Limbo' not only reflected and inflamed the concern about the direction in which the street seemed to be heading but showed how Lygon Street (and what it represented) had become firmly entrenched in the local psyche. No longer just the migrant-coloured shopping strip of decades past, Lygon Street had become an integral part of a wider Melbourne story. It had become so much a part of so many lives that people felt like they 'owned' the street and actually gave a damn about what happened to it.

There is little doubt that the next wave of 'immigrants' to give Lygon Street's melting pot another hearty stir was the surge of food joints that swept into the street in the late 1970s and early 1980s, obliterating much of the old retail culture in its path. In 1974, there were thirty-six restaurants, cafés, takeaway shops and amusement parlours in Lygon Street. By 1983 there were sixty-one. This meant that one in four businesses on the street was an eating place, in comparison to the one in ten ratio that was the common mix in other inner-city shopping strips at the time. Add the fact that other buildings along the street, including a church, had been demolished to make way for motels (the Downtowner and Lygon Lodge) it seems to show that, for the first time, Lygon Street was shifting from its traditional role of servicing the needs of local residents and was instead courting customers from much further afield. This next stage of Lygon Street's journey, it seems, was to be more about tourism and entertainment than groceries and dry-cleaning.

In many ways a shift such as this was simply a matter of survival for Lygon Street traders. The number of families living in Carlton was declining, particularly as the Italians had started migrating from the crowded inner-city suburb in increasing numbers, heading for larger houses on more land in Melbourne's outlying suburbs. The new, noticeably more upmarket, demographic that was populating Carlton (the dreaded 'yuppies' of the 1980s) was sprucing up the terrace houses that had once been condemned as slums and were doing so with fewer or no children in tow, so there was less need for multiple grocery stores, fruit shops, butchers and chemists on Lygon Street. And there was no room for those who stuck to their old-school ways. As Bob Watts, owner of Watts Corner Shoe Store, says:

If I was only relying on the local trade I would have gone broke. Most of the trade I get comes from outside the area now and we have a reputation for specialising in particular types of footwear that bring people to us. The locals began to abandon Lygon Street in the 1980s and even the people who were living in North Carlton never really came down here after that. In the 1950s and even the 1960s it was different because there were a lot of people living around, in houses and boarding houses. There were just more locals around.

Gil Boffa, who was the secretary of the Carlton Traders Association in the early 1980s, was interviewed by *The Age* newspaper in 1983 and summed up the feeling of those with businesses on the street.

The Traders Association would like … more opportunity for people to have their passeggiata, *their walk up and down, to sit down and watch the passing parade. All the great streets have that facility. The traders also want a balance between retail shopping for daytime people as well as allowing the area to flourish as a night-time place. A tension has existed for some time because traders feel that a lot of potential retail outlets are being swallowed up by restaurants. They have no objection to restaurants per se, but what it does is diminish the size of the shopping centre and make it less and less viable. Then, because there are less shops, people are less attracted to the area.*

Though there was a general air of regret at the passing of an increasingly idealised version of Lygon Street that had existed in previous decades, there were few people — pro or con — who didn't see that change in the street was inevitable. But it was the direction of this change that was to be the street's main concern over the coming period. One of the flashpoints for this concern came late in 1980 when developers lodged plans with Melbourne City Council to demolish and redevelop the landmark 1871 Holdsworth Building and the structures behind it, including the renowned Pram Factory Theatre. This development was to become Lygon Court.

The reaction to this plan — which was to include a multi-storey commercial and residential tower that, depending on the version of events you read, would be anywhere from four to nine storeys high — was swift and loud. Petitions, black bans, Supreme Court writs and appeals all rallied support and drew attention to the proposed development. One of the traders who would be affected by the scheme, Ian Goss, owner of Café Paradiso was quoted in the *Herald*, saying, 'the most frightening aspect is that it will encourage other owners in Lygon Street to believe they are sitting on potential multi-storey properties. If they follow suit, the Lygon Street we know will be destroyed.'

297

The fracas over the Lygon Court development and the fear for the future of the street was the catalyst for the 1984 Lygon Street Action Plan, a joint undertaking by the Melbourne and Metropolitan Board of Works, the Melbourne City Council and the State Government's Ministry for Planning and Environment. The plan, which took two years to complete, aimed to address Lygon Street's 'dual roles as a focus for local community and a renowned entertainment area for residents and visitors from throughout the metropolitan area and interstate'. It also provided another sure sign of the influence and significance that Lygon Street now wielded. The street had enough clout to get both government and private forces rallying together in order to preserve and exploit its unique characteristics. This was a first for any street in Melbourne, another in a string of firsts for Lygon Street that have consistently kept it in the public eye.

Not all — in fact not many — of the recommendations in the ninety-six-page Lygon Street Action Plan were ever acted upon. This did not stop the document having a significant effect on Lygon Street's future, both in the type of businesses that were allowed to operate and in the way the street looked and functioned. Parking, traffic flow, signage and street landscaping were all covered in the Action Plan but the most significant and long-lasting effects it was to have on the street were the preservation of the beautiful and unique Victorian streetscape and the brake that it was able to apply to the runaway train of restaurants and cafés that threatened to turn the street into a trashy one-note samba of lookalike eateries.

But it was not just officially sanctioned action plans that kept Lygon Street safe from the over-ambitious schemes of hovering, avaricious developers. The traders and residents on Lygon Street had become used to being ever-watchful and on hand to prevent the more underhanded attempts to get certain buildings ready for demolition. Dealings with the Housing Commission of Victoria in previous decades had made Lygon Street's residents and traders alert to the ways and means of some developers who noticed only dollar signs where others saw buildings of historical significance or, even less quantifiable, a functioning community.

From the early 1970s until 1980, Joanna Pace and her husband Ottorino lived with their four children (from Otto's previous marriage) in the dwellings above their two shops in Lygon Street's Holdsworth Building. Their shops had been the site of the renowned Holdsworth Funeral Parlour until the early 1970s, a fact that apparently made some of their cake and pancake chewing customers a little pale and uneasy when they learned of the site's somewhat morbid history. But the Paces were not superstitious people and the living situation suited them at the time. Joanna says that Otto was not particularly happy to be living above the shops, believing it to be 'a step backwards' but with family to raise and two businesses to run (the Pancake Place and Ottorino Pace Pasticceria Gelateria, otherwise known as Carlton Continental Cakes) they had little choice in the matter. Joanna actually enjoyed living on Lygon Street because 'it had such a good community feel and we made friends that will be friends forever'. It was also good for business and, as it turned out, fortunate for the Holdsworth Building.

There were all sorts of people putting forward designs for high-rises and if those designs went through it would have destroyed the street forever. It would have been horrible, so it is incredibly important that it didn't get up and the buildings we have weren't lost. There was all sorts of skulduggery going on in Lygon Street at that time. A truck went into the veranda out the front and damaged it and though I don't know whether it was deliberate there were a lot of people around at the time who certainly thought it was.

One morning at about five o'clock I woke up and I heard all this chopping going on, so I leapt out of bed and there was a team chopping down the veranda. So I rang up the police, I rang up the council, I rang up everybody I could think of and it ended up on the front page of The Age. *They were able to make them stop chopping but part of the veranda was wrecked and it remained in a dilapidated state for a long time. But nobody gave up, everybody kept an eye out and it was very good because that veranda was one of the last of its kind in Victoria.*

But in the end there was little anyone could do to halt the street's seemingly unstoppable popularity, the inexorable march towards 'entertainment precinct' status and the inevitable development and higher rents that would spell the end for many of Lygon Street's remaining old-school businesses. The Lygon Court development went ahead, though the original high-rise dominated plan had shrunk under the glare of publicity and the ensuing heritage overlays. The facade — including the embattled veranda — and part of the Holdsworth Building was preserved, but there was plenty that was lost for those who pined for the area's bohemian glory days. The Pram Factory was sold very early in the piece and, almost like it had been cut off at the roots, the Australian Performing Group disbanded (though one of its offshoots, Circus Oz, carried on to become one of Australia's most acclaimed and sought-after art exports). Where the Pram Factory once stood is now the entrance to a 170-space car park and a Safeway supermarket. Businesses like Café Paradiso, with its renowned back courtyard overhung with grapevines, and the Pancake Place closed in 1986, while Brunetti's (which had replaced Otto Pace's pasticceria in 1979) relocated around the corner to Faraday Street.

Readings Bookstore also moved but remained in Lygon Street, eventually moving to its current larger premises across the road (the former Commonwealth Bank) in 1988. The Albion Hotel was also a victim of the new development, the former bloodhouse and bohemian hangout par excellence succumbing to the times and morphing into swanky retail space.

But while there was much gnashing of teeth about Lygon Street losing its village atmosphere and becoming an over-priced restaurant and fashion strip, the changes at this time seem to be just another example of Lygon Street's ability to adapt to the times. As Carlton's main commercial artery it had always reflected and responded to the changes going on around it. New developments with multi-level car parks built into their basements and fluoro-lit supermarket aisles replacing floodlit emoting actors may not have been everybody's cup of tea but they were simply reflecting a pragmatic approach that catered to the crowd that was increasingly using the strip. And despite the wailing, there was obviously enough of 'old'

Lygon Street left to keep the regulars returning so they could sit in their favourite haunts among the dark wood, smoke stains and the faded posters for theatre happenings long past and agree with each other about how much better things were in their day.

Many of the surviving long-term business owners on Lygon Street were less worried about the bohemia-killing development that was occurring and more concerned with the type of crowd Lygon Street had begun to attract. The 1980s in particular, saw the gulf widen between how people used Lygon Street during the day and how it was used at night. This was perhaps where the true battle for the heart and soul of the street was to take place.

The presence of massed restaurants, cafés and amusement parlours — particularly those that opened 24 hours — rapidly transformed Lygon Street into Melbourne's busiest, noisiest and most exciting entertainment precinct. The transformation had started gently with places like Notturno and L'Alba burning the midnight oil and catering to a crowd that had a fairly democratic mix of local residents and business owners, shift-working nurses and doctors from the nearby hospitals and happy night owls, relieved at the prospect of a Melbourne that didn't go all dark and quiet as soon as the clock struck midnight. But as Lygon Street's reputation grew as nightlife central, the mix began to change and the street's reputation as an all-inclusive, family-friendly place was replaced by one that was raucous and edgier, with more than a hint of darkness and danger.

Some who had known the street for a long time, like Tiberio Donnini, believe things took a turn for the worse with the massed, two-day celebrations that descended on Lygon Street after Italy won the World Cup in 1982.

It was during the 1980s and into the mid-1990s that Lygon Street got really ordinary. It became really ugly there for a while with that nightclubbish group that moved in. It all coincided with 24-hour coffee places. Those places attracted the hoons and the gooses. At the start, it was us that used to patronise these places, it was our area and it was all about locals. It was nice to go and have a coffee late at night. After we won the World Cup in 1982 and all those imbeciles came down to Lygon Street burning things

and driving around, that was the beginning of the end. It became an ugly version of a nightclub, it had nothing to do with Italy. That was when all the old Italians in the area started to sell up.

Others saw the celebrations differently. Giancarlo Giusti the founder of Grinders Coffee remembers the street as being 'full of young people of all nationalities all coming together in Carlton'. Gil Boffa, who was quoted after joining in the celebrations on the street that night thought that the massed revelry showed that Lygon Street was something special, that it was functioning as more than just another strip of shops.

It wasn't because there were old buildings but because of the sort of people that are part of Carlton. You have a cross-section, a melting pot of Melbourne. You have intellectuals and pseudo-intellectuals, artists and pseudo-artists. You've got Italians. You've got playwrights. You've got posers and poofters. You've got the whole lot, but they all have a feeling of belonging and they all say — this is my suburb.

Lygon Street's 1982 World Cup party seemed to set something of a precedent for impromptu gatherings in the street. And the ever-louder laments about Lygon Street becoming less about Italy and more about being a large open air nightclub seemed to be borne out by the 1983 celebrations that hit the street after Australia's win in the America's Cup yacht race. No feasible explanation has ever been given as to why Little Italy would be the logical place for a huge, drunken party to celebrate victory over the United States of America in an obscure, elitist sporting event, but it seems Lygon Street had become the default setting for spontaneous gatherings of this nature during the 1980s. Many of the traders were less than impressed that Lygon Street had been thus anointed.

Joanna Pace, who was working at Casa del Gelato as the America's Cup celebrations got into full swing, says that it was 'a horrible night'.

It was terrible. We had to shut our doors because people were coming in and throwing champagne at us, spraying it around. It was just not an Italian thing at all. Italians consider drunkenness disgraceful and here we had a street full of it.

It was around this time that Lygon Street was also attracting a reputation as a place for hoons to gather and flaunt their low-slung, rumbling muscle cars. The long, wide, flat stretch of Lygon Street proved to be an ideal venue for drag races between hotted up vehicles and soon the weekend night air was filled with the smell of burning rubber and exhaust smoke, the sound of revving engines and the screech of tyres. The noise and potential danger of the behaviour made many people, particularly families, begin to avoid Lygon Street altogether. Beverly Caprioli believes that the hoons did severe damage to Lygon Street's reputation that took many years to fix.

It became a noisy street with all the hoons racing their cars up and down. On Saturday nights there would be police helicopters hovering and police cars blocking off streets just to try and stop them. The air would be thick with burnt rubber. It wasn't a family-oriented place for a while. I mean if I had had the choice I wouldn't have come here in those years myself. It was dangerous and it was likely you would get run over. I used to sit outside and take down registration numbers of the cars and then I would ring the police. How else were we going to stop these people? We did whatever we could.

Saturday night was the worst. The hoons used to all gather over at the coffee shop over the road and you felt like going over and bashing their heads together, for ruining the street. The problem went on for a few years and in the meantime we lost a lot of people to other streets like Brunswick Street. Slowly we got the families back but it took a lot of years for people to return and some people never did. But, then again, we had loyal regular customers that never stopped coming so they couldn't scare everybody away.

The Lygon Street Action Plan helped in ridding Lygon Street of its drag-racing hoons. Footpaths were widened, trees were planted in Lygon Street for the first time and a 'pedestrian refuge' was installed in the middle of the street. The street became too narrow for drag racing and the hoons moved off, first to Cardigan Street, one block away and then out of Carlton altogether. Lygon Street continued to vibrate to the rumble of muscle cars and their sound systems on weekends but the pace had been slowed to a 'look at me' cruise.

Part of what attracted this hoon culture to Lygon Street and what kept a certain element of it there even when the drag racing left was the rise in profile of organised crime in Lygon Street. The element of danger combined with the common sight of immaculately turned-out gangsters and their often erratic behaviour kept the street buzzing and edgy.

There had always been an element of the illegal in Lygon Street whether it be the sly grog shops and brothels of the early days, the presence of Squizzy Taylor in the 1920s and 1930s, the illegal wine and card games of the 1950s and 1960s or the quite open drug deals that took place in the Albion Hotel or Johnny's Green Room in the 1970s. But it was during the 1980s that, crime-wise, things became more hardcore. With the emergence of the 'Carlton Crew', a crime syndicate that was closely allied with Lygon Street, serious violence, standover tactics, protection rackets and drug dealing came into play. The central figure in all of this was Carlton-born Alphonse Gangitano, also known as 'the prince of Lygon Street'.

Though he came from a respectable family (his parents owned a travel agency in Carlton), Alphonse Gangitano, it seems, was looking for something a little faster even as a youngster. Chopper Read claims to have given a sixteen-and-a-half year old Alphonse Gangitano his first sawn-off shotgun in Johnny's Green Room, just off Lygon Street, and it seemed Alphonse never looked back.

***

Focaccia

Makes 2 loaves

***

1½ tablespoons dried yeast
2½ teaspoons caster sugar
1 kg (2 lb 4 oz/8 cups) plain flour
230 ml (7¾ fl oz) extra virgin olive oil

***

Dissolve the yeast and sugar in 250 ml (9 fl oz/1 cup) warm water, and sprinkle over 2 tablespoons of the flour. Stir to combine, then leave in a draught-free place for 10 minutes, or until the yeast is foamy.

Sift the remaining flour into a mixing bowl, stir through 2 heaped tablespoons of salt and make a well in the centre. Add the yeast mixture to the well, using your hands or a fork, working from the inside to the outside, incorporating the flour as you work. Gradually add 100 ml (3½ fl oz) of the oil and 250 ml (9 fl oz/1 cup) water and continue mixing until a dough forms (you may need to add a little extra water if it is too dry). You can also do this with an electric mixer and a dough hook attachment, just be sure to add the water in small increments.

Transfer the dough to a lightly oiled bowl, cover with plastic wrap and set aside in a warm place for 1–2 hours, or until the dough has doubled in size (the time will vary, depending on the temperature of the room). Punch the dough down, knead lightly, then return to the bowl, cover, and rest for a further 45 minutes, or until doubled in size again.

Preheat the oven to 220°C (425°F/Gas 7). Lightly oil two 35 x 25 cm (14 x 10 inch) baking trays. Divide the dough into two portions and press into the prepared tins, patting into place with your fingers, to a thickness of about 3 cm (1¼ inches). Allow the dough to rest in the tins for 30 minutes. Press down with your fingers as you go to make indentations in the dough — this will make small pockets to capture the oil. Sprinkle each focaccia with the remaining oil and some sea salt. Bake in the oven for about 15 minutes, or until the base is golden and crisp.

309

Variation: Finely sliced garlic, chopped black olives and rosemary sprigs can be scattered over the top of each focaccia just before baking, or dark grapes, such as muscatels, can be pressed into the dough just before baking.

Almond Kipfel

Makes 55–60

***

250 g (9 oz) unsalted butter, at room temperature
50 g (1¾ oz/¼ cup) caster sugar
300 g (10½ oz/2 cups) plain flour
55 g (2 oz/½ cup) ground almonds
1 small egg yolk
icing sugar, for dusting

***

These traditional Italian almond shortbread biscuits rolled in sugar are made in the shape of a horseshoe and are a popular item at the iconic Brunetti's on Lygon Street.

Preheat the oven to 180°C (350°F/Gas 4). Lightly grease and line two baking trays with baking paper.

Using an electric mixer fitted with a paddle attachment, beat the butter and sugar on medium speed for 5 minutes, or until light and fluffy.

Sift the flour into the butter mixture, add the ground almonds and fold together. Add the egg yolk and mix to form a soft dough.

Transfer the dough to a lightly floured work surface. Knead lightly until the dough comes together into a ball. Divide the dough into two equal portions and roll each portion into a log shape with a 2 cm (¾ inch) diameter.

Cut the rolls into 6 cm (2½ inch) pieces then shape the ends to form a crescent. Arrange the biscuits on the prepared trays and bake in the oven for 15 minutes, or until lightly browned.

Remove from the oven and allow the biscuits to cool on the trays for about 5 minutes. Dust the warm biscuits with the icing sugar to coat both sides, then transfer to a wire rack to cool completely.

Almond kipfel can be stored in an airtight container for 7–10 days. Any unbaked logs can be wrapped individually in plastic wrap and frozen until required. Simply defrost at room temperature before cutting and baking.

Torta alla Panna Charlotte

Serves 8
(Makes 1 cream charlotte or 2 sponge cakes)

✳✳✳

7 large eggs
250 g (9 oz) caster sugar
250 g (9 oz/1¾ cups) plain flour
2 teaspoons baking powder
1 teaspoon natural vanilla extract

ZABAGLIONE
2 large egg yolks
60 g (2¼ oz/¼ cup) caster sugar
125 ml (4 fl oz/½ cup) marsala
2 tablespoons brandy
300 ml (10½ fl oz) pouring cream

90 g (3¼ oz/1 cup) flaked almonds, toasted
60 g (2 oz/½ cup) finely chopped dark couverture chocolate

✳✳✳

The classic sponge used in this cream charlotte forms the basis of many of Brunetti's cakes. If served as the basis of any other dessert it is usually brushed with a sugar liqueur syrup. If you are making it to eat on its own or to use in a different recipe there is also a tempting chocolate variation for you to try.

Preheat the oven to 180°C (350°F/Gas 4). Grease and line the base and sides of two 22 cm (8½ inch) round cake tins with baking paper, ensuring that the paper comes up over the sides, as the cake rises during baking.

To make the sponge cakes, put the eggs and sugar in a heatproof bowl and place over a saucepan of simmering water and whisk together until just warm. Remove from the heat, transfer to an electric mixer and beat on low speed for 5–8 minutes, or until the mixture is cooled, very thick and resembles a mousse.

Sift the flour and baking powder together in a mixing bowl, then sift again onto the egg mixture. Add the vanilla extract and fold through using a rubber spatula until all the ingredients are just combined.

Divide the batter evenly into the tins. Bake for 20–25 minutes, or until the cakes spring back when pressed gently. Let the cakes cool on a wire rack for 10 minutes, then remove from the tins and allow to cool completely. (The sponge cakes can be made in advance and covered in plastic wrap and stored overnight in the refrigerator for up to 3 days. They can also be wrapped and frozen for up to 3 months.)

To make the zabaglione, place the yolks and sugar in a heatproof bowl and place over a saucepan of simmering water. Using hand-held electric beaters on medium speed, beat the yolks and sugar together until combined, then gradually beat in the marsala and brandy. Continue beating for 8–10 minutes, or until the mixture is thick and foamy and has doubled in volume. Remove from the heat and cool.

Beat the cream until stiff peaks form, add the zabaglione mixture and beat until well combined.

To assemble, spread one of the sponges with half of the zabaglione. Sprinkle over half the toasted almonds and all of the chocolate. Carefully position the second sponge on top, spread with the remaining zabaglione and sprinkle with the remaining almonds. Refrigerate, preferably overnight, before serving.

Variation: To make a chocolate sponge, sift together 200 g (7 oz/1⅔ cups) plain flour with 50 g (1¾ oz) unsweetened cocoa powder. The charlotte can be made using the chocolate sponge cake and soaking the cake with espresso coffee and brandy, then layering with the zabaglione.

Gelato Bacio

Makes 1.25 litre (44 fl oz/5 cups)

***

1 litre (35 fl oz/4 cups) full-cream milk
450 g (1 lb/2 cups) sugar
1 vanilla bean, split lengthways, seeds scraped
5 large egg yolks
200 g (7 oz) nutella or Gianduja
50 g (1¾ oz/½ cup) roasted hazelnuts, coarsely ground,
plus extra to serve
60 g (2 oz/½ cup) dark couverture chocolate chips,
plus extra to serve

***

This simple hazelnut gelato is delicious and one of the most popular ice creams at the Gelo Bar.

Put the milk, 225 g (8 oz/1 cup) of the sugar and the vanilla seeds into a large saucepan over medium heat and bring to the boil.

Whisk the egg yolks and remaining sugar in a bowl for about 2 minutes, or until pale and thick. Slowly pour in the hot milk, stirring to combine. Return the mixture to the saucepan and cook over low heat, stirring with a wooden spoon, until the mixture thickens enough to coat the back of the spoon. Remove from the heat and strain into a bowl. Allow to cool.

Stir the nutella through the cooled custard until combined and refrigerate for at least 2–3 hours, or preferably overnight.

Churn the custard in an ice-cream machine and freeze according to the manufacturer's instructions. Add the hazelnut and chocolate 10 minutes before you finish churning.

Alternatively, freeze the custard in a shallow baking tray for 2 hours, or until set but not frozen. Place the ice cream into a food processor and blend to aerate it. Stir in the hazelnuts and chocolate and return to freezer to freeze completely.

LYGON STREET   THE HEART AND SOUL

Sicilian Almond Macaroons

Makes about 100

***

500 g (1 lb 2 oz/5 cups) ground almonds
750 g (1 lb 10 oz/3½ cups) caster sugar, plus extra to serve
2 teaspoons natural vanilla extract
1 teaspoon natural orange extract
6 large egg whites
100 g (3½ oz/⅔ cup) almond kernels
icing sugar, for dusting

***

Macaroons are delicate almond-based biscuits with a fudgy centre and this recipe is a favourite from the Gelo Bar. You need to start this recipe the day before you wish to serve it.

In a large bowl, mix together the ground almonds, 500 g (1 lb 2 oz/2¼ cups) of the sugar, the vanilla and orange extracts, and 3 of the egg whites. Cover the bowl with plastic wrap and refrigerate overnight.

Preheat the oven to 180°C (350°F/Gas 4). Line two baking trays with baking paper. Bring the almond mixture to room temperature (remove it from the refrigerator 30 minutes before preparing the meringue mixture).

In the bowl of an electric mixer, whisk the remaining egg whites until soft peaks form. Gradually add the remaining sugar, whisking until stiff peaks form. Using a rubber spatula fold the meringue mixture into the almond mixture.

Shape heaped teaspoons of the mixture into balls using wet hands and arrange the balls on the prepared trays. Sprinkle a little extra caster sugar over the balls, then press an almond into the top of each macaroon. Bake for 10–15 minutes, or until golden. Remove from the oven and allow to cool on the trays for 5 minutes, before transferring to a wire rack to cool completely.

Alphonse's Carlton Crew were a scary collection of ex-boxers and ex-bouncers who helped collect the protection money and the cash from the video gambling machines, jukeboxes and cigarette machines that were installed by the Carlton Crew in businesses along Lygon Street and other parts of the city. Police believe that the money raked in from these machines helped fund Alphonse Gangitano's alleged forays into cocaine and heroin trafficking. Violence was never far from Alphonse and there are multiple stories of kneecappings, shootings and vicious assaults. Apparently the Carlton Crew modelled themselves on American movie gangsters like those from *The Godfather* and *Scarface* and they would dress and talk like Al Pacino, complete with American accent and whole slabs of plagiarised wiseguy dialogue.

For those not directly in the line of racketeering, however, the Carlton Crew seemed just another — albeit colourful — part of the Lygon Street landscape. Beh Kim Un from vegetarian restaurant Shakahari remembers seeing the Lygon Street gangsters around the place.

We had real mafia around here. They weren't just the small-time petty crims and that made a difference. They behaved like gentlemen, they always dressed well, in beautiful suits, and they always hung around in a group. We didn't really go into any of the places where they went. It was a bit scary. I knew they were part of the mafia thing but I never really knew who any of them were until they started to get shot.

After Alphonse Gangitano was shot in 1998, his funeral procession, according to one report 'ended with a stately procession down Lygon Street, the strip he and his soldiers had terrorised and stood over for years'.

Though there is still the occasional flare-up of gang-related violence in the area around Lygon Street (such as the 2004 shooting of underworld hitman Andrew 'Benji' Veniamin at Rathdowne Street's La Porcella pizzeria by Carlton Crew-linked Mick Gatto) the days of Lygon Street being 'terrorised' by the Carlton Crew seem to have dwindled as new crews moved on to stake out fresh turf elsewhere in the city.

Lygon Street losing the direct focus of organised crime is, perhaps, indicative of a more general shift that was happening in Melbourne at this time. The 1980s and 1990s saw the rise in popularity of other centres and streets throughout Melbourne that began offering eating, shopping and nightlife experiences that had once been Lygon Street's virtually exclusive territory. One suburb over, Fitzroy's increasingly colourful Brunswick Street had taken on the mantle of Melbourne's bohemian centre, while Chapel Street in South Yarra and St Kilda's Fitzroy and Acland Streets became the preferred hang-outs of the young and the stylish. Arguably, many of these strips emulated a 1970s-era 'Lygon Street model', replacing Lygon Street as the obvious place to head for a night out, an Italian meal or a place to shop for ingredients and produce that could not be found anywhere else. Hand-made tortellini, extra virgin olive oil and fresh mozzarella may have made their most public debut on Lygon Street but they were now easily available in most corners of the city.

***

But for all the reports of Lygon Street having lost it and for all those who abandoned it in search of the next big thing, there were still plenty of places that continued to feed off the street's traditional energy and many signs that the bohemian cosmopolitan spirit had not been completely lost.

La Mama theatre remained in its former factory building behind the Del Monaco clothing store, even after the former Lygon Street tailor shop was leased out to other interests. The Del Monacos still own the factory in which La Mama, under the direction of Liz Jones, continues to present new Australian plays and poetry in a venue that has remained reassuringly downmarket and unstintingly true to its idealistic roots. La Mama is virtually unique in Australia as a place that nurtures new theatrical talent at a grassroots level and it continues to provide a vital stepping stone for emerging artists — be they playwrights, technicians, directors, actors or musicians — to get a first shot, and invaluable experience, of performing their work in public. With a second theatre under its direction (the Carlton Courthouse Theatre around the corner in Drummond Street) La Mama's continuing influence is certainly on the record. Not only does the theatre's presence in Carlton carry on the artistic presence that has always attached itself to Lygon Street but, by presenting around forty new shows every year, La Mama continues to foster a pool of talent that will flow into all areas of arts in Australia for years to come. But without the late Rose Del Monaco's enthusiasm for the theatre it may have fallen by the wayside like most of its contemporaries. It provides a prime example of old Lygon Street looking out for the new.

One of the most reassuring signs for many fans of old Lygon Street was the demise of the Lygon Street branch of McDonald's. When the chain restaurant first applied to open in Lygon Street in the mid-1980s, the move was met with outrage, a plethora of conspiracy theories about covert American takeovers of the street and a concerted lobbying effort against the golden-arched hamburger joint, led by the Carlton Traders Association. But even though the Melbourne City Council initially denied it a permit on the grounds that there were already too many restaurants on the street, the Planning Appeals Tribunal overturned that decision and allowed McDonald's to open. It was to be a short-lived stay.

The official McDonald's line in 1988 was that they had to close because they were too successful. The shop, apparently, was too small to cope with demand and so they had been forced to move the business to a larger premises in Clifton Hill. Business owners on Lygon Street gleefully beg to differ.

Joanna Pace was President of the Traders Association at the time and says the franchisee would 'come and cry on my shoulder because nobody was going in there except late at night, between one and three in the morning'.

'He came and asked me what he should do and while I felt sorry for him, I didn't think McDonald's belonged on Lygon Street and by the way it was traded out, I think a lot of other people felt the same way too.'

While much of the news about Lygon Street during this period was about these battles for its heart and soul, there were plenty of other traders who, like always, were getting on with business. Recommendations in the Lygon Street Action Plan to limit the number of new restaurants on

CROSSFIRE
MELBOURNE
Thurs. 16 Dec.
Fri. 17 Dec.
Latrobe University
Sat. 18 Dec. arvo.
Station Hotel, Prahran
Sat. 18 Dec. nite
BUCKEYE and PINTO
VALHALLA
VALHALLA

the street, slowed the spread somewhat, particularly between Elgin and Grattan Streets where a diverse mix of old and new businesses catering for both residents and tourists were peacefully coexisting and flourishing, much as they always had. But along the southern stretch of Lygon Street, now deemed a 'tourism and entertainment precinct' the number of restaurants continued to grow. In 1995 there were around seventy-five restaurants and cafés on the street, a number that increased to ninety by 2002. The widened footpaths saw street-side dining flourish, while more of the older businesses along the entire stretch — butchers, grocers, tailors — succumbed to brutal commercial reality and made way for the upmarket and chain clothing stores that could afford to pay the rent.

But there were still plenty of good news stories to be had about food on Lygon Street. The Twins takeaway shop on the corner of Lygon and Elgin Streets achieved the same sort of legendary status of restaurants in the past, introducing hordes of students and late night revellers to the joys of the perfect souvlaki and the immaculately constructed hamburger.

Toto's was sold to a Lebanese family, the Mazloums, in 1984 but continued to attract the crowds that still flock to eat in Australia's first commercial pizzeria. The University Café, with a slight name change to Universita, expanded into a former Lebanese takeaway shop next door and was, according to Beverly Caprioli, the first restaurant in Melbourne to have a licensed street-side café.

We had everybody in Melbourne ringing us and asking us how we went about it and mostly I'd just say, 'with great difficulty'. I celebrated the night we got the licence with a scotch that I never usually drink. I was out there with my scotch when these two police walked past and came over to me and asked me what I was drinking. I had the licence in the window and I said I'm having a scotch. They said, 'Well you're not licensed to', and I said, 'Well I am', and pointed to the licence in the window, which they went and read. I baited them a bit I think but they were actually really interested in how I had got it.

The Donnini family, who have an eponymous restaurant on Lygon Street today, run by Tiberio's son Marco, also continued to make an impression on the area with their award-winning Donnini's restaurant in Drummond Street and their fresh pasta shop on Lygon Street, which they opened in 1981. The Donnini family no longer owns the pasta shop but it continues to operate under their name, both on Lygon Street and at three other locations across Melbourne. Tiberio Donnini believes that both businesses continued on the family tradition of bringing something new both to Lygon Street and the dining culture as a whole.

We were the first to sell sauce in the pasta shop. We were noticing that people would come in and they would buy a kilo of tortellini and then say, well what do we do with it? It was a bit like giving them a car without the engine and so we were basically making sauces for our customers because that was what they were asking for. At Donnini's in Drummond Street we were the first restaurant to actually mix the pasta and the sauce together. Before us, you would just get the pasta with the sauce spooned on top or you would order spaghetti saltati which was a dish that mixed sauce and pasta. We must have been doing something right because we received an award from the Italian government in 1981 as the best Italian restaurant in the southern hemisphere.

Brunetti's pastry shop was changing with the times too. After moving his pastry shop around the corner to Faraday Street in order to dodge the wrecking balls that appeared after the Lygon Court development was given the go-ahead, Piero Brunetti went about turning his name into something of a Carlton — and Melbourne — icon. When he sold the business in 1991 to his friend and fellow pastry chef Giorgio Angele and his sons, there was the usual round of hand-wringing, but the Angele family (who used to supply cakes to Lygon Street cafés like Café Sport in the 1960s) retained the name and have expanded the business that includes Brunetti's original pasticceria and gelateria but now also includes a cavernous Roman-style café, restaurant and large and immensely popular pavement seating area.

As Silvana Mercogliano says, 'People don't go to Brunetti's because it has the best cakes in the world. People go there because it has the feel of Italy. Everybody goes there, young and old. It is the place to be seen. It is like an event.'

***

Another event that kept Lygon Street on everybody's radar was the Lygon Street Festa. From its beginnings in 1978, the Festa attracted larger and larger crowds (estimated to be around 600,000 over two days in the early 1990s) and outlived many other street festivals that followed in its wake.

With the enormous crowds also came problems beyond that of trying to fit everybody into the street. There was politicking and infighting between various groups of traders, resentment that the Festa was no longer about Lygon Street businesses and that, like the street itself, the Lygon Street Festa was in danger of losing its Italian flavour.

Silvana Mercogliano says that in the beginning, the Festa was not about making money but something that would bring people into Lygon Street to experience what it was all about. 'And then people started to make money from it and it became something else. They would bring in souvlaki vans and put them in front of restaurants. It was like the street didn't exist.'

The Festa survived in many different formats until 2005. There is talk of reviving it but there are many, like Leo Donati, who believe 'the street doesn't need it. It was great in the beginning but I'm glad it's gone.'

In 1998, *Age* food writer and restaurant critic John Lethlean in an article entitled 'Lygon In Limbo' wrote:

Have we all grown up, those of us who had our first espresso at the Café Sport, our first gelato limone at the original Brunetti's and tasted our first spaghetti vongole in the Paradiso? Of course. But so has Melbourne.

And that's the point. With few exceptions, Lygon Street seems to have been forgotten in the process. As a place for drinking, casual eating and fine dining, it is mostly stuck in a time warp ... Lygon Street seems to talk only to students and tourists, with an Italian persona too often personified by Ferrari flags and red gingham tablecloths ...

***

329

Ragu

Serves 4–6

***

3 tablespoons olive oil
1 brown onion, finely chopped
2 garlic cloves, crushed
1 carrot, finely diced
1 tablespoon chopped fresh rosemary
500 g (1 lb 2 oz) minced (ground) beef
100 g (3½ oz) proscuitto or pancetta, finely chopped
2 tablespoons tomato paste
2 tablespoons chopped fresh oregano
125 ml (4 fl oz/½ cup) red wine or dry white wine
400 g (14 oz/1⅔ cups) tomato passata

***

This Tiamo Ragu is a classic Bolognese-style sauce which has achieved fame status on Lygon Street — it is best cooked the day before you wish to serve it to allow the flavours to intensify.

Heat the oil in a large saucepan over medium heat. Add the onion, garlic, carrot and rosemary and cook for 6 minutes, stirring often, until the onion is soft. Add the minced beef and proscuitto and cook, stirring often, for 10 minutes, making sure to break up any lumps with the back of a spoon. Add the tomato paste and oregano, mixing well, and cook for a further 5 minutes.

Add the wine and tomato passata to the pan and bring to the boil, then reduce the heat to very low, cover, and simmer for 1 hour. You may need to add a little extra water if necessary. Season with salt and pepper, to taste. Remove from the heat, allow to cool, then refrigerate overnight.

Reheat over medium heat to warm through, then stir through your favourite fresh pasta (see recipe, page 114).

Variation: You can also make this ragu using the same amount of minced (ground) lamb or by combining 250 g (9 oz) minced (ground) pork with 250 g minced (ground) veal, if you prefer.

Swordfish

Serves 4

***

4 x 200 g (7 oz) swordfish steaks
2 tablespoons olive oil
½ red onion, finely chopped
2 garlic cloves, finely chopped
2 tablespoons capers, rinsed and drained
2 tablespoons chopped flat-leaf parsley
2 tablespoons oregano leaves
steamed green beans, to serve

***

These swordfish steaks are served with a warm onion, caper and herb salsa — a simple, yet classic meal which has proved a popular favourite on the Tiamo menu over the years.

Season the swordfish with the salt and pepper. Heat 1 tablespoon of the oil in a large frying pan over high heat and cook the swordfish cutlets for 2 minutes. Turn over and cook the other side for a further 2 minutes, or until the fish is just opaque. Remove the fish from the pan and set aside.

Put the remaining oil in the pan with the onion, garlic and capers and cook for 1 minute over high heat, or until fragrant and lightly golden. Return the fish to the pan, add the parsley and oregano and baste the fish in the onion mixture to coat.

Remove from the heat and serve the swordfish with the warm salsa scattered over the top. Serve immediately with steamed green beans on the side.

Gnocchi with Leek Sauce

Serves 4

✳✳✳

1 portion gnocchi (see recipe, page 268)

LEEK SAUCE
3 leeks, white part only
cornflour, for dusting
500 ml (17 fl oz/2 cups) vegetable oil, for frying
60 g (2¼ oz) butter
¼ teaspoon ground nutmeg
1 cup sparkling white wine, such as Prosecco or Champagne
200 ml (7 fl oz) thick cream
2 tablespoons finely chopped flat-leaf parsley
2 tablespoons freshly grated Parmigiano Reggiano cheese, to serve

✳✳✳

Rinse the leeks well under running water. Finely dice two of the leeks and set aside. Cut the remaining leek into fine julienne strips. Roll the julinned leek in cornflour to coat.

Heat the vegetable oil in a saucepan over high heat to 180°C (350°F), or until a cube of bread dropped into the oil browns in 15 seconds. Deep-fry the julienned leek for 1 minute, or until golden. Remove from the oil with a slotted spoon, drain on paper towels and set aside to use as a garnish.

Melt the butter in a frying pan over low heat. Add the diced leek, cover the pan and cook the leek for about 15 minutes, or until soft but not brown. Season with the nutmeg, 1 teaspoon salt and freshly ground black pepper, to taste. Add the sparkling white wine and simmer with the lid on for 10 minutes, or until reduced by half. Add the cream and parsley and stir to combine. Remove from the heat and process in a blender until smooth. Return the leek sauce to a clean pan and keep warm over low heat until the gnocchi is ready.

Bring a large saucepan of salted water to the boil and add the gnocchi. Cook for 2 minutes, or until the gnocchi rise to the surface. Remove the gnocchi with a slotted spoon, add to the pan with the leek sauce and toss gently to coat. Serve with the grated cheese and garnish with the deep-fried leek.

Crèma al Caramello

Serves 8

* * *

**320 g (11¼ oz/1½ cups) sugar
1 litre (35 fl oz/4 cups) full-cream milk
1 vanilla bean, split lengthways, seeds scraped
4 large eggs
3 egg yolks**

* * *

Preheat the oven to 170°C (325°F/Gas 3).

Place 200 g (7 oz) of the sugar in a heavy-based saucepan with 125 ml (4 fl oz/½ cup) water and stir over low heat until the sugar dissolves. Increase the heat, bring to the boil and cook for 10 minutes, without stirring, until a rich golden caramel forms. Quickly pour the caramel into eight 125 ml (4 fl oz/½ cup) ramekins or dariole moulds and swirl to coat the base and sides. Place the caramel-lined ramekins in a deep roasting tin and set aside.

To make the custard, put the milk and vanilla seeds in a saucepan and bring to the boil.

Whisk together the eggs, egg yolks and remaining sugar in a bowl until combined. Slowly pour the boiling milk into the egg mixture and stir until smooth. Strain through a fine sieve into a jug, then pour the custard into the prepared ramekins.

Pour enough hot water into the roasting tin to come halfway up the sides of the ramekins. Place in the oven and cook for 30–40 minutes, or until just set but still a little wobbly in the centre. Remove the ramekins from the tin and allow to cool. Refrigerate for at least 6 hours, or overnight.

To serve, dip the base of each ramekin briefly in hot water, run a knife around the outside of the custard and carefully invert onto serving plates, to serve.

It was a common perception at the end of the 1990s that Lygon Street's condition was terminal and, like the people who had written the street off in previous decades, the lament went up that it would never be the same again. In some ways it was true. Lygon Street had been through some rougher than usual handling in the previous two decades and such handling could not help but change what it was. But that, as it turns out, is the point.

The Carlton Moviehouse (known both affectionately and derisively as 'the bughouse') might have gone, but in Lygon Court, Cinema Nova does a roaring trade on an ever-increasing number of screens while also hosting readings and book launches by big name authors organised by Readings Bookstore across the street when there are simply too many punters to fit into the always busy shop. Café Sport and Genevieve's are no longer but places like Balzarri and Carlton Espresso are waving the flag for the new Lygon Street style with menus and attitudes that hark back to the traditional values of quality flavour-filled ingredients treated with a minimum of fiddling that were really what put Lygon Street on the feeding map in the first place.

And the old guard continues to do what it has always done best. Cafés like Trotters and Tiamo channel Lygon Street's past. Tiamo, one of the longest stayers on the street, is a place that has, along with fellow icons like the University Café and Jimmy Watson's, come to represent a particular Lygon Street look, style and attitude. The food at Tiamo is simple, humble and receives no awards and accolades, and the décor (particularly in the original Tiamo 1) is dark, worn and student-scruffy but there are queues of people waiting for tables every night. There are people who would consider a visit to Carlton wasted if they did not stop in for a coffee or a glass of wine or a spaghetti bolognese at Tiamo either before or after they caught a film at the Nova or went browsing in Readings. Tiamo represents both time warp and timelessness on Lygon Street, something that can probably come from having been run by the same family for three generations.

***

There may only be one butcher shop and one fruit shop left from the Elgin–Grattan stretch that once saw multiple butchers and greengrocers but those that have remained are packed with fiercely loyal devotees who would do their shopping nowhere else. And the new immigrants, most noticeably Africans, make their way from the Housing Commission towers to do their grocery shopping in Lygon Court's supermarket, carrying on a modern day version of a traditional connection between Lygon Street and freshly arrived migrants. As Giancarlo Giusti, who sold his landmark Grinders coffee business to Amatil Coca-Cola in 2005, says:

The people are complaining and saying, 'Oh Carlton is not like it was anymore.' Of course it is not anymore. Of course we don't see Carlton of a hundred years ago. We have to change. Every day changes just like the people who come to Carlton change. We have to go on.

But while we do go on there is still something about Lygon Street that makes those who have experienced it at a certain point in time pine for the past, and become quite fierce about protecting their own part of it.

Pat Knox, who is in her fifth decade on the street, remembers the competitive nature of some of her customers when Poppy Shop celebrated its fortieth birthday.

There was a bit written in the paper about me being here for forty years and suddenly there was a competition among my customers about who had been coming here the longest. One would say, I've been shopping here for thirty-two years and then someone else would pipe up and say, well, I've been shopping here for thirty-eight years. It got a bit snippy for a moment. There have been so many familiar faces over the years. I mean there was a woman who came into the shop the other day and I said to her, 'I haven't seen you in ages,' and she said, 'Well, I've been living in England for twenty years, so no wonder.' It is like being on this street for so long. Things change gradually and all of a sudden you're in a totally different place. Lygon Street is still good, but it is different.

There is little doubt that Lygon Street is less Italian than it once was. Many of the businesses with Italian names are no longer owned by Italians and the cultural mix of restaurants and cafés now reaches into every corner of the globe. Down the Queensberry Street end of Lygon Street, international students from RMIT and the University of Melbourne — the majority of whom are from Asia — have adopted the strip and businesses have followed suit, keeping it lively and pumping every night of the week with a decidedly Asian flavour.

Further north, as Lygon Street moves into East Brunswick, an eclectic mix of shops, cafés, bars and restaurants have begun to colonise what has, for many years, been the most neglected part of the street. There is a definite bohemian, artisan air to the new businesses that are sprouting in this less crowded, less touristed part of Lygon Street with its (for now) cheaper rents, absence of chain stores and old-time businesses like the Abruzzo Club. It is almost as if Lygon Street needs a dose of the alternative and the artisan as part of its identity and this once forgotten East Brunswick stretch has become the perfect fertile soil for this part of its identity to take root.

It is difficult to put all these new eating places, bakeries and green-grocers into any one box (as was possible in other eras and areas of Lygon Street) because they have not arrived here with any particular wave of immigrants. What they do have in common, other than a reluctance to pay commercial rent in Carlton perhaps, is that they have a serious and committed attitude to good food. The always crowded Gelo Bar dishes out what many believe is the best gelati in town while bars like The Alderman and bakeries like Sugarloaf are drawing a wider following than just those from the immediate neighbourhood. Places like Rumi, a modern Middle Eastern restaurant occupying the site of a former pizza parlour, add other flavours and accents to the street and continue a tradition, started more than half a century ago, when the steak and eggs Mexican Café became the University Café, of small, modest eateries dishing up tasty and surprising food. Rumi shows that the melting pot continues to bubble away nicely, even in Lygon Street's farthest reaches.

***

But despite all the movement and changes from the deep south to the far north, Lygon Street remains Melbourne's Little Italy.

This comes not just from the many Italian restaurants and businesses that continue to ply their trade in Lygon Street but from a concerted effort by the Italian community to commemorate the incredible influence Italian migrants had — and continue to have — both on the street and in the surrounding area.

The Italian Assistance Association CO.AS.IT (Comitato Assistenza Italiani), an organisation formed in 1967 to provide welfare services to Italian migrants, has its headquarters on Faraday Street opposite Brunetti's and houses the Italian Historical Society and an Italian language school among a myriad of other activities. Argyle Square's Piazza Italia, built by Italian and Australian stonemasons on the site of the old bowling club in 2005, is another lasting monument to the Italian influence.

Though the past decades have seen Lygon Street change dramatically under an accompanying barrage of often fiercely negative publicity, the street, in many ways, remains true to what it has always been. It is still the main commercial artery of Carlton and its main focal point. It still brings people of all races and backgrounds together. It still feeds people well. It still manages to provide for the locals who need bread, milk, meat, vegetables, medicine, dry-cleaning and newspapers. And it still manages to have a grip on the imaginations of those that know it.

Lygon Street has changed. Businesses, social experiments, ethnic influences and iconic people and places have come and gone. But all have left their mark and have added their own particular flavour to the melting pot. It is something that has always happened in Lygon Street. And so it should always continue to be.

***

Baked Eggplant with Capsicum Sauce and Yoghurt

Serves 6

***

YOGHURT SAUCE
500 g (1 lb 2 oz/2 cups) thick Greek-style yoghurt
1 garlic clove
2 teaspoons freshly squeezed lemon juice

CAPSICUM SAUCE
125 ml (4 fl oz/½ cup) olive oil
1 kg (2 lb 4 oz) red capsicums, seeded and cut into
1 cm (½ inch) dice
1 brown onion, cut into 1 cm (½ inch) dice
1 garlic clove, thinly sliced
400 g (14 oz/1⅔ cups) tinned diced tomatoes

2 eggplants
vegetable oil, for deep-frying
1 heaped tablespoon pine nuts, toasted
1 handful coriander leaves

***

This baked eggplant takes on Middle Eastern flavours and is a wonderful reflection of the food at Rumi, one of the new-comers to the restaurant scene on Lygon Street.

To make the yoghurt sauce, tip the yoghurt into a very clean tea towel or 20 cm (8 inch) square of muslin (cheesecloth) and tie the ends together to form a bag. Sit the bag over a bowl to catch the escaping liquid and refrigerate for 2 hours or until the yoghurt is slightly thickened.

Meanwhile, grind the garlic and ½ teaspoon salt into a paste using a mortar and pestle. Whisk the garlic paste into the drained yoghurt with the lemon juice. Cover with plastic wrap and refrigerate until needed.

To make the capsicum sauce, heat the oil in a large saucepan over low heat. Add the capsicum, onion and garlic and cook gently for 30 minutes, or until the capsicum and onion are soft. Add the tomatoes and simmer for about 1½ hours, or until a thick sauce forms. Season to taste with salt and keep warm.

Meanwhile, peel the eggplants using a vegetable peeler and cut each eggplant in half lengthways. Cut each half into 2 cm (½ inch) thick slices. Preheat the oven to 220°C (425°F/Gas 7).

Heat the oil in a large heavy-based saucepan to 180°C (350°F), or until a cube of bread dropped into the oil browns in 15 seconds. Lower the eggplant wedges into the oil, in batches, for 5–6 minutes each, or until dark brown, then drain on paper towels.

Add the deep-fried eggplant to the pan with the capsicum sauce and stir to combine. Transfer to an 18 x 22 cm (7 x 8½ inch) ovenproof dish and bake for 10 minutes. Remove from the oven, scatter with pine nuts and coriander, and serve with the yoghurt sauce on the side.

347

Hot Yoghurt Soup with Chicken and Pistachio Dumplings

Serves 6

***

DUMPLINGS

100 g (3½ oz) minced (ground) chicken
2 tablespoons chopped pistachio nuts
½ small brown onion, finely diced
½ teaspoon ground allspice
½ teaspoon ground cinnamon
¼ teaspoon ground nutmeg
500 g (1 lb 2 oz) gyoza wrappers

SOUP

750 g (1 lb 10 oz/3 cups) thick Greek-style yoghurt
1 egg yolk
2 tablespoons short-grain white rice, boiled in salted water
for 15 minutes, then drained
½ teaspoon dried mint

***

To make the dumplings, combine the chicken mince, pistachios, onion and spices together in a large bowl, mixing well.

Cut each gyoza wrapper into circles with a 5 cm (2 inch) diameter biscuit (cookie) cutter.

Place a teaspoon of the chicken mixture in the centre of each wrapper, fold into a half-moon shape and seal the edge with a scant amount of water. Bring the ends of the half-moon shape into the middle and press together to join, then twist to create a tortellini-shaped dumpling.

Whisk the yoghurt, egg yolk, cooked rice and mint in a large saucepan. Bring to a simmer over medium heat and add the dumplings. Cook for 3–4 minutes, or until the dumplings start to float. Ladle the soup and dumplings into individual bowls, to serve.

351

Epilogue

SATURDAY MORNING ON LYGON STREET, JANUARY 2008

At the entrance to Lygon Court, under the veranda of the Holdsworth Building, a tattoo-sporting busker in shorts and a pork pie hat picks up his piano accordion and begins to play. Nearby, a flower-seller pulls a dripping bunch from her crowd of buckets and hands them to a well-groomed couple in designer sneakers already laden with bulging recyclable shopping bags who have, with the flowers, reached the end of their shopping for the morning. Caffeine depleted, they haul their load towards Trotters, negotiating their way around a hunched old woman in a hand-knitted cardigan pushing a shopping trolley. Miraculously, for such a sunny day, the couple snares a coveted streetside table and as they settle, they eye the window of Donnini's Pasta shop next door with its trays of fresh pasta sitting on wooden shelves, perhaps contemplating a change in tonight's menu. The small, moodily gloomy shop is no longer owned by the Donnini's but the owners, the Omizzolo family who once ran a fruit shop further down Lygon Street, have maintained the authentic old-school food shop feel.

On the other side of Trotters, Leo Donati, the only butcher left on Lygon Street, is at work in his immaculate shop. There is opera playing, art on the walls (including some John Kelly cows) and a steady stream of customers, nearly all of them regulars who chat about their families and meat to the suave and charismatic Leo as he trims lamb and chops shanks on the marble counters. One customer, Leah Jablko, shopping with her husband Abe, is telling Leo about the milk bar her parents used to own further up Lygon Street near the old Rising Sun Hotel.

Across the street at Jimmy Watson's a small crowd sits under orange umbrellas, enjoying the sunshine that is brilliantly reflected from the whitewashed facade. There is a group of ten or twelve older men, all drinking white wine, chatting to each other in Italian and calling out 'ciao, ciao' as some arrive and others depart. A steady stream of people head into Watson's, some to eat, some just to sit in the courtyard and soak up the sun and the chardonnay, others to pick up a few bottles for the evening's dinner party.

Down the lane that runs beside Readings Bookstore a small group of students sporting baseball caps and shoulder bags study hand-written notices taped to one of the bookstore's windows. Some are scribbling in notebooks, others are feeding numbers into their phones. Most are looking for somewhere to live or for someone to share their house. A piano player is searching for a room. A make-up artist student and single mum with a three-year-old girl is looking for another mum or kid-friendly housemate to apply for a lease. There are ads for feng shui classes, Spanish classes and the Drawing Models' Union. Most of the room vacancies for students are in houses well away from gentrified Carlton but by the way the small crowd is constantly replenished, the legendary Readings notice board must still be coming up with the share-house goods.

Three of the students drift away from the window and head around the corner to Tiamo's, glancing towards the street where an immaculately detailed Commodore glides past, its open windows spilling huge perineum-vibrating hip hop beats. On this day, Tiamo 1, the original dark wood, smoke-cured student hangout is the only shop open of the three shopfronts Tiamo now occupies. Lygon Street's second-last remaining butcher, Frank Lucchiari's Excell Meat Company, is papered over and in the process of being turned into an extension of Tiamo 2. Tiamo 2, once Mrs Varrenti's grocery store, is papered over too. A crowd of streetside tables stretches the length of the three shops, sheltered by the original veranda and the canvas awnings that bridge the gap where the footpath has been widened. It seems fitting that Tiamo (originally one of Lygon Street's original break-through cafés, the Black Pearl) should now occupy three places on Lygon Street because the Succi family is now three generations deep on Lygon Street.

A few doors up, past some (more) upmarket clothing stores, King & Godfree is open for business, as it has been for well over a century. Past the terrazzo entrance with its inlaid K&G coat of arms and the attendant line of wine specials is the deli and food section and, behind that, a whole room — formerly the grocery store — packed full of wine. The iron gates that guard the entrance to the cellar are closed and locked but you can peer through and see the stairs leading down to the cellar and imagine all the treasures that might — or might not — be down there in the dark.

Around the corner in Faraday Street, next to the former Carlton Moviehouse (now a travel agent), is a building in the process of being renovated. Above the door of the corner shop you can still see the original red lettered sign, Genevieve Licensed Café. If you peer through the dusty windows there is nothing but a shell inside. There is something slightly forlorn about the site, as if it is the Tomb of the Fallen Bohemian, but head past the throng at the enormous Thresherman's Bakery, cross Lygon Street and you come to Carlton's Bohemian Eternal Flame — La Mama theatre, still looking suitably shabby at the back of a car park. The theatre's hand-painted signs still advertise the latest shows, making people pause for a moment before crossing the road to enter the pasticceria maelstrom that is Brunetti's on a sunny Saturday morning. All walks of life, all accents, all ages, all permutations and combinations seem to be squashed into the overflowing tables that run along the whole five-shopfront length of the Brunetti behemoth. There is a mosh pit at the cake counter but the rest of the crowd, well dressed and studiously nonchalant, sips espresso and café latte, nibbles biscotti and panini and check each other out behind de rigueur Italian designer sunglasses. Every second person is on the phone. One woman suddenly cranes around and waves at the friend she is talking to, down the opposite end of the footpath, both of them laughing at discovering themselves in the same place. A father is being pestered by his young daughter to go to the Poppy Shop and, worn down, he knocks back his espresso and, like thousands of parents over the last forty years, is dragged across the road to where Pat Knox's ever-colourful window gives an irresistible hint of all the treasures that lay waiting inside.

Past the Victorian-era building housing the Commonwealth Bank, its three magnificent old window arches now sporting shiny ATMs, is the Universita or, as its old neon sign above the veranda stubbornly continues to insist, the University Café. A couple with two elegant dalmatians are finished with the paper and their coffee. Watched by the dogs, he heads inside to pay, past the original three-group Gaggia espresso machine displayed in the front window. This is the machine that Nando Donnini believes his skin is still attached to, so many coffees did he pull. Across the road from the Universita, almost like it is keeping an eye on it, is Donnini's restaurant, run by Marco Donnini, the fourth generation of the family to work on Lygon Street. Lena Donnini still helps out in the kitchen a couple of days a week and Tiberio is often seen about the place.

There is the faint sound of Italian pop music in the air, coming from Mondo Music, a shop that has been open since the late 1960s, that not only deals in pop music, from Italy and elsewhere, but does a good line in Italian soccer paraphernalia. Its pink neon sign and drifting tunes are, like the neon sign of Nino Borsari on his bike just down the street, part of another era, visible reminders of the layers of Lygon Street's history.

On both sides of the street, as far as the eye can see, there is a sea of outside tables sheltering under wide verandas. A family group, all sporting shorts, sneakers, oversized T-shirts and holding gelati piled onto double cones strolls out of Ottorino and Joanna Pace's Casa Del Gelato looking up and down the street, trying to decide which direction to stroll next. It truly is a pretty streetscape, particularly on a clear and sunny day, and it is easy to see why people have always been attracted to the strip and why the old-time names like Il Gambero, Copperwood, Key On The Wall, Di Mattina, Papa Gino's, Toto's and Notturno have been increasingly joined by names like Starbucks and Esprit, Borders and fcuk. A melting pot indeed.

Down the southern end of Lygon Street, past Argyle Square and the bleak-looking Piazza Italia, deserted in the middle of the day except for some pigeons, the swarm of restaurants becomes more insistent. The council's plan to turn this part of the street into a tourist and entertainment hub has apparently succeeded, particularly if your idea of entertainment begins and ends with eating out. The material of Italian cliché (that is, red gingham) is everywhere here and tired-looking touts stand outside the wall-to-wall pizza and pasta joints hoping to lure the strolling, menu-browsing tourists into their large and fairly empty restaurants. Things are livelier at night when the lights are dim and the interiors seem atmospheric rather than tired, but you can't help but feel that these almost identical restaurants are locked in a Darwinian battle where only the fittest will survive.

Still, these massed eating houses remain a source of income — as Lygon Street restaurants always have — for the students from Melbourne University and RMIT, if the numbers of young, groovily coiffed Chinese, Malaysian, Indian and Singaporean waiters and waitresses that are slinging pizza and cannelloni to the tourists this lunchtime are anything to go by.

On the corner of Queensberry Street, the once lavish houses in the grand Lygon Buildings have been divided up into student accommodation and the shops below cater to the student crowd. Lambs Greek restaurant holds the prized corner position as it has for more than a quarter century while Thai, Malaysian, Indian and Sri Lankan restaurants are evenly spaced between Italian joints and gelati shops.

In the midst of all the tourist-oriented restaurants is Balzarri, a quietly stylish restaurant that is bringing something more than lasagne and marinara pizza to Lygon Street. It is not alone in trying to break through the Lygon Street clichés. Further up, past Bob Watts' old-style shoe store and the University Hotel (where the former front bar is now a 7-Eleven) the staff at La Parisienne Pâtés help well-heeled foodies make their selection among a sea of terrine, sausage, pâté and rillettes while a block away in the window of one of Lygon Street's newest favourite cafés, Carlton Espresso, is a blackboard sign that reads: 'Sono in Spiaggia. Gone to the beach. Re-open 18th Jan'. A disappointed regular slumps slightly when she reads the sign and then wanders off to find the next best thing. Nearby, another sign in the window of the Carlton Yacht Club bar riffs on Giancarlo Giusti's famous sign at Grinders: 'We may not speak Italian but we speak a damn good Martini' and it seems that the cycles of the street, its village atmosphere, its sense of humour and its awareness and appreciation for the like-minded businesses are all travelling as well now as they ever did, helped by the ghosts of people and businesses past.

Some of the ghosts have been given official recognition. Formerly nameless lanes that run off Lygon Street and the streets around it now pay tribute to those who helped make the street what it is. Del Monaco Place, Sartori Lane, Markov Place, Goldhar Place, King & Godfree Lane, La Mama Place. The shiny street signs join the present and the past.

Further north on Lygon Street new shoots have appeared. The old Rising Sun Hotel, where Carlton urchins like David Campbell once sold newspapers, has been transformed by John Portelli into the Enoteca Vino Bar. There are people lunching in the chic Vino Bar while others browse through the incredible range of olive oil, cheese, antipasto ingredients, Italian wine and liqueurs. It is a meticulous selection and like the Lygon Food Store when John worked there, you will find cheese that has been treated with painstaking daily attention and ingredients and labels that cannot be found anywhere else in the country.

And still further north is the East Brunswick stretch of Lygon Street, a slightly shabby group of shops, some of them empty, some neglected and dusty but others showing definite signs of new life. There is a car yard, a shop selling water tanks, another selling bathroom appliances. Up the road a little is the Abruzzo Club, and there is a coffee lounge called Sahara Nights. But there are also smart new places like Rumi, which is packed out every night and dishes up modern Lebanese food, and other cafés with names like Small Block and Ginger Lee, small bars like The Alderman, a bakery called Sugar Loaf and a new greengrocer, Smith & Maloney. The crowd moving among these places is young, stylish and studiously low-key. There are no chain clothing stores and the only gelati available is at the immensely popular Gelo Bar that, every warm night, resembles a scene from small-town Italy.

Lygon Street on this sunny Saturday in January 2008 is beautifully alive with the past, the present and the future. It is not like it once was, but it never has been. It is the function of a melting pot to blend all available ingredients so that they appeal to many people on many different levels. And Lygon Street has done that because, as it has proved since its earliest days, it is a unique and truly great big melting pot.

***

Bibliography

- Bach, S 1979, 'The Kadimah 1911–1961', BA (Hons) thesis, Department of History, Monash University, Melbourne.
- Brown-May, A 2001, *Espresso, Melbourne Coffee Stories*, Arcadia, Melbourne.
- Church, J 2005, *Per L'Australia, The Story of Italian Immigration*, Miegunyah Press, Melbourne.
- Finn, E 1976, *The Chronicles of Early Melbourne (1835 to 1852)*, Heritage Publication, Melbourne.
- Grimshaw, P & Law, A 1988, *Among the Terraces: Family Support in Carlton*, Carlton Forest Project, Melbourne.
- Grimshaw, P & Stafford E 1988, *Among the Terraces: Carlton People & Social Change*, Carlton Forest Project, Melbourne.
- Holmes, K 1988, *Among the Terraces: Work In Carlton*, Carlton Forest Project, Melbourne.
- Jones, FL 1964, 'Italians in the Carlton Area: The Growth of an Ethnic Concentration' *Australian Journal of Politics and History*, Vol. 10, Victoria.
- Lindsay, N 1985, *My Mask* (1896), Angus and Robertson, Sydney.
- Logan, WS 1985, *The Gentrification of Inner Melbourne*, UQP, Brisbane.
- Lowenstein, W 1978, *Weevils in the Flour*, Scribe Publications, Melbourne.
- Medding, P (ed) 1973, *Jews in Australian Society*, Monash University, Melbourne.
- Poliness, G 1989, *Jimmy Watson's Wine Bar*, Globe Press, Melbourne.
- Sagazio, C 1988, *A Walk Through Italian Carlton*, National Trust, Melbourne.
- Sparrow, J & J 2001, *Radical Melbourne — A Secret History*, Vulgar Press, Melbourne.
- Sturt, M 1988, *Among the Terraces: Carlton's Early Beginnings*, Carlton Forest Group, Mebourne.
- Wynn, A 1968, *The Fortunes of Samuel Wynn: Winemaker, Humanist, Zionist*, Cassell Australia, Stanmore, NSW.
- Yule, P (ed.) 2005, *Carlton, A History*, Melbourne University Press, Melbourne.
- Zable, A & O'Brien IM & Light H & Malgorzewicz H 1993, *Bridging two Worlds: Jews, Italians and Carlton*, Museum Victoria, Jewish Museum of Australia, Italian Historical Society, Melbourne.

Index

363

Acknowledgments

Firstly, I would like to pay tribute to the tireless efforts, unique talents and remarkable passion brought to this project by Maureen McKeon. She was not just the source of many of the book's great recipes but an astonishingly thorough and generous research assistant, fact checker and sounding board. She is a person who works above and beyond the call of duty.

I would also like to thank the team at Murdoch Books: Kay Scarlett who got the ball rolling, Jane Lawson who kept it going, Reuben Crossman who made it look so good and Amanda McKittrick, the tireless hunter of visuals. A special shout out to my incredibly sympathetic editor Jacqueline Blanchard, a most perceptive, patient and humorous woman.

A heartfelt thank you also goes to the following people for the generous sharing of their time, talent, stories and recipes that gave the book its shape and colour:

David Campbell, Tiberio Donnini, Elena Donnini, Nando Donnini, Silvana Mercogliano, Salvatore Mercogliano, John Portelli, Rosemary Portelli, Luigi Buono, Adelina Pulford, Emma Downey, Fabio Angele, Fernando Cappelluti Beverly Caprioli, Giancarlo Caprioli, Giancarlo Giusti, Tom Lowenstein, Evan Lowenstein, Heymie Wald, Victor Hecht, Elsie Valmorbida, Mark Rubbo, Tony Knox, Stephanie Alexander, Pat Knox, Allan Watson, Simon Watson, Ramone Villotet, Beh Kim Um, John Dunham, Leo Donati, Bob Watts, Tony Bilson, Joanna Pace, Italian Historical Society Melbourne, CO.AS.IT (especially Rose and Pierro), Jewish Museum of Australia, Susan Faine, Raymond Capaldi, Paula Campi, Rita Erlich, Gianni Omizzolo, May Graham, Roberto Bortoletti, Joseph Abboud, Maria D'Aversa. And, of course, photographer Dean Cambray.

And finally, to my beautiful, funny and endlessly patient daughter, Michaela Teschendorff Harden, who so cheerfully put up with daddy during the process — thank you, sweetie.

Published in 2008 by Murdoch Books Pty Limited

Murdoch Books Australia
Pier 8/9, 23 Hickson Road
Millers Point NSW 2000
Phone: +61 (0) 2 8220 2000
Fax: +61 (0) 2 8220 2558
www.murdochbooks.com.au

Murdoch Books UK Limited
Erico House, 6th Floor
93–99 Upper Richmond Road
Putney, London SW15 2TG
Phone: +44 (0) 20 8785 5995
Fax: +44 (0) 20 8785 5985
www.murdochbooks.co.uk

Chief Executive: Juliet Rogers
Publishing Director: Kay Scarlett

Publisher – Food: Jane Lawson
Project manager and editor:
Jacqueline Blanchard
Concept and design: Reuben Crossman
Photographer: Dean Cambray, including
 food on pages 275, 338, 345
Food editor: Maureen McKeon
Food Photographer: George Seper
Food Stylist: Mary Helene Clauzon
Food Preparation: Joanne Glynn
Production: Kita Goerge

Additional photographs supplied by:
pp. 12, 17, 19, 28, 33, 40 (top), 68-69, 84 (top),
84, State Library of Vicotria; p. 22, Museum
Victoria, p. 67, National Library of Australia;
pp. 40 (bottom), 49, 50, 51, 62, Jewish Museum
Australia; p. 93, Allan Watson; pp. 110, 128,
154, 213, 217, 246, CO AS IT; pp. 174, 190,
Sylvia Mercogliano; p.191, Leo Donati;
pp. 236, 280 (top left), La Mama Theatre;
p. 260, John Poretlli, p. 280 Lygon Street
Festa Organisation.

National Library of Australia Cataloguing-in-
Publication Data
Harden, Michael, 1963
Lygon Street: stories and recipes
from Melbourne's melting pot
9781741962321 (hbk.)
Includes index, bibliography.
Cookery--Victoria--Carlton, Jewish cookery,
Italian cookery, Carlton (Vic.) – History.
641.5099451

A catalogue record for this book is available
from the British Library.

Colour separation by Splitting Image Colour
Studio, Melbourne, Australia.
Printed by 1010 Printing International Limited
in 2008. PRINTED IN CHINA.
Reprinted 2009 (twice).

IMPORTANT: Those who might be at risk from
the effects of salmonella poisoning (the elderly,
pregnant women, young children and those
suffering from immune deficiency diseases)
should consult their doctor with any concerns
about eating raw eggs.

OVEN GUIDE: You may find cooking times vary
depending on the oven you are using. For fan-forced
ovens, as a general rule, set the oven temperature to
20°C (35°F) lower than indicated in the recipe.